GANGLAND UK

THE INSIDE STORY
OF BRITAIN'S MOST EVIL
GANGSTERS

GANGLAND UK

CHRISTOPHER BERRY-DEE

JOHN BLAKE

Published by John Blake Publishing Ltd,
3 Bramber Court, 2 Bramber Road,
London W14 9PB, England

www.johnblakepublishing.co.uk

First published in hardback in 2008
Paperback edition published 2009

ISBN: 978 1 84454 832 3

British Library Cataloguing-in-Publication Data:

A catalogue record for this book is available from the British Library.

Design by www.envydesign.co.uk

Printed in Great Britain by CPI Bookmarque, Croydon CR0 4TD

3 5 7 9 10 8 6 4

Papers used by John Blake Publishing are natural, recyclable products made from
wood grown in sustainable forests. The manufacturing processes conform to the
environmental regulations of the country of origin.

To *the memories of:*

Damilola Taylor, aged 11, murdered 27 November 2000;
Letisha Shakespeare, 17, and Charlene Ellis,
18, murdered 2 January 2003;
And Gary Newlove, 47, murdered 10 August 2007.

Contents

	Prologue	ix
	Introduction	xvii
1	Early British Gangs	1
2	The Brothers Gunn	13
3	Goldfinger – Mr Kenneth James Noye	35
4	The Kray Brothers	61
5	The Richardsons	107
6	Thomas 'Tam' McGraw and the Scottish Gangs	131
7	The Essex Boys	151
8	The Adams Family	165
9	The Wembley Mob	177
10	Bert Wickstead – Gangbuster	185
11	The Securitas Crew	193
12	The Great Train Robbers	213
13	Street Gangs UK	229
14	Triads UK	251
15	Our Journey Through Gangland UK	259

Prologue

If this book does not wake Britain up, nothing will, for it has been researched and written while gang-related crime in the UK has reached epidemic proportions to become a social disease. Indeed, we are suffering a global pandemic and, like any deadly virus, it causes suffering, death and destruction on a massive scale, in which the un-inoculated suffer the worst. The cause is gangland crime, and it is here to stay in the UK, for there is no current antidote.

The incubation of this social disease goes back a century or more and, despite the warnings, the writing was always on the wall. Ever resourceful law enforcement agencies across the world have been more than eager to stamp it out. There have *always* been a handful of 'bent' coppers to be 'bought' by the gang masters; the majority of police officers, though, are genuinely dedicated to 'protect and serve'.

'Hamstrung' is the word to describe law enforcement

today in the agencies' fight against the criminal underworld and, wherever one looks, the problem is always the same – lack of social commitment by government, who offers mealy-mouthed promises to tighten up on gang-related crime. This approach is merely window-dressing whose sole aim is to appease the populace when votes are required. The truth is that police forces up and down the country are shackled by lack of funding, overtime restrictions, top-heavy civilian management – and they are managed by pen-pushers and penny-counters who do nothing but extract valuable financial resources from an already restricted law enforcement budget.

At the time of writing, the present Home Secretary, Jacqui Smith, is planning to slash the numbers of British policemen and women by some 12,000 officers; British police are fighting over decent pay scales; British prisons have become so overcrowded that magistrates and judges are being 'advised' not to send anyone, other than the most serious of offenders, to jail. And current Government figures show that four out of five people convicted of carrying knives are not being sent to prison.

Until now, guidelines have suggested that a high-level community order should be imposed on those caught and convicted of carrying knives – the weapon of choice for wannabe gangsters. Other options are to impose a fine of up to £1,000 or sentence the offender to up to 12 weeks' custody. But, according to 'new' guidelines issued by the Lord Chief Justice on 20 February 2008, yobs who slash victims with a knife could receive no more than a community service order; new advice issued to the judiciary said that an offender who carries out a common assault with a weapon should *not* necessarily be handed more than a community sentence.

In Hampshire, a total of 160 people were found guilty of possessing a blade when they appeared before magistrates in the county in 2006, but only 29 of them were sent to prison, according to Ministry of Justice figures. And this comes *after* figures were released showing the number of people convicted of carrying a knife in the county rocketing by 65 per cent compared with the previous decade. In all courts, a total of 37 people, aged between 10–17, were convicted of carrying knives in Hampshire in 2006, up from 33 in 2005. And that's just Hampshire… what about the real, hardcore counties, towns and cities?

The writing on the wall? Today, following the guidelines of their American counterparts in gangland crime, many British inner-city gangs mark the territorial boundaries of their turf with graffiti – a bit like street dogs pissing their mark against a pub wall. But the Government has done *exactly* that, too! This Government, along with previous governments, has consistently failed to address the social disease that is street crime – which inevitably leads many of the so-called 'shot-callers' into organised crime. Street crime is, and has always been, the breeding ground of many of the characters featured throughout this book.

Most of the 'big-time' gangsters in this book would pour scorn on the scum who infest our streets today. Many of those from the 'old school' would give the young street hooligans the thrashing of their lives if they overstepped the mark. The Krays, the Richardsons, the likes of Kenny Noye… they would take these yobs and chavs and give them a lesson in the subtle art of 'social communication' that they would never forget, starting with, 'Don't piss in your own backyard.'

But the message from the 'official' graffiti – the message sent out to youngsters today from Government, and now the judiciary – is that street crime, and young gang crime, *does* pay.

I do not think that there could be anyone above the age of consent in the UK who does not recognise the name Anthony Edward 'Tony' Martin. A small-holder, after being plagued by burglars at his farm in Norfolk, on the night of 20 August 1999, struck back at his assailants using lethal force.

Two yobs, persistent burglars the pair of them, broke in and were surprised by Tony who held a shotgun. Brendon Fearon, 29, and Fred Barras, 16, attempted to flee, being the gutless cowards they were, both suffering gunshot injuries. Fearon was shot in the leg, Barras fatally in the back. A third accomplice, 33-year-old Darren Bark, drove off in the getaway car. All from Newark-on-Trent, Fearon was sentenced to three years in prison, and Bark to 30 months, with an additional 12 months arising from previous offences.

On 23 August 1999, Martin was charged with the murder of Barras, and the attempted murder of Fearon – wounding with intent to cause injury to Fearon, and possessing a firearm with intent to endanger life. Tony Martin was given a mandatory life sentence.

The case became a *cause célèbre* for some as a result of Tony shooting the two burglars. The issue attracted considerable media interest and polarised opinion in the UK to a greater degree than usual. To some, he is seen as trigger-happy and unstable, who wilfully killed a fleeing boy using an illegally held shotgun. To others – the majority of decent citizens anxious to protect their properties, as well as the lives of themselves and their families – he is a wronged man and an example of how the British legal system supposedly punishes victims and rewards criminals.

Over the years, Martin had been burgled several times, losing £6,000 worth of furniture. He complained to the police and complained about police inaction over the robberies. Some have expressed doubts that those incidents had, in fact, taken place at all. Police interests are arguably best served by this allegation. But can they always be trusted?

That was in 1999, and again the wheel has turned full circle, with a similar case occurring in Skelmersdale, Lancashire. On 17 February 2008, 25-year-old Liam Kilroe was on bail, and on the run, after having been charged with two robberies. A quick glance at his criminal CV makes one wonder what on earth the authorities were thinking when they let him back out on to the streets.

A 34-year-old storekeeper, Tony Singh, was attacked at 9.40 pm after a 13-hour day minding his corner shop. Kilroe appeared at the window of the businessman's Ford Focus car, smashed it with the handle of his knife and demanded the shop's takings. Mr Singh fought back and, during the struggle, the knife ended up embedded in Kilroe's chest. He died from this single wound. At the time of writing, Mr Singh was arrested and could have faced a possible murder charge.

Kilroe's CV puts this all into perspective: 1999 –

Assault; 1999 – Burglary; 2002 – Possession of Cannabis; 2002 – Possession of an offensive weapon; March 2002 – Robbery of a store in Skelmersdale, threatened a woman worker with a knife and stole £170.00; Robbery of a newsagent's in the same town, another female worker threatened, £50 taken; Robbery of a post office in the same town, again using threats of violence, £8,000 stolen; Sentenced to four years in a young offenders' institution; October 2006 – armed robbery at another Skelmersdale post office, struck the postmaster on the head with an imitation firearm and fled empty-handed; November 2006 – Armed robbery in Croston, Lancashire, threatened a woman with a handgun and stole £8,000; February 2008, dies after a bungled mugging.

Mr Singh's desperate act of self-defence came just a week after a gang of three youths were jailed for beating and kicking to death 47-year-old Garry Newlove, a father of three who confronted them while they were smashing up his wife's car on 10 August 2007.

Recidivist offender Adam Swellings, 19, Stephen Sorton, 17, and Jordan Cunliffe, 16, were found guilty of murder at Chester Crown Court. Two youths, aged 15 and 17, were acquitted. Later, as the killers faced inevitable life sentences, Mrs Helen Newlove said it was 'a shock' to have learned of the release on bail of Swellings on 10 August 2007 – the day her husband died.

Helen added, 'We knew Swellings had previous convictions, but it was a shock to hear he had been released that day. I'm absolutely disgusted. These magistrates, it's unbelievable. They let him out and they walk the streets. He's not taken a blind bit of notice of the conditions of bail. He's gone out, got drunk and taken drugs and my husband has been left dead... Until this Government puts into place an effective deterrent, the youths of today know all too well they can play the system and get away with it. As far as I'm concerned, life should mean life. After all, the tariff for murder is mandatory, but why, as the justice system does not uphold this sentence?'

The gang roamed the streets drunk on cheap, strong cider and high on cannabis looking for trouble. More often than not, they found it. They threatened anyone who crossed their paths and terrorised a young schoolgirl. She told how Swellings – nicknamed Swellhead – said he would kill her.

Another local resident, electrician Steve Ormerod was subjected to an almost identical attack that had left Garry Newlove dead. They knocked him to the ground and kicked him repeatedly. On the night they murdered Garry, they were 'bladdered' on booze. Stephen Sorton alone had downed around ten bottles of Stella Artois and a 3-litre bottle of cider.

The official police response to all of this? 'Local officers are frustrated because they do not have the time, the resources or the infrastructure to provide the support we would like to give residents.'

Excuse the language, but it is a fucking disgrace.

Introduction

'Gil. You've got to liven him up, put the fear of
God into him, mate, and he knows it's only down to
you that he's walking about and breathing fresh air.'

TERRENCE 'TERRY' ADAMS, TO HIS ENFORCER,
GILBERT WYNTER MI5 TAPES (1997)

According to a 2006 report published by the Home
Office, almost half-a-million British youngsters belong
to teenage gangs. The fear is that some youngsters could
graduate to the adult gangs involved in drug-dealing and
serious theft found in most major cities and members of
gangs were far more likely than other youths to have
been expelled from school, to have friends who have
been in trouble with the police and to be regularly
drunk. Today, in a society where cans of lager can be
cheaper than bottled water, many of Britain's youth have
a bleak future.

Current statistics show that almost half-a-million
youngsters regularly break the law and intimidate their

communities. Many have taken illegal drugs, carry weapons and have been involved in serious violence, as well as vandalising property and frightening passers-by. Indeed, with an already over-stretched police force, and a criminal justice system reluctant to incarcerate young offenders, aligned with an overcrowded penal system, the rule of law in our society is seriously under threat.

More than a third of youths have committed at least one serious offence – including assault, burglary, mugging, stealing a car or selling hard drugs. Nearly two-thirds have committed a serious offence of some sort; more than a quarter have committed a criminal offence; and more than a quarter have committed a series of crimes. One in eight carries a knife, underlining fears over increasing numbers of stabbings on Britain's streets but, unlike the USA, only one in a hundred have carried a gun. Illegal drugs have been taken by 45 per cent, while 11 per cent have used a Class A substance such as heroin, crack or cocaine. Four in ten gang members said they had threatened or frightened victims, 29 per cent had used force or violence, 36 per cent had written graffiti and 31 per cent had vandalised property. These are the serious gangsters of tomorrow.

The average gang was found to have about 15 members, making them a formidable and intimidating force on any street. Similar numbers of girls and boys are involved in gangs, with 14 or 15 being the prime ages for membership. About half were mainly male, 40 per cent comprised both sexes, and 10 per cent were all or mainly female. 60 per cent were all white, 31 per cent were racially mixed, 5 per cent were Asian-only and 3 per cent black only. A third said their group had a name. Almost

40 per cent had a leader, and 15 per cent had rules for members. Almost 90 per cent had a specific place – such as a park, street corner or square – where they hung out.

The Home Office has determined gang membership to be more common among youths from less affluent families and, to a lesser degree, among those not living with both parents. It was also discovered that youngsters were often prompted to join gangs after they had become victims of crime themselves. But this is nothing new. As we shall learn from the older criminals and gangsters featured throughout this book, their formative years and social imprinting was exactly the same as the modern-day hooligan, so no surprises there.

One 21-year-old thug has said that 'being in a gang means something. You matter if you got a gang... you're important. You look after each other.' Gang life came to an end for this youth six years ago when he was placed in a young offenders' institution for murder.

It would be fair for the reader to ask at this point a question along the lines of: 'So, what has all this got do with a book called *Gangland UK*?' Well, it has everything to do with such a book because the facts contained in these pages should send out a clear message to every parent whose children are gravitating towards gang-related crime. Every single gangster or robber featured within these pages has come undone. Many have been murdered. Most have been imprisoned for long periods of time, and a good few are locked away for the rest of their lives. So, the gangsters are not role models in any shape or form for the youths of today.

Many look back at the Krays with some form of reverence, but this book exposes them for what they truly were and, compared with other criminals featured here, they were not that 'big-time' after all – unless one imagines that walking into a pub and blasting a man's head off in cold blood to be something of a social achievement.

Today, we live in a society where a delinquent regards an ASBO as a badge of honour, and something to be proud of. In most inner-city areas, a significant number amount of council housing and state benefits are handed out willy-nilly to bone-idle parents who are too lazy to pry themselves away from their plasma TVs; their kids run the streets, out 'til all hours, keeping boredom at bay through petty crime and generally making a nuisance of themselves until, eventually, they fall foul of the law. Do the parents care? Some do, but in many cases, not at all. And the same can be said of all the parents of the criminals featured in *Gangland UK*.

I would suggest that every mature, old-fashioned crook who is mentioned in this book might give the kids of today a little hard advice: 'Sonny, you little shit, crime just don't pay… ' but let's hear it straight from the horse's mouth – from the villains and gangsters themselves.

1

Early British Gangs

'*I am the porter that was barbarously slain in Fleet Street... by the Mohocks and Hawkubites was I slain, then they laid violent hands upon me. They put their hook into my mouth, they divided my nostrils asunder, they sent me, as they thought, to my long home, but now I am returned again to foretell their destruction.*'

REVEREND DIVINE IN THE PAMPHLET CALLED *THE SPIRIT* (C1715)

Gangs have been a fairly consistent feature of the urban landscape of Britain. In the 17th century, British gangs routinely vandalised urban areas, were territorial, and were involved in violent conflict with other gangs. From time immemorial, wherever there have been large populations of people, there have always been groups of ill-doers who prey on the law-abiding and innocent. In the memorable words of historian Christopher Hill: 'The 17th century lived in terror of the tramp.'

The Mohocks was such a gang that brought mayhem

to the streets and alleyways of London during the early 18th century. Taking their name from the Mohawk native American Indian tribe, they attacked men and women, disfiguring their male victims and sexually assaulting the females.

The Mohawks (originally meaning 'man-eaters') were the native people of New York, but how a bunch of British thugs adopted their name in the 18th century is anyone's guess. Today, the Mohawk, or Mohican, is a hairstyle which consists of shaving either side of one's head, leaving a strip of long hair down the middle.

The gang was also known as the 'young bloods', which was later shortened to 'bloods'. This name is possibly the origin of the British sense of the adjective 'bloody', which was not considered particularly impolite until that time. However, while they entertained themselves by cutting off noses, hands and inflicting all manner of pain and suffering on others, they were claimed by many to be 'young gentlemen' because they didn't rob anyone. Matters came to a head in 1712, when a bounty of £100 – a huge sum in those days – was issued by the Royal Court for their capture.

On the Monday, 6 June 1712, Sir Mark Cole and three other gentlemen were tried at the Old Bailey for riot, assault and beating the watch (the forerunners of our police force). A paper of the day asserted that these were 'Mohocks', that they had attacked the watch in Devereux Street, slit two persons' noses, cut a woman in the arm with a penknife so as to disable her for life, rolled a woman in a tub down Snow Hill, misused other women in a barbarous manner by setting them on their heads, and overset several coaches and chairs with short clubs, loaded with lead at both ends, expressly made for the purpose.

In their defence, the prisoners denied that they were Mohocks, alleging that they were 'Scourers' and had gone out, with a magistrate's sanction, to scour the streets, arrest Mohocks and other offenders, and deliver them up to justice. On the night in question, they had attacked a notorious gambling-house, and taken 13 men out of it. While engaged in this meritorious activity, they learned that the Mohocks were in Devereux Street, and on proceeding there found three men desperately wounded, lying on the ground; they were then attacked by the watch, and felt bound to defend themselves. As an instance of the gross misconduct of the watch, it was further alleged that they, the watch, had on the same night actually presumed to arrest a peer of the realm, Lord Hitchinbroke, and had latterly adopted the practice of doing their rounds by night accompanied by savage dogs. The jury, however, in spite of this defence, returned a verdict of guilty. The judge fined the culprits the sum of three shillings and fourpence each.

Among other gangs – notably the Muns, the Tityré Tūs, the Hectors, the Scourers and the Nickers – were the Hawkubites, who actually preceeded the Mohocks by several years, beating up women, children, watchmen and old men in London's streets after dark during the reign of Queen Anne. Reverend Divine's pamphlet of around 1715 clearly expresses the threat from such a gang:

'From Mohock and from Hawkubite,
Good Lord, deliver me!
Who wander through the streets at night,

Committing cruelty.
They slash our sons with bloody knives,
And on our daughters fall;
And if they murder not our wives,
We have good luck withal.
Coaches and chairs they overturn,
Nay, carts most easily;
Therefore from Gog and Magog,
Good Lord, deliver me!'

Kent has always proved to be a fertile breeding ground for gangsters, and was the home of a notorious gang who started out as soldiers, having returned home penniless after the Napoleonic Wars. They started smuggling around 1817, and perhaps well before that date. The route was across the English Channel between Boulogne and the beach at Sandgate. Similar landings were at Deal and St Margaret's Bay, north of Dover.

Known as The Aldington Gang, they roamed the Romney Marshes, and their headquarters and drop-off for their contraband was The Walnut Tree Inn, which still stands today.

Built during the reign of Richard II (1377–99), the inn started life as no more than a timber-framed, wattle-and-daub hut with a thatched roof. In the mid-15th century, a small bedroom was added at a higher level – reached by ladder – and, by the turn of the 16th century, a number of improvements had been carried out and the main dwelling was enlarged. Ale was brewed there in the 17th century and a licence to sell ales and ciders was granted. High up on the southern side of the pub is a small window, through which the gang would shine a signal to their confederates on Aldington Knoll. The ghost of George Ransley, a bygone smuggler, is reputed to haunt the inn and many strange happenings have been reported.

The Aldington Gang was probably the last major gang to have existed in Kent. It is believed that they were also known as The Blues on account of the colour of the clothing they wore and the blue flares used for signalling.

In February 1821, 250 highly organised men took part in unloading a galley laden with spirits, tobacco and salt. Three groups of smugglers had gathered; one to unload and transport the cargo, and two groups of 'batmen'. Batmen stood guard when a run was taking place to fight off anyone who tried to interfere, and they drew their name from the long clubs, or bats, they carried. They were spotted by a few local blockade men, as the main blockade force of Customs & Excise had been lured away by the smugglers.

The incident became known as the 'Battle of Brookland'. It took place between Camber and Dungeness where the smuggling party was spotted by the Watch House at Camber and a fight took place over Walland Marsh. Although the gang were successful in unloading the goods, they were harried right across the marshes until they reached Brookland, where the smugglers turned and fought back. It was a bloody business. Five men were killed in the fighting, twenty or so more were wounded. In the confusion of the battle, the gang's leader, Cephas Quested, turned to a man close by, handed him a musket and ordered him to 'blow an officer's brains out'.

Unfortunately for Quested, who was out of his mind on drink, he handed the weapon to a Customs & Excise midshipman who immediately turned the gun on Quested and arrested him. After being sentenced, Quested was taken to Newgate and hanged for his activities on Wednesday, 4 July 1821.

Another leader of this gang was a George Ransley. Ransley was certainly known for his organisational abilities, and some say he was a giant of a man, standing well over 6ft in his socks. Others argue that he was hardly more than 5ft. Some say he was a likeable rogue; others lived in absolute fear of him. No one will ever really know the truth, but there was no doubt that he could be as ruthless as he needed to be to achieve his ends.

Ransley was born in 1792 at Ruckinge, a small village founded in Saxon times, which lies on the northern edge of Romney Marsh. He started work as a ploughman, then a carter, all admirable work when he wasn't servicing his wife, Elizabeth, which was pretty frequently by all accounts. They had ten children. However, the Ransleys were not quite the law-abiding citizens they claimed to be. The local churchyard contains a simple grave to mark the last resting place of two of George's brothers, convicted of highway robbery in 1800. They were hanged from a gibbet on nearby Penenden Heath.

For his part in the scheme of things, the story goes that George found a stash of spirits hidden by smugglers and, with the proceeds of the sale, bought his house The Bourne Tap from where he frequently sold the spirits he later landed. Another place frequented by the gang at this time was an Augustine priory in Bilsington – still standing today – which was actually used as a store house.

Ransley took over the gang of smugglers after the Battle of Brookland. He employed a doctor, with an allowance paid to a man's family if he was ill. It was a policy that avoided the capture of injured men by the Revenue's forces and helped to ensure loyalty.

The success of smuggling, or any gang-related business, is dependent upon the good will of the local people, and the gang started to lose this special relationship as they extended their ruthless activities beyond that of the publicly acceptable crime of smuggling and turned on rural communities. In fact, several of the gang became burglars, and this, in turn, drew the attention of the Bow Street Runners – the nearest thing to a police force at the time.

In July 1826, the gang was caught on the beach at Dover and a midshipman, Richard Morgan, who was a quartermaster with the blockade, was killed. He was much liked in Dover, and he had spotted the gang trying to run the cargo ashore. After firing a warning shot, the gang turned on him, resulting in his death and the wounding of a seaman who was with him.

The shooting shocked the local community. It was a foolish act which brought about the downfall of George Ransley. A reward was offered for information and several people eventually claimed a part of it.

In October 1826, Ransley and seven others were arrested at Aldington by the Bow Street Runners on suspicion of murder but, as the killing took place in the dark, there were no positive eyewitnesses as to who had squeezed the trigger. Eventually, a total of 19 men were captured and stood trial at Maidstone Assizes in January 1827. They were all found guilty of charges that carried the death penalty, but their lawyer, described as a 'local gentleman from Maidstone', managed to get their sentences commuted to transportation. George Ransley was shipped out to Tasmania, where his knowledge of farming stood him in good stead. As a reward for good behaviour, his wife and ten children were allowed to sail out and join him. After being granted a pardon, he started farming 500 acres at River Plenty, Hobart. At the then ripe old age of 77, he passed away at New Norfolk on 25 October 1856. His wife, Elizabeth, survived him by just a few years, dying aged 76. A fascinating insight into this former smuggler's family tree can be found at: http://sharjarv.tripod.com/gedfiles/gen01344.html.

There is always an edge of romanticism attached to tales of smuggling gangs from days of yore and, although an extremely brutal gang with a brutal reputation to match, the Aldington Gang were not, it is claimed, without a sense of humour. One Revenue officer who was blindfolded and had his legs bound was told he was to be thrown over a cliff. He managed to cling on to tufts of grass as he fell and hung with his legs dangling in the air for some time. It was not until his blindfold slipped that he realised that his feet were a matter of inches above the ground. The 'cliff' was only 7ft high! And there is a story that, as a result of a fight *between* gang members one night, one of the gang was murdered and the body disposed of down a well at the side of an inn. It is said on some nights the sounds of scuffling and a body being dragged outside can still be heard – but maybe that's just the drink talking.

*

The Nottingham suburb of Bestwood conjures up a pot-pourri of images – the medieval history of Bestwood Park, the industrial history of the quaintly named Papplewick Pumping Station, the ancient colliery, as well as the sometimes troubled housing estate at Bestwood.

And Bestwood has a *real* story to tell. Its principal characters include Charles II and his somewhat empty-headed actress lover, Nell Gwynne; the founder of the Raleigh cycle company, Sir Frank Bowden; and richly embroidered CV of borough engineer, the splendidly named Marriott Ogle Tarbotton, whose remarkable achievements include building Nottingham's aforesaid Papplewick Pumping Station.

Ogle stands out as a man who laboured day and night with fevered enthusiasm on the tricky subject of the disposal of human waste, to the extent that he designed and built the city's first sewerage system. It was a matter that so consumed him that he passed away, exhausted, aged 52, within weeks of its completion.

And who could forget, of course, our legendary Robin Hood and his Merry Men. Supposed residents of nearby Sherwood Forest, they allegedly stole from the rich to give to the poor, yet Mr Hood and his band of followers turned out not quite to be what the myth would have us believe – they were true rascals indeed!

Despite the world renown of Nottinghamshire's most idolised gang leader, one cannot find a single reference to Robin Hood – a.k.a. Robin of Loxley – in any criminal records, past or present. We don't know where he was born or where he is buried, suggesting that he may never have been born at all. We don't know what he looked like – tall, short, fat or thin – the colour of his eyes, his hair, or whether he was straight or gay. Hollywood would have us believe that he wore a daringly short, rather close-fitting waisted Lincoln green jacket and skin-tight tights, as well as a rakish cap, sporting a 2-metre ostrich plume tucked into the headband, and footwear that any self-respecting Shakespearian actor would die for – dun-coloured suede booties, or thigh-high, black leather boots.

In consequence, there remains an enormous amount that we can't verify about Mr Hood. We don't know how many people he robbed, nor how many people he and his band of followers killed. We don't even know his real name. His life, according to many notable authorities, bore a striking similarity to accounts of the life of one Fulk FitzWarin, a Norman nobleman who was disinherited and became an outlaw and an enemy of the tight-fisted King John of England, who argued with the Pope, disputed with his own barons, and died from dysentery, most likely brought upon from a surfeit of poisoned ale, peaches and plums.

In the oldest of legends, Robin's enemy, due to his role as a bandit, was the Sheriff of Nottingham. But in later versions (if any one of them are based on a shred of fact) the sheriff is despotic and gravely abuses his position, appropriating land, levying excessive taxation, and persecuting the poor – not unlike some senior local government officials today.

In some versions, Robin is a yeoman. In later versions, he is described as the nobleman, Earl of Loxley, who, like the venerable Fulk above, was unjustly deprived of his lands.

In other stories, Robin had served in the Crusades – although no one has defined precisely, somewhat conveniently, which specific Crusade this was – and, upon returning to England, he discovered that everything he owned had been pillaged by the dastardly sheriff.

If this was the case, it's not hard to see that Robin

might be excused his dastardly conduct – he'd given up his day job, borrowed a substantial amount of money to buy a first-rate steed, floated across the English Channel in nothing short of a large coffin, and ridden 1,000 miles deep into the Byzantine Empire to fight a war that for centuries seemed to have no beginning and, at that time, no foreseeable end. Exhausted, Robin would have ridden all the way back to France, re-negotiated the dangerous English Channel to Dover, then dragged his emaciated horse 251 miles north to his Nottingham wattle-walled cottage. Upon his arrival, he would have found his home empty, having been pillaged by pals of the local sheriff.

So, in some tales, Robin is the champion of the people, fighting against corrupt officials and the oppressive order that protects them, while, in others, he is an arrogant and headstrong rebel, who delighted in bloodshed, cruelly slaughtering and beheading his victims.

Today, Nottingham has another so-called Robin Hood with his own band of Merry Men – a vicious outfit who will never be offered star billing as 'principal characters' on Nottingham's official website. The faces that stare out at us, courtesy of a police charge room camera, are hooded-eyed Colin Gunn, and his brother, David, a ruthless crew who brought terror and mayhem to Nottingham by performing their civic duty carrying out murder, robberies, burglaries and beatings – on men and women – as well as torture, extortion, racial abuse, prostitution, drug distribution and the corruption of police officers. Single-handedly, they turned Bestwood into a place where no decent person dared to live.

The Sheriff of Nottingham in this case is replaced by a disconsolate Chief Constable, Steve Green, whose officers – Charles Fletcher and Philip Parr – had been lured knee-deep into corruption and conspiracy to the degree that that they received 7 years and 12 months in prison respectively. At his wits' end, Mr Green eventually set up a band of 'Untouchables' to snare the gang that held the local populace in their iron grip of fear.

In their early years, the Gunn brothers might have modelled themselves on Robin Hood. Maybe they identified themselves with the Kray brothers. But, in reality, what we do find are two completely nasty pieces of work who were prepared to make nightmares come true.

2

The Brothers Gunn

*'There are a lot of bodies – dead and alive –
that have the hallmark of Colin Gunn...they shoot
someone just to get respect.'*
A SENIOR NOTTINGHAMSHIRE POLICE OFFICER

The Gunn brothers grew up in Bestwood, one of the
many sprawling, low-rise estates in Nottingham. Built
in the late 1940s and early 1950s, it once was one of the
city's nicest areas. With its modern, three-bedroomed
houses and inside toilets, you were considered lucky if
you moved there.

Not any more. Even though the Gunns are now
behind bars, Bestwood residents still live in fear of the
two men, and many on the estate refuse even to mention
their name.

In their youth, the brothers were model kids, even
featuring in a church magazine for chasing and catching
a purse-snatcher. Then things changed. Their teenage
years were littered with criminal convictions, including

violence, burglary and handling offences. In their early twenties, their 'bling-bling' jewellery and expensive cars were a magnet for every disaffected youth in the area as they bragged about the millions they had stashed away. Colin Gunn drove a car with the number plate 'POWER'.

Gun crime had arrived in Nottingham in early 2000, some time before the Gunns arrived on the scene and, in keeping with many other cities, it was predominantly a phenomenon of the African-Caribbean community. But by the end of 2002 and into 2003, it was becoming increasingly clear to police fighting on that front that there was another dynamic in the city, one that was causing more insidious problems –gun crime was emerging in the white community, and the Gunns were at the heart of it.

Chief Constable Green said, 'We increasingly formed the view that in the centre of all that was Colin Gunn. I think that led us to conclude that we would never resolve the gun crime until we confronted the Colin Gunn problem.' And what a problem it was turning out to be.

The Gunns had soon caused Nottingham to be nominated fourth place in the country's gun crime league and, if we are to give the brothers any credit, the statistics are impressive and speak for themselves. In 2002, at the height of their notoriety, 54 guns were fired, causing 36 injuries. After the Gunns' arrest in 2005, the figure plummeted to 11 guns fired and just 5 injuries.

In 2002, there were 21 murders involving firearms in Nottingham; that equates to 24 per cent, compared with 8 per cent nationally. After their arrest, the tally dropped to 14 homicides, of which 0 per cent were gun related, compared with 7 per cent nationally.

During the police operation to capture the men, £10.1 million in assets were seized, along with a staggering £73.5 million in drugs. Police carried out more than 80 operations and arrested more than 100 people to get to Colin Gunn, who was by now serving 35 years after being convicted, in June 2006, of the murder of an elderly couple whose son had killed a friend of the Gunn family.

41-year-old Gunn, a shaven-headed bodybuilder, was charged with conspiracy to commit misconduct in a public office. Police officers Charles Fletcher and Philip Parr were also found guilty of conspiracy to pervert the course of justice.

Gunn and his gang (including his brother, David, who also has an extensive history of serious crime, and is now serving 8.5 years for conspiracy to supply amphetamines) based their operations on the Bestwood Estate. They ruled by fear and intimidation. They were involved in selling drugs and guns, torturing and murdering those who crossed them.

The Gunns even threatened senior police officers with death, and they paraded their wealth, boasting of their millions to unemployed teenagers. But police found it impossible to implicate Colin Gunn as the mastermind as he rarely got his hands dirty by ordering his henchmen to carry out beatings and murders. Detectives also suspect that Colin had been involved in many murders and punishment beatings on both men and women.

Police also believe that Colin Gunn ordered the shooting of a social worker who dared to give evidence against his gang, but the cops have no evidence to prove those allegations. On Monday, 17 May 2004, 50-year-old Derrick Senior was shot after he helped to convict a gang that had racially abused and beaten him in the Lord Nelson pub in Bulwell, including tearing out one of his dreadlocks. Senior, who should have sought police protection, but didn't, claimed that he would not give in to criminals. He was shot several times as he reversed out of his drive on the Heathfield Estate three days after his abusers had been convicted.

Senior had been having a drink with a female friend when a group of drunken men started picking on her. When he went to her defence, they turned on him, dragging him into a corner of the pub by his dreadlocks. He suffered a fractured eye socket and a broken rib during the attack. He was racially abused and the drunks paraded the dreadlock around as a 'trophy'. Robert Watson, 25, Joseph Graham, 23, Lee Marshall, 24, and John McNee, 24, were jailed for racially-aggravated assault.

On the day of the attempted murder of Mr Senior, John McSally, 50, a gangland 'enforcer' for Colin Gunn, rode up on his motorbike and opened fire, yelling, 'You grassing bastard.' Senior was hit in the chest, stomach and legs, but survived after playing dead, slumping over the steering wheel of his car.

On Friday, 1 June 2007, McSally, of Plaza Gardens, Basford, was jailed for life for shooting Senior. Gunn had offered Senior a 'substantial amount of money' to withdraw his testimony against the four drunks, but he refused. Sentencing McSally, Mr Justice Pitchers said, 'You are an incredibly dangerous man – ready, for money, to kill without a second thought.' Ordering McSally to serve at least 35 years, the judge added, 'Even by the warped standards of those who enforce their will by violence, these were evil offences.'

McSally, allegedly acting on Gunn's orders, had also shot gang associate 46-year-old Patrick Marshall outside the Park Tavern pub in Basford on 8 February 2004. Marshall was Colin Gunn's odd-job man, but he had got on the wrong side of him after going on a £100,000 cocaine run to Lincolnshire without his boss's permission. Then word spread around that Marshall was trying to get a gun to shoot associate 'Scotch Al' after a feud. Marshall contacted McSally, who found a gun and went to meet him. But instead of handing him the weapon, McSally blasted him in the head in the pub car park. The getaway car was recovered by police and had Colin Gunn's overdue phone bill inside it and three photographs of his brother, David. McSally is now serving a life sentence for this offence. His co-accused, Craig McKay, denied any involvement in the shooting and was cleared by a jury.

Today, tales abound on the Bestwood Estate about Gunn's ruthless streak. It is said that he once broke the arms of one of his own men after he drove badly and 'disrespected' him. People were shot through their hands for carrying out burglaries on the estate without his permission. People moving to the estate were visited and told that Gunn ruled the roost. Many were too scared to stay.

A senior officer said, 'These are not normal villains. They would shoot someone to get respect. They are extremely vicious and brutal people. The smallest slight to Gunn would end with a severe beating. Some of his guys are just psychopaths. There are a lot of bodies –

dead and alive – that have the hallmark of Colin Gunn. I don't think there is anyone who is grateful for ever having met him.'

Police realised that, if they were to bring down Gunn, they would have to establish a new way of working. Knowing that at some stage they would come across corruption in the force, they set up operations within operations, like a Russian *matrioshka* doll. These were kept so secret that officers outside the squad had no idea that they existed.

To capture Gunn, officers identified his lieutenants, thugs and drug-dealers and started at the bottom, taking them out one by one, piling the pressure on Gunn to encourage him to get involved personally. Chief Constable Green told his men, 'Shake these criminals to the core and lock them away in any way that is ethical and lawful.' The main operation was called Stealth, and beneath that, cloaked in secrecy, was Utah, which had been set up solely to catch Gunn.

It soon became known that Gunn was heavily involved in the murders of 55-year-old textile worker John Stirland and his wife, Joan, 53, who were tracked down and murdered at their seaside bungalow in Trusthorpe, Lincolnshire, on 8 August 2004. Mrs Stirland's 22-year-old son, Michael O'Brien, had shot dead an innocent man outside a Nottingham pub in 2003. The victim, 22-year-old shop-fitter Marvyn Bradshaw, was a friend of Jamie Gunn, Colin's nephew. It later emerged that Bradshaw, a family man with no links to crime or gangs, was killed after being mistaken for someone who had assaulted O'Brien in The Sporting Chance pub with an ashtray.

There had been a 'lock-in' during the night in

question. Customers were inside enjoying a late drink and, at the door, a young man was refused admission. He was Michael 'JJ' O'Brien. He had already been turned away from two other pubs for wearing trainers and a tracksuit top.

A scuffle took place and O'Brien, a small-time drug-dealer, who had already served jail time, now the worse for wear with drink, was hit in the face with an ashtray. O'Brien, who was with his mate, 31-year-old Gary Salmon, retreated to Salmon's flat nearby, where they changed into dark clothes and balaclavas. They also picked up a single-barrel shotgun to commit what was to become the seventeenth shooting in Nottingham that August.

Back at The Sporting Chance, four men left the premises and climbed into a silver Renault Laguna car. At the wheel was Marvyn Bradshaw. Sitting beside him was his longtime friend Jamie Gunn. As the car edged out of the car park, a shot was discharged and Bradshaw, hit in the head, slumped sideways. He died later in hospital; having been shot from such close range, death from the head wound was inevitable. The lad had most certainly been killed in a case of mistaken identity. Indeed, neither he nor Jamie Gunn had been involved in the ashtray incident.

After the shooting, the two men returned to Salmon's flat where O'Brien boasted to two teenage girls, 'I shot him... he was a bad man.' Scared to death, they contacted the police. The loud-mouthed O'Brien's bragging proved to be his downfall, and that of his parents, too.

As the result of the shooting, the Stirlands were forced to flee their Nottingham home after several shots were fired into their living room. Thugs had warned the couple to leave the area or 'stay and face the consequences'. They immediately packed up a few possessions and left without telling friends where they were going.

First, they moved to Humberside, but it is believed that they may have been forced, once again urgently, to abandon their new home because they turned up at a second address, a bungalow in Trusthorpe, on the Lincolnshire coast, in December 2003, with only the clothes they stood up in.

In April 2004, they told Nottinghamshire Police that they had moved and senior officers in Lincolnshire were made aware of the problems and their background.

In July, their son, 23-year-old O'Brien, was sentenced to life for murdering Marvyn Bradshaw. O'Brien rubbed salt into the wounds of the dead man's parents, taunting them from the dock, 'I'm not bothered, I'm a bad boy. It means nothing to me. Your son looked like a doughnut with a big hole in his head. I know where you live.' Before being escorted away, he threw a beaker of water towards Mr and Mrs Bradshaw, screaming, 'I will do my time standing on my head.' Quite understandably, Colin Gunn was livid when he heard of this.

Three days later, 53-year-old Mrs Stirland rang Nottinghamshire Police to say that fresh threats had been made against her and her family. Lincolnshire Police were informed the next day. Despite this, when she rang Nottingham Police at 11.30am on Sunday to say that there had been a prowler in her garden the previous night, the police did not consider it immediately necessary to inform their neighbouring force. Instead, an officer Mrs Stirland knew rang her back at 2.00pm. After a seven-minute conversation, the officer called Lincolnshire Police to tell them of the prowler, but did not ask for a patrol car to drive past the bungalow. She did not want to call 999 because she didn't want police cars swooping on the house and alarming her neighbours.

Within minutes of speaking to the Nottinghamshire officer, and almost three hours after first reporting the prowler, the Stirlings were shot dead. Two men wearing blue boiler suits were seen in the vicinity of the murder scene. Witnesses described them walking or running away from the bungalow while a black Volkswagen Passat was parked nearby with its hazard lights flashing. The car was later found ablaze in a quiet country lane. The two men were spotted close by. The car had been stolen on 31 July, from Nottinghamshire.

Chief Constable Green said, 'The ruthlessness with which Gunn tracked the Stirlands down after they fled Nottingham was characteristic of a man who led a bloodthirsty and violent regime.'

But, the question now was: how had Gunn tracked down the Stirlands so quickly? A former Nottingham neighbour explained that the couple's rented address had become local knowledge in the city after a family friend, who lived on the same estate, accidentally met the Stirlands in Mablethorpe, just four miles from the bungalow.

Another rumour was that the couple's daughter had been followed when she visited her parents the day before they were killed. Or was it because, just two weeks before they were murdered, the couple took the risk to returning to Nottingham to attend the wedding of Mr Stirland's son, Lee, and his fiancée Adele?

More revelations were to follow. According to Nottingham residents, Mrs Stirland, a children's care nurse at the Queen's Medical Centre, had previously been heard in a Nottingham pub praising her convicted son. She told fellow drinkers that O'Brien had vowed to take revenge on the people who put him away, which would have done nothing to endear her, her husband and her mindless son to Mr Colin Gunn.

However, now the true facts can be revealed. In an effort to track down the Stirlands, Colin had contacted a former BT worker, Stephen Poundall, in a bid to find the couple's address. In turn, Poundall spoke with past colleagues, Anthony Kelly and Andrew Pickering, who ran a computer search. They found the address and passed it on to Poundall, although they had no idea why he wanted it. Kelly and Pickering later admitted computer misuse and were sacked by BT, as well as being handed down suspended jail sentences.

Aged just 19, Jamie Gunn never recovered from the shock of seeing his friend die and, a year later, on 2 August, just three weeks after O'Brien's conviction, he was found dead in his mother's bed by a younger brother and sister. Jamie had died of pneumonia. He had stopped eating and begun drinking heavily and his immune system was weakened. Jamie had died as surely as if O'Brien had killed him, too.

The Gunns decided to give Jamie a proper send off, and the funeral was as lavish as that of any Mafia family member. On Friday, 13 August 2004, 1,000 mourners descended on the hilltop surrounding the Arnold parish church of St Mary in Bulwell; 700 of them crammed into the 17th-century church, while another 300 stood in the drizzle outside. A horse-drawn, glass-sided hearse waited at the gate below, alongside two motor hearses bearing flowers, including huge wreaths saying 'Jamie', 'Brother' and 'Jim Bob'.

As crime writer James Cathcart reported for the *Nottingham Evening Post*, 'There were three of the most stretched kind of stretch limousines, plus three big funeral Daimlers, a convoy of bulky, dark 4x4s and a conspicuous black Mercedes two-seater... Hard-looking men with stubble for hair stood smoking and chatting quietly in the churchyard, their jackets straining across their shoulders. The style, as well as the scale of the funeral, would have suited a Kray brother, rather than a teenage bouncer unknown to the world outside Nottingham before his death... just a mile away, on Hucknell Road, a demolition team was tearing down the last recognisable traces of The Sporting Chance.'

Colin Gunn is now serving life for conspiracy to murder the Stirlands. His fellow plotters, Michael McNee and John Russell, will serve 95 years before they are considered for parole. After being sentenced on Friday, 30 June 2006, the verdict went down very badly among Gunn's supporters on the Bestwood Estate. That weekend, around 30 people started a mini-riot, setting fire to cars and causing £10,000 worth of damage.

Colin Gunn was also arrested in connection with the murder of Marian Bates, a 64-year-old Arnold parish jeweller, who was shot dead at point-blank range while shielding her daughter Xanthe from two crash-helmeted robbers at 1.30pm on Tuesday, 30 September 2003. Her bespectacled 67-year-old husband, Victor, picked up a fencing foil to try to protect his wife but was attacked with a crowbar. Wearing washing-up gloves, the men escaped with a pathetic haul of two rings, one pendant and three pairs of earrings worth £1,120.00.

Although Colin Gunn was never charged with any involvement in the raid on the couple's shop, his name has been linked to the investigation a number of times. It is thought that he feared he would be implicated immediately after the shooting and sought the services of corrupt trainee detective, Charles Fletcher, to find out what he could about the investigation less than 24 hours after Mrs Bates had been murdered.

Indeed, Gunn's common-law wife, Victoria Garfoot, had previously been stopped by police driving a maroon-coloured Peugeot in July 2003. She told police that the car belonged to Colin Gunn. Three months after that incident, the *very same* Peugeot was used as the getaway car for two gang members – 19-year-old Craig Moran and Dean Betton, 23, who were known associates of the Gunn clan and who were accomplices in the bungled raid on the Time Centre jewellers on Front Street.

Betton, from Broxtowe, and Moran, a Bestwood resident, were jailed for 13 years each for conspiring to rob the jewellery shop. Peter Williams, the teenager who accompanied the gunman into the Time Centre, was convicted of murder and jailed for life, with a minimum tariff of 22 years. Then aged 19, Williams had a string of convictions and should have been electronically tagged at the time of the raid – he hadn't been. Moran's girlfriend, Lisa Unwin, 23, from Bestwood, Nottingham, was found guilty of conspiring to pervert the course of justice, along with Moran, by providing him with a false alibi.

In describing the robbery to a jury, Victor Bates

explained that two men came into the shop, pointed a gun at him and pulled the trigger. At first, the pistol failed to fire, but a few moments later his wife was lying on the floor with a bullet in her chest.

'My wife moved forward quickly and stepped in between the gunman and my daughter, Xanthe, and the swine shot her in cold blood. He just shot her from about three feet – and she went down heavily... like a lump of bricks.'

Victor said that he tried to kill the intruder with a fencing foil he had hidden in the shop, but he failed. 'I was intent on killing him but he started whirling around like a Dervish and I couldn't get a clear shot at him. I would have made justice very summary if I could have. The other guy, who was small, whacked me on the wrist with the crowbar and then hit me in the head – and missed my eye by about an inch. I was dazed and went down stunned – he fractured my cheekbone and cut my face.'

Clearly now upset, Mr Bates added, 'I feel like a fool – when you are faced with a gun, you don't think about a prearranged act like falling on the floor and feigning a heart-attack. You blame yourself for not taking strict security provisions. I wanted to help my wife but I couldn't – I think I knew she was dead. She was a very well-known girl and very popular and hadn't got an enemy in the world – it makes it all the more frustrating that it should happen to her.'

The actual shooter of Marion Bates is widely believed to be young Gunn associate James Brodie, who has never been traced. He disappeared the day after the murder and is presumed dead, according to police. One theory is that Brodie, a heroin addict, was executed on the orders of

Colin Gunn within 48 hours of the murder for fear of him implicating those higher up the pecking order. Rumours abound as to how he met his grisly end, including tales of his body being dumped in sewage works or his remains fed to pigs on a north Nottinghamshire farm.

Police intelligence led a team of body-searchers to the Willows Fish Farm, Wanlip Road, Syston, Leicestershire, where divers and forensic specialists looked for clues. Police divers dredged a stretch of water, while a team of forensic archaeologists surveyed a pit of quicksand.

Barrie Simpson and his colleagues, who are more used to excavating mass graves in Iraq and the former Yugoslavia, used 'non-invasive methods' so that they didn't disturb the ground. Simpson, an honorary research fellow at the University of Birmingham, and part of a national network of academics called the Forensic Search Advisory Group, said, 'It [the ground] is like an underground room. Just as a fingerprint officer searches a room for fingerprints, we search for evidence like this. We specialise in the search, location and recovery of buried items. It could be a weapon, body or ransom money.'

Such ground-probing radar searches are so non-evasive they could even have uncovered part-buried footprints left at the time Brodie went missing, so Barrie Simpson and his team carefully made shallow probe holes on a bank surrounding the quicksand which were sniffed in turn by the dogs.

When nothing was found by lunchtime, the team moved to an area of woodland next to the fish farm entrance, where they looked for changes in the vegetation which would have indicated unnatural disturbance, and so might have suggested that something could have been buried underneath.

'A burial will affect how vegetation grows,' said Mr Simpson. 'Sometimes it increases, sometimes it decreases.'

The police found nothing, and today a £10,000 reward for information leading to the whereabouts of James Brodie remains uncollected. The reward, however, does not specify 'dead or alive'. Anyone with any information was (and at the time of writing, is) asked to contact police on 0115 844 6994, or call Crimestoppers anonymously on 0800 555 111.

By now, a joint investigation between the National Crime Squad and police professional standards department were tracking the Gunn gang's movements. Even PC Charles Fletcher and PC Phil Parr were being watched by a covert team.

When Colin Gunn was arrested, police found two A4 pieces of paper which he had absent-mindedly dumped in his mother's waste bin in Raymede Drive on the Bestwood Estate. They contained police intelligence about Gunn himself and cars he was linked to. The paperwork had to be secretly removed from the bin by DCI Ian Waterfield to keep the inquiry under wraps. The items were a direct link between Gunn and his middle-man, 33-year-old Jason Grocock. Crooked PC Fletcher had faxed intelligence reports from Radford Road Police Station to Grocock, then manager of Limeys discount clothes shop in Bridlesmith Gate, Nottingham. He then passed the inside intelligence to Gunn and others.

Trainee detective Charles Fletcher, 25, and Phillip Parr, 40, later admitted at Birmingham Crown Court to separately disclosing data on serious inquiries, including the details of the murder investigation of Marian Bates, to the Gunns. Fletcher also admitted two charges of conspiracy to pervert the course of justice.

Over a two-and-a-half year period, beginning in December 2002, Fletcher trawled police data bases to find information. He also sought information about the double murder of Joan and John Stirland. In return, the bent cop received discounts on designer suits from a Nottingham fashion store.

Grocock was convicted of conspiracy to commit misconduct in a public office and two further charges of conspiracy to pervert the course of justice. He received three years' imprisonment.

40-year-old David Barrett was convicted of two charges of conspiracy to commit misconduct in a public office and was sentenced to three years. Darren Peters, 38, and Javade Rashid, aged 40, were convicted of the same charge and were sentenced to four years and six months respectively, and a fifth person cannot be named for legal reasons.

Chief Constable Green said, 'When we put in place the operation to dismantle Gunn's empire we wanted to get justice for every victim of the evil of Colin Gunn. We haven't finished that quest for justice.'

And in March 2008 Colin Gunn's legal advisor indicated that his client's own quest for justice was not yet over. It was reported that Gunn intended to appeal against his convctions on the basis that his conversations with lawyers while in jail may have been bugged.

A Bestwood community leader, who does not want to be named, said, 'A church article is where the Gunns got this

Robin Hood reputation. They were once good guys, genuinely. But as time went on, they chose their paths, although even today the perception around here is that they are nice guys because they don't cause, or want, any trouble on their doorstep.'

As with the Krays in 1960s London, many residents say that the Gunns only hurt those who deserved it, but the truth is somewhat different. The reputation of Bestwood as a no-go for strangers has forced house prices down and it is populated by those who have been moved into council houses or cannot afford anywhere else.

The community leader said, 'The fear factor remains. A lot of people say he [Colin] would look after them. It's how the IRA operated. Gunn made sure crime was low so he could go about his business undetected and without police being around. A lot of people regarded him as a sort of Robin Hood character but then most of them had no idea he was involved in such serious stuff as murder. They will be shocked to find out and think his reputation will change.

'There is no doubt that he [Colin] is a nasty piece of work. The way he worked was that so much of the fear is fuelled by rumour and urban myth. There are rumours of people going missing. There have been rumours that Colin is coming out, that David has already been seen out and about. David is a different kettle of fish. You can at least talk to him. Colin has had a reputation for being a nutter... he hits you first then talks to you.

'Everyone is waiting to see what happens now there is a vacuum and there are a couple of families on the estate who people are looking at. But the Gunns have long arms and are still running the place through their associates, fuelling the fear with rumours that they are coming out.'

It is a very remote possibility that Colin Gunn will ever be released from prison. Since he was jailed, there has only been one fatal shooting in Nottingham – a result that has seen the city slip down the gun crime league. 'Undoubtedly, it's a safer place,' says Mr Green, adding, 'from the day they were arrested and taken off the streets, the city of Nottingham was transformed, and long may it remain so. I would think a fool would say gun crime is dead, but what the figures show, and what the feel of the city shows, is that it's a very different place to what it was a few years ago.'

So if we are to use any yardstick by which to measure the lives and crimes committed by the Gunn brothers, the 'adventures' of our legendary Robin Hood may be a good place to start, for most certainly the Gunns were not in the same league as their more 'celebrated' London counterparts, the Kray brothers.

For the most part, the Gunns are a pair of intellect-ually-challenged common thugs. From a sink-estate background, perhaps they glimpsed the opportunity to enter 'the Big Time', when it became obvious that the Sheriff of Nottingham (Chief Constable Steve Green) was well and truly committed to dealing with the African-Caribbean – or 'Yardie' – crime problem that was over-whelming his city.

There seems to be some confusion as to exactly when the Yardies arrived in the UK. The Yardie phenomenon was first noted in the late 1980s and their rise is linked to that of crack cocaine in which many trade. However, this pre-dates the event that gave them their name.

'Yardie' is a term stemming from the slang name given to occupants of government yards in Trenchtown, a neighbourhood in West Kingston, Jamaica. Trenchtown was originally built as a housing project following devastation caused by Hurricane Charlie in 1951. Each development was built around a central courtyard with communal cooking facilities. Due to the poverty endemic in the neighbourhood, crime and gang violence became rife, leading the occupants of Trenchtown to be in part stigmatised by the term 'Yardie'. Today, in the UK, they drive top-of-the-range BMWs, flaunt designer gold 'bling-bling' jewellery and carry automatic guns as a weapon of choice. In terms of a reputation for ruthless violence, they could one day rival the Triads or Mafia.

But if the Gunns thought they could even begin to emulate these 'gangstas', in terms of drug and arms dealing, as well as robbery, a lifestyle synonymous with violence – impulse shootings and gangland-style executions used to sort out internal squabbles – then they had to be living in cloud cuckoo land.

To further debunk their pseudo Robin Hood image, the Gunns most certainly did not rob from the rich to give to the poor. To begin with, the investigation into the Gunns and their activities cost millions of pounds, all of which was provided courtesy of the taxpayer. For that matter, they hadn't even had the intelligence to rip off the rich – theirs was not a world of international banking frauds, credit-card-cloning, international car-ring enterprises or links with Eastern European master criminals. In reality, the Gunns robbed, brutalised, dealt in drugs, threatened, extorted, bullied, corrupted, terrorised, tortured, murdered and conspired, all with the sole aim of filling their own wallets at the expense of others.

And the seat of the Gunns' empire? A rundown council house on the Bestwood Estate, Nottingham, with their communications centre only a short walk away... at their mum's house.

And how did the Gunns spend their ill-gotten gains? No Rolexes or Bentleys for them, but they could muster up a clapped-out old car or two, and drink themselves stupid in a few local pubs – one of which has since been demolished in remembrance of Colin's patronage.

Perhaps Colin Gunn's crew could bear comparison with Robin's Merry Men? Unfortunately not – they turned out to be a bunch of semi-illiterate hoodies, who would 'grass' up their own grandmothers to save their own skins. Two crooked cops, one of whom sold his soul for measly discounts on cheap suits. It should also be remembered that Robin's legendary band of men managed to live in hiding undetected in Sherwood Forest, leaving the Sheriff exasperated at every turn. Colin Gunn, however, intellectually challenged as he was, managed to leave a critical paper trail that led the Sheriff's men to his own front door.

Levity aside, the Gunns have caused mayhem within the confines of the City of Nottingham. Sure, they plundered and murdered and, in some respects, they 'took care of business' on their own doorstep. They committed crimes which the city would rather forget – indeed, my many requests for the local newspaper and the local police to contribute to this chapter have been ignored. One may wonder why.

At the end of the day, it is the people of

Nottinghamshire who have had to foot the bill for its law enforcement agency's efforts to bring the Gunns to justice. It has been a million-pound expenditure, one that has been funded by decent, law-abiding, citizens. And one view prevailing among many in the area is that if the police had adopted a proactive approach – akin to the old Bobbies on the beat – to dealing with local crime when the problem first arose, instead of consigning finite financial and manpower resources to form filling and office filing, the problems caused by the Gunn brothers may never have escalated to such destructive proportions.

In retrospect, the lack of inner-city, proactive, three-strikes-and-you're-out policing and hardline law enforcement was a major contributory factor in giving the Gunn brothers licence to continue as they did. And some connected with the Gunns' history in Nottingham believe that the police must bear some responsibility in the murders perpetrated or sanctioned by the Gunns. It also beggars belief that two Nottinghamshire police officers and two BT workers were part of this criminal enterprise.

The vacuum left by the Gunns on the Bestwood Estate will be filled by other wannabe gangsters. The police, with one eye on their ever-diminishing budget, and the other eye focused on looking after more affluent areas – the better addresses always receive a faster response time – may inevitably allow the lessons from Brothers Gunn to slip conveniently into local folklore.

Robin Hood? Somehow, during the writing of this chapter, I have kind of warmed to the guy... tights and all. Do Colin Gunn and his cronies bear comparison?

No comparison at all.

3

Goldfinger — Mr Kenneth James Noye

*'I took the knife and did him. Old Bill or not,
he had no fucking business being here.'*

KENNY NOYE TO DC FINLAYSON ON HIS ARREST FOR
STABBING DC JOHN FORDHAM

At the time of writing, Kenneth James Noye, Britain's
most infamous villain, is 60. The essential difference
between him and other gangland figures such as the
Krays and the Richardsons is that he had the vision and
the means to infiltrate legitimate business.

And the comparisons between Colin Gunn and Kenny
Noye are as chalk and cheese – an untaxed, beaten-up
Skoda or a top-of-the-list Land Rover, with which Kenny
Noye, as we shall soon learn, was uniquely linked. Kenny
had class by the truckload; the Gunns had none.

Noye would regularly drink at the Hilltop Hotel near
his home where the then aristocracy of gangland, the
Krays and the Richardsons, the Haywards, Frankie
Frazer and others would gather to quaff Dom Perignon

and watch the cabaret. The Gunns mixed with juvenile chavs, watched the occasional porn video, urinating the proceeds of their crimes against a pub wall.

Kenneth Noye Esquire dealt in millions of pounds of gold bullion, while Mr Gunn, according to his police arrest paperwork, wore a few items of over-the-top 'yellow metal jewellery on his person'.

Kenny Noye built up a solid reputation as a 'fence' who could shift anything, and he was an 'armourer', who could provide guns through his pal Sidney Wink. And while Colin Gunn lived on a rundown estate, Kenneth Noye owned a 20-acre private estate in West Kingsdown, a civil parish and a small village near Sevenoaks, Kent. Colin did own some property – a garden shed. He did not have a villa overseas, as did Kenny, who owned a hilltop mansion in Altanterra, Spain.

Colin Gunn was married to Lisa Unwin, upon whom he showered food vouchers, milk tokens, and allowed her the use of a beat-up old car. Mr Noye, on the other hand, bought his wife, Brenda, a squash club, and lived what only can be described as the lifestyle of the *nouveau riche* – sporting expensive clothes, jewellery and limos – and had several 'tabloid-stunner' female companions on the go. These included his exotic South American mistress, with her equally exotic name – Mina Al Taiba.

Kenny Noye was slim, well-proportioned and handsome. Colin Gunn was not what you would call good-looking. He was shaven-headed, with a phsyique not built for speed, except in short, breathless bursts when running from the law. The former, one might introduce to one's daughter; the latter, you would hide the dear girl in a cellar, probably for many years.

GOLDFINGER – MR KENNETH JAMES NOYE

Mr Gunn used low-life thugs to do his dirty work, while Mr Noye used a worldwide web of heavy-hitters to do his bidding. Gunn didn't have a bank account, while Noye had more banking options than the Inland Revenue.

The doorbell of Kenny's Hollywood Cottage, in West Kingsdown, Kent, triggered a stereo blasting out Shirley Bassey singing the theme tune to the James Bond film *Goldfinger*. The Gunns favoured hammer-on-the-door-til-you-get-a-response'.

In 1997, after being arrested by Scotland Yard for receiving stolen goods, Kenney joined a Freemason's lodge which had a large number of police officers among the Brotherhood. He mixed with 'premier league' villains such as John 'Little Legs' Lloyd, and the legendary Freddie Foreman. He had enough folding money to be able to fly to Miami with £50,000 to invest in land. One deal alone resulted in a net profit for Noye and his associates of £600,000.

But the real money came from gold smuggled in from Africa, Kuwait and Brazil. Between 1982–84, Kenny ran smuggling operations worth a staggering £35 million, and his own cut was just under £4.5 million.

Kenny Noye stabbed an undercover cop to death. He was acquitted of this 'murder' because DC John Fordham, wearing a balaclava and clothing reminiscent of an extra in *Mission Impossible*, was in the dead of night effectively trespassing, without even a warrant to enter Noye's Kent estate. A 'startled' Kenneth Noye allegedly feared for his life.

Freemason Kenney Noye also stabbed a young man to death following a road-rage incident on the M25. And for this offence, he is serving a life term in a supermax prison facility 'somewhere in England', according to the Home Office. Actually, he is at HMP Full Sutton, near York.

Yet, strangely, both criminals now share a few things in common. They both used corrupt police officers. They are now post-conviction brothers-in-arms, serving life sentences in prison cells, and their chances of release are minimal.

Neither of them could be described as contemporary Robin Hoods and, essentially, whatever course their criminal career paths may have followed, and however rich or pathetic their lifestyles, they have both been reduced to the same outcome. They went into prison wearing smart suits, and they'll most probably be released wearing the wooden variety. In a nutshell, they are both fucked!

Yet if one were to thrust both men on to a reality TV show and judge them for their antisocial talents – on, say, *Crim Idol* – Kenny would be voted back for the finals. He would have survived the first auditions because of his panache, cheeky smile and cold-blooded attitude. He would have survived 'boot camp'; his accomplishments – already established in the Brinks Mat robbery – easily outstripping any that a panel of judges could have hoped to have completed in several lifetimes.

Colin Gunn? A pathetic wannabe by comparison. If Col had got as far as appearing before the judges in the first place, they would have sent him packing, and before the studio doors had closed, his mother would have stormed back in, protesting vehemently that Col would go on to do great things. History proves that he didn't.

*

1947 was the year of the first known sightings of UFOs by Kenneth Arnold, whose attention – while flying over Washington – was drawn to nine luminous disks in the form of saucers. It was then that he uttered the immortal words: 'God dang! What the holy shit was that?' Shortly afterwards, on Wednesday, 2 July, it is said that a UFO crashed near Roswell, New Mexico, disgorging strange little men over a small area, the incident giving rise to worldwide panic that we were about to be invaded by aliens.

Still up in the air – albeit at an altitude of a mere 70 feet – this time over California, designer Howard Hughes performed the maiden flight of the *Spruce Goose*, the largest fixed-wing aircraft ever built. On 2 November 1947, after a series of taxi tests with Hughes at the controls with co-pilot Dave Grant and a crew of two flight engineers, accompanied by nine invited guests from the press corps, the Hercules lifted off from the waters off Long Beach. The aircraft singularly distinguished itself by lumbering along for just under a mile before it landed – never to fly again.

Chuck Yeager did much better. He flew a Bell X-1 faster than the speed of sound, the first man to do so in level flight, or, for that matter, any sort of flight.

In the UK, significant events were conservatively confined to terra firma. The Gatwick rail crash on 27 October 1947 raised a few eyebrows when the *Flying Scotsman* express from Edinburgh Waverley to London King's Cross derailed, killing 27 people; two bumbling electric commuter trains collided in fog, killing 32 people near South Croydon railway station; the Thames inconveniently flooded; and the country was gripped with excitement when Gravesend, Liverpool Edge Hill and Normanton held by-elections.

However, of more interest to us was that Kenneth Noye was born in Bexleyheath, Kent, on Saturday, 24 May 1947. On the Taurus-Gemini cusp, his astrological strengths are to be expressive, incisive and socially involved; his weaknesses are identified as being self-centred; caustic and closed. He is all of those things... and much much more.

As a youngster, he was a perky and mischievous lad. By the time he had reached 12, he was a strikingly good-looking boy, 5ft in height with a well-defined face, strong eyebrows and deep, dark, narrow brown eyes. Some of the boys in his class were jealous of his good looks; subsequently, he was sometimes bullied in the play-ground between classes. However, he rapidly learned to defend himself and the bigger, older boys rapidly learned to leave Kenny Noye alone.

Within a few years, Kenny had embarked on juvenile crime. Breaking and entering and interesting himself in dodgy deals, he became fascinated by the tough, edgy characters in their sheepskin coats who seemed to have endless bundles of £5 notes in their pockets. According to Wensley Clarkson, author of *Killer on the Road*, 'These twisted values intruded upon young Noye's life with increasing frequency and made him fairly confused about morals... He was also developing a terrible temper. If he didn't get what he wanted, he often became violent.'

Those close to him noted that he had a hair-trigger reaction which would be provoked by the smallest incident. Instead of taking a deep breath and walking away from potentially difficult situations, Kenny would steam straight in. He was fearless.

By the age of 14, Kenny Noye was operating a successful stolen bicycle racket, charging younger children protection money at school, doing an early-morning paper round and selling programmes at the greyhound track where his mother worked.

Aged 15, he found himself Saturday employment in the men's department of Harrods in Knightsbridge, and started dressing more smartly. As a result, Kenny Noye became fascinated by all the rich and famous people; he watched their wallets closely and they style of clothes they bought, and he would return home to dream about his future.

It is doubtful that Kenneth Noye was aware of this at the time, but within his small frame and sharp mind were all the ingredients – the building blocks, if you like – to form a first-rate criminal. Good-looking, amiable when it suited him, yet hard as nails – he had the ambition to devise cunning schemes to amass all the folding money he could lay his hands on, and dress himself as 'class'. Working at Harrods, mixing with those who had 'real 'class, was an education to him, in much the same way as a lowly butler often pretentiously assumes the airs and graces of his lordly employer.

And, to give Kenneth credit, by the age of 18 he was earning enough money to make his first material dream come true. Graduating from being a 'Mod', and tearing around on a scooter, he bought himself a bright yellow Ford Cortina Mark 1. He had sprung up to 5ft 8in tall, he was fairly muscular and looked older than his age. He started visiting some of the legendary clubs and bars in and around the Old Kent Road, where, keeping in the background, his education was furthered observing some of the most infamous criminals of the mid-1960s. He was intrigued. He wanted some of the action – the big cars and mohair suits. He wanted respect.

Perhaps even the Great Train Robbery in 1963 played a part in his ambition; south-east London at the time was a hot-bed of cutting-edge criminal activity, where the status of such criminals put them on a par with film stars. But his first serious brush with the law was when he was arrested for handling stolen vehicles, and he ended up with a one-year sentence in a Borstal near Shaftesbury, Wiltshire.

If it had been the intention of the sentencing magistrate to make an example of young Kenny Noye by handing him a stiff prison term, it backfired. Noye took the inconvenience in his stride. He made contacts, took down names, addresses and phone numbers of his fellow cons. He listened to what they had to say, kept his own counsel, and was determined to learn from their mistakes. He vowed that when he was released he would run his own 'business'. No one would grass him up in the future and, with this in mind, he believed that he would never be outwitted by the Old Bill again.

Upon his release from Borstal, Kenny met a young, blonde girl. Petite and neatly dressed, Brenda Tremain had good looks and a forthright personality. The couple were soon mixing with the wheelers and dealers at their local pub, The Harrow. Perched midway along the relentlessly grey, grimy and desolate Northern Road at Slade Green, The Harrow was a large, downbeat, smoky old pub, which, at the time, was run by a close family friend. It was, and still is, the sort of place that favours locals and is unlikely to draw outsiders, bar the lost or perversely curious.

One particular acquaintance was Micky Lawson, who owned a used car showroom opposite the Tremains' family home. From The Harrow, the two men gravitated to pubs in south-east London – the Frog and Nightgown, The Connoisseur, the Prince of Wales and The Beehive in 'Del Boy' Trotter's Peckham, and it was inevitable that Noye would start mixing with some of the hardest gangsters in London. In the 1960s, this was the Richardsons' manor.

The Richardson gang was a tight-knit group of pug-ugly villains and blackguards less well-remembered than their rivals, the notorious Krays. Nevertheless, in their heyday, the Richardsons were held as being one of London's most infamous and sadistic gangs. Also known as 'The Torture Gang', their socially responsible 'speciality' was pinning victims to the floor with 6in nails and amputating their toes with bolt cutters.

The gang's leader was Charlie Richardson. He and his younger brother, Eddie, turned to a life of villainy when their father abandoned the family home leaving them penniless. Charlie's 'legit' side of the business included investing in scrap metal, while Eddie operated a fiefdom of fruit machines. These businesses were merely fronts for underworld activities which included extortion, murder, fraud, theft and handling stolen property.

Eddie was a persuasive entrepreneur who seemed to have no problem in convincing pub landlords to buy one of his machines. He would make an initial sales pitch and, if the offer was politely declined, the landlord risked heavies smashing up his premises before his very eyes. With a number of bent coppers on the Richardson's payroll, complaining to the Old Bill was not an option.

However, the lawless Richardsons preferred the method of investing in 'long firms'. A company would be set up by an acquaintance of the brothers. Trading would start, building up a good credit rating, and then the company would place a large order on credit and sell the goods. Quite naturally, the Richardsons would pocket the money and the company would disappear into thin air, often leaving the unwitting supplier totally ignorant that he had just made a large donation to the Richardson gang, who, in turn, contributed a percentage of the proceeds to the police fund to keep the cops off their backs. Nice work if you can get it.

Perhaps the greatest influence on Kenny's life around this time was Billy Haywood, a brutal mobster who had secured a place in gangland folklore by fighting a pitched battle with the Richardsons over who should control local protection rackets. Known as 'The Battle of Mr Smith's Club', one of Haywood's men, called Dickie Hart, was shot dead during the mêlée; Haywood won, however, effectively taking down the Richardsons' empire at a stroke.

It was Haywood who impressed upon Noye that the more astute criminals were the middle-men – the handlers of stolen property and money – rather than those who actually got their hands dirty. This confirmed what Noye had more or less figured out for himself while in Borstal, so he lapped up Haywood's counselling like a cat gorging itself on cream.

And there was something else that Noye had figured out on his own, something that was also endorsed by Billy Haywood. Always a 'watcher of people', Kenny had noticed that the small-time crooks spent most of their illicit gains gambling on the dogs, the horses, in pubs and clubs, pissing their money up against a wall, and buying what we might call today 'bling-bling' trinkets – heavy gold bracelets, neck chains, rings and the like. The brighter lads invested, and many invested significantly in property, mini-cab firms, launderettes, sometimes even the stock market.

The 1960s was a crucial time in Noye's life. Even before he had been sent to Borstal, he'd been mapping out a criminal career. His chance meeting with Brenda Tremain in her local pub, The Harrow, and a chance meeting with Micky Lawson, who introduced him to the south-east London pubs, all contributed to Noye's education. His mentor – the utterly fearless, yet criminally astute Billy Haywood – and the constant shoulder-rubbing with scores of London's real tough guys, all cemented together his ambitions for the future. But he had a fatal flaw, and it was to prove his Achilles heel – his short fuse.

Noye had been drinking in a Peckham pub, and his drink was knocked over. Rightly, Kenny asked for it to be replaced. The request was denied. The two men exchanged words and the comparatively diminutive Noye walked out to the sound of hisses and boos. Thinking that Noye was a coward, the customers returned sniggering to their drinks… it was a bad move.

Rather than slink away from the pub with his tail in between his legs, Noye had gone to his car to pick up an 'equaliser' – a double-barrelled, 12-gauge shotgun.

Moments later, he burst through the front door and aimed it at the men who had insulted him. The bar went as quiet as the grave; no one dared move. Slowly, Noye brought the weapon round, stopping momentarily at each one in turn. Then he pointed it at the ceiling and pulled the trigger. The shot blasted a hole in the plaster, showering the men with debris. Then he calmly walked out without a further word being said. The message sent a signal around the manor – cross Kenny Noye and you could end up dead.

From then on, Kenny Noye started earning serious money from fencing stolen property – car parts, shipments of whisky, cigarettes and cigars. Among the criminal fraternity, his word and his money were good. He was someone to be trusted, and he never missed a trick, but he needed a front for his growing enterprise, somewhere away from prying eyes and off the beaten track.

He found such a location in a quiet Kent village called West Kingsdown, and there he started his own haulage company, which he ran from a battered caravan behind a local garage. And the parish had another bonus, too – there was only one copper whose principal duties extended to riding around on his bike or napping in a panda car. The local force were totally oblivious to the success of Mr Noye's growing haulage company, which soon expanded to more than a dozen lorries.

Kenny and Brenda married in August 1970. They had bought a dilapidated bungalow on 20 acres of prime land in West Kingsdown's Hever Avenue. They set the bungalow on fire, claimed on the insurance and set about constructing a huge, mock-Tudor mansion. This was followed by the building of Hollywood Cottage – ten bedrooms, an indoor swimming pool, jacuzzi, huge snooker room, all protected by the most comprehensive of security systems. Noye was now a millionaire.

For the next decade, Kenny Noye went from strength to strength, give or take one or two brushes with the law. During this time, though, he had set his sights on gold bullion, and a lot of it was stolen – 10 tonnes of it to be precise – in what has become known as 'The Brinks Mat Robbery'.

The scheme had been masterminded by one Brian Robinson, and the heist occurred at around 6.40am, on Saturday, 26 November 1983, when six armed robbers broke into the Brinks Mat's Unit 7 warehouse on a trading estate near Heathrow Airport. The men thought – as they had been told by insider guard Anthony Black, brother-in-law of Robinson – that the haul would be £3 million in cash. How wrong they were, for when they got inside they found themselves looking in amazement at ten tonnes of gold bullion worth the best part of £26 million.

Of course, it proved to be a terrible ordeal for the Brink's-Mat staff, who feared for their lives. Petrol was poured over one man's genitals, and he was threatened with being set ablaze or being shot if he didn't comply by neutralising the alarms and opening the vault – which he did.

The vault turned out to be a treasure trove. For several moments, the robbers were unable to speak. They were looking at 60 boxes, which contained a total of 2,670 kilos of gold worth £26,369,778. Over in a corner was a stack of several hundred thousand pounds in used banknotes. In a safe was a pouch containing $250,000 in travellers' cheques. In anther safe was yet another pouch filled with polished and rough diamonds valued at £113,000.

The gang had expected rich pickings, but not a haul beyond their wildest dreams. As Wensley Clarkson observes in his book, 'Their audacious plot, ruthless in its conception and brilliant in its execution, had just landed them the biggest haul in British criminal history.'

The 1963 Great Train Robbery, which netted the villains £2.6 million, paled into insignificance, even considering inflation, when compared with this Brink's-Mat raid. No doubt, the Great Train Robbery was a coup. It involved cunning and intricate timing – the stopping of a mail train in the dead of night precisely at a particular railway bridge in Buckinghamshire, the unloading of mail bags containing the haul, and conveying it away in a small fleet of vehicles to a place called Letherslade Farm, where it was divided up, with each crook going their separate ways. But the Brink's-Mat gang, with balls of steel, hoovered up their entire proceeds and carried it all away in a single truck. For that, they deserve the Nobel Prize for Planning and Execution.

Scotland Yard soon discovered the family connection between Messrs Black and Robinson and, under interrogation, Black soon grassed up his accomplices. Tried at the Old Bailey, Robinson and principal accomplice Michael McAvory earned themselves 25 years' imprisonment. Black got six years, and served three.

Enter Kenny Noye. Prior to his conviction, McAvory had entrusted part of his share to an associate called Brian Perry. Perry recruited Kenneth Noye (who had links to a legitimate gold dealer in Bristol) to dispose of the gold. Noye melted down the bullion and recast it for sale. However, the sudden movements of large amounts of money through a Bristol bank came to the notice of the Treasury, who informed the police. Noye was placed under police surveillance and, in January 1985, 'it all came on top', as they say in Kenny's world.

With all of the Brink's-Mat robbers behind bars, police focused on Noye and they shadowed him everywhere he went. It was obvious that he was the key to the distribution of the gold and, if they were going to achieve anything, they would have to move closer to him rather than simply tail him from place to place.

Early in January 1985, eight C11 officers from the Specialist Surveillance Unit took up covert positions near Hollywood Cottage but, apart from Noye's comings and goings, nothing much happened until 26 January.

It was a bitterly cold evening when, at 6.15pm, DC John Fordham, 43, and DC Neil Murphy, dressed in rubber wetsuits, camouflage clothing and balaclavas, climbed over a wall into Noye's property and made their way to a copse and shrubbery in front of the large barn. Fordham was also equipped with a pair of light-intensifying, night-sight binoculars, a webbing scarf, gloves, a camouflaged forage cap and a green webbing harness to keep the larger of his two radios in position while crawling through the undergrowth.

The officers were now just 60 yards from the house when one of Noye's three Rottweilers appeared out of the darkness and started snapping at the 'intruders'. Noye heard the commotion, grabbed a leather jacket from behind a chair and headed for the front door. Outside, he walked to his Ford Granada and picked up a knife and a torch.

The Rottweiler was still barking, and Noye heard someone call out halfway down the drive, 'Dogs!' Neil Murphy made a beeline for the boundary fence of the property and climbed up to take stock of the situation. He tried to attract the attention of the dogs but, in doing so, attracted the attention of Noye, who flashed the torch beam in his direction.

'Keep those dogs quiet,' shouted Murphy.

Noye froze. A second later, a hooded figure appeared a few feet away. A scuffle ensued and Noye, fearful that he was about to be murdered by the stranger, stabbed DC Fordham eight times. The officer died shortly afterwards.

At the resulting trial, the jury found Noye not guilty on the grounds of self-defence. And there is some logic to this as former Kray henchman Freddie Foreman has said, 'Put yourself in Kenny's position. If you went into your back garden tonight and someone leaps out of the ground in a mask and that, what would you think? You would suspect they was there to rob you and your family.'

In 1986, though, he was found guilty of conspiracy to handle the Brink's-Mat gold, fined £700,000 and sentenced to 14 years in prison, although he had to serve only 8 years before being released in 1994. For several years, Noye slipped in and out of the country from Spain, where he had built several large villas; then, on Sunday, 19 May 1996, Noye stabbed to death 21-year-old electrical engineer Stephen Cameron during a so-called 'road-rage' incident at the M25/M20 intersection near Swanley, Kent.

Noye immediately fled the country. The police tracked him to south-east Spain and, on 28 August 1998, he was arrested at the El Campero restaurant in Barbate on the

Atlantic coast and deported back to Britain. Tried and convicted in 2000, he received a life sentence. Eight years later, he won permssision to bring a legal challenge over the refusal of the Criminal Cases Review Commission to refer his conviction back to the Court of Appeal.

The life of Kenneth Noye has been one of malevolence and corruption. It is an example of how someone eagerly embracing crime as a profession can accumulate enormous wealth and frightening power. It is also a stark reminder of how vulnerable society can be when faced with such a single-minded predator.

Compared to the Gunn brothers, Kenny Noye operated at Premiership level, rather than at Conference. Hard as nails and highly astute, Kenny Noye was in a class of his own. A Freemason with a taste for the finer things in life – beautiful young women, expensive homes and international travel – his only real downfall, which has ensured that he could spend the rest of his life in prison, was his quick and violent temper. Had he not brutally stabbed to death Stephen Cameron in front of his beautiful blonde fiancée, 19-year-old Danielle Cable, in 1996, he would have still been enjoying his accumulated millions today.

Despite being acquitted of the murder of DC John Fordham, and the possible excuse of self-defence that convinced the jury at the time, Noye cannot be excused for the killing of young Stephen Cameron and leaving him to bleed to death by the side of the road. This was an entirely vicious, rage-filled crime, and it is right to point out that dark side to Kenneth Noye, rather than perpetuate the myth of the 'gentleman master criminal', a dapper, cheeky chappie, who loves his mum and looks out for those less fortunate than himself.

Pending the outcome of his possible appeal for the 1996 murder of Cameron, Kenneth Noye is currently expected to serve at least 20 years of his life sentence, but he will still continue to amass a fortune from his financial investments and, if he is ever released, he will return to society a multi-millionaire. He was 53 when he was locked up and he cannot be considered for release until 2020, when he'll be in his mid-seventies.

Robin Hood? Kenny Noye was far from it. However, what we cannot take away from him is the undeniable fact that he operated for a time at the very pinnacle of the UK underworld.

And what of the legacy of Mr Kenneth Noye? Many of his former associates have met 'unfortunate' ends... although there is no suggestion here that Kenny played any part in their deaths or maimings. Indeed, it's worth remembering that those who live by the sword, die by the sword.

• John Marshall

Just after Noye's disappearance following the murder of Stephen Cameron in May 1966, 34-year-old car dealer John Marshall was found shot dead in his black Range Rover at Round Hill in Sydenham, south London. It was Marshall who had supplied Noye with stolen vehicle licence plates, including the registration plates used on the Land Rover Discovery linked to the road-rage killing of Stephen Cameron.

Marshall vanished after leaving his £250,000 home at Little Burstead, Essex, at about 10.00am on 15 May to meet 'business contacts'. His car is believed to have crossed the Queen Elizabeth II Bridge into Kent at about midday. He didn't return home and failed to keep other appointments that day. He was reported missing that night by his wife, Toni, who would normally contact him regularly throughout the day.

Seven days after he vanished, on 22 May, his body was found in straw in the unlocked trunk of his Range Rover by a police officer at Round Hill. He had been shot twice in the head and chest execution-style. The only thing clear about the weapon was that it wasn't a shotgun. The Range Rover's keys, a grey Head sports bag, two mobile phones and a Patek Phillippe 18ct gold watch with a blue face were missing. However, £5,000 cash that he had taken with him the morning he disappeared was still in the vehicle.

Marshall had also been an accomplice of Pat Tate (see below).

• **Danny 'Scarface' Roff**

Roff was shot dead outside his home in Bromley, Kent, in March 1977. A cold-blooded criminal, he and accomplice Jeremiah Parker held up a sub-post office at gunpoint in Evelyn Street, Deptford, in June 1987. The money the two men got from the raid, and many others like it, helped them start new lives on the Costa del Sol in the 1990s. They may have escaped British justice in their sunshine hideaway but they could not escape the violent retribution of other mobsters.

On a warm evening in 2006, Parker, 43, was enjoying a drink with friends at The Point bar in Nuevo Andalucia, Marbella, with a mainly British crowd. He was standing on the terrace when a hitman walked up and fired five bullets into him.

By this time, Roff had already met his maker. After one failed attempt on his life, which left him in a wheelchair, his past caught up with him outside his luxury home in Bromley, Kent. The 36-year-old was shot dead by two hooded executioners. The bullets hit his head and chest as he was moving from his Mercedes to his wheelchair.

Roff was widely believed to have been the man who shot dead Great Train Robber Charlie Wilson at his Marbella villa in 1990; it was also believed that his own murder was a revenge killing.

Roff was also the prime suspect for the January 1993 contract killing of 55-year-old property tycoon Robert Urquhart – a good friend of Noye – outside his Marylebone home when he was shot dead by a gunman who escaped on a motorcycle.

• **Keith Hedley**
Hedley was murdered by alleged bandits on his yacht in Corfu in November 1996.

• **Pate Tate, Craig Rolfe and Tony Tucker**
All were shot to death by shotgun blasts into their Range Rover along a farm lane in Rettendon, Essex, during the night of 6 December 1995. Engineer Michael Steele and mechanic Jack Whomes were convicted solely on the word of police supergrass Darren Nicholls. The case highlights police corruption and is presently under review by the Criminal Cases Review Commission.

While in jail at Swaleside, Noye had befriended Tate, a tattooed, muscle-bound, 18-stone drug-dealer from Essex, who acted as his protector. At Tate's suggestion, Noye invested £30,000 on an Ecstasy shipment, making a quick £70,000 profit. Police claim that Ecstasy from this part of the batch could be forensically linked to the death of teenager Leah Betts. The claim was another attempt to implicate Noye.

Leah was a schoolgirl from Latchingdon in Essex. She is notable for the extensive media coverage and moral panic that followed her death several days after her 18th birthday, during which she took an Ecstasy tablet, then collapsed four hours later into a coma, from which she did not recover. Subsequently, it was discovered that water intoxication was the cause of her death.

• **Sidney Wink**
Wink was a gunsmith and dealer who put a pistol to his own head and squeezed the trigger in August 1994.

• **Nick Whiting**
Whiting came unstuck when he was stabbed nine times and shot twice with a 9mm pistol in 1990. A car dealer, he went missing from his showroom in West Kingsdown in 1990. His body was later recovered from Rainham Marshes in Essex.

• **Stephen Dalligan**
Dalligan was shot six times in the Old Kent Road in 1990.

• **Daniel Morgan**
Morgan was at the centre of one of Britain's most enduring murder mysteries. In March 1987, private detective Daniel Morgan was found in the car park of the Golden Lion public house in Sydenham, south London,

with an axe embedded in his skull. Morgan's business partner, with whom he had fallen out, was friendly with a number of police officers who have since been implicated in the killing. Allegations of police involvement were made at the inquest but, in spite of hundreds of statements, hours of covert surveillance and four investigations that identified several key suspects, no one has ever been charged.

The inquest, which took place in April 1986, and ended with a verdict of 'unlawful killing', heard allegations of involvement by Metropolitan Police officers, and allegations of attempts to cover up that involvement. It also heard that Jonathan Rees, Daniel Morgan's business partner in their private detective company, Southern Investigations Ltd, had talked about having Daniel killed and arranging for police officers at Catford CID to be involved in the murder and its subsequent cover-up.

Morgan had enjoyed a number of careers, and he also 'enjoyed' a falling out with his business partners in the PI business. Things came to a head when Southern Investigations was asked to provide security for a car auction company in Charlton, south London. Though Morgan didn't want the work, his partner, Jonathan Rees, took the job on, using some of his police contacts to moonlight while off duty.

On 18 March 1986, Rees was in charge of the night's takings for the auction – some £18,000. He took the money to a local bank, but discovered that the night safe had been glued shut. Some say this was a most convenient state of affairs, one that demanded that Rees take the money home, where, as coincidence would have it, he was sprayed in the face with a 'noxious liquid'.

As might be expected, no one was ever arrested for the robbery. Indeed, many – including the car auction company, which demanded the return of its money – today believe that the gluing-up of the night safe, and the attack on Rees, was a sham.

For his part, although he alleges he was a victim, Rees agreed to repay the money on the proviso that it came from the Southern Investigations company account. Morgan smelled a rat. He refused the offer, arguing, diplomatically, that the loss had been down to Rees alone.

Rees was now in a fix. Desperate to take control of the company and its finances, he tried on several occasions to have Morgan arrested for drink-driving, knowing that if he lost his licence he would have to give up working at the agency, but to no avail.

At the inquest, Kevin Lennon, the company's bookkeeper, stated that Rees told him, 'I've got the perfect solution for Daniel's murder. My mates at Catford [CID] are going to arrange it... when he is gone, Sid Fillery will replace him.' Fillery was, at that time, a serving DS, and a 'friend' of Kenny Noye.

In the hours following Morgan's death, a murder inquiry was launched, headed by DS Douglas Campbell. One of the lead detectives assigned to the case was none other than DS Fillery.

In 2004, Roger Williams, MP for Brecon and Radnorshire, told the House of Commons that a full judicial inquiry was 'the only way of obtaining a fresh and independent scrutiny of the murder and the circumstances in which successive investigations into it have come to nothing'.

Roger Williams told the House of Commons, 'Not only was Sid Fillery among the officers, but he played a key role in the initial murder inquiry during the first four so-called 'golden' days before he was required to withdraw from the murder squad for reasons of personal involvement with the primary suspect, Jonathan Rees. During those four days, Fillery was given the opportunity to manage the first interview under caution with Rees, and to take possession of key incriminating files from the premises of Southern Investigations Ltd, including Daniel's diary, which has never since been found.'

Rees, Fillery and two other police officers were subsequently arrested in connection with the murder, but no charges were ever brought. Fillery went on to take up joint ownership of Southern Investigations Ltd.

• George Francis

Francis was the ninth man linked to the Brinks Mat gold bullion heist to be murdered. He had survived a previous attempt on his life when he was shot at in a pub he owned in Kent in 1985. 18 years later, he was executed by a hooded gunman at 5.00am on 14 May 2003.

A career criminal, the 63-year-old, who had homes in Beckenham and Kent, was shot four times in the face, back, arm and finger as he opened his business in Lynton Road, Bermondsey. He was at the gates of his haulage company Signed, Sealed & Delivered, and was gunned down as he leant into his car to get a newspaper. His body was found slumped in the front seat with his legs hanging out of the front passenger door.

Francis was killed after he tried to collect a £70,000 debt from a business contact. After the shooting, it was found that a CCTV camera at the yard had been repositioned so that it did not capture any footage of Francis's death.

54-year-old Terence Conaghan from Glasgow, and John O'Fynn, 53, from Hoddesdon, Hertfordshire, were found guilty of murder. Harold Richardson, aged 59, of Towncourt Lane, Petts Wood, was found not guilty.

Francis, who had served a jail term in 1997, knew Richardson through a number of business deals. Richardson, in turn, knew O'Flynn in the same way, while O'Flynn had known Conaghan for a number of years.

A cigarette butt was found in a drain at the scene of the shooting. DNA linked it to O'Flynn. A pair of glasses were found on the ground, which were later found to have a one-in-a-billion DNA link to Terence Conaghan. A 9mm Luger bullet, of the same type used to kill Francis, was also found near the building. CCTV images also captured Conaghan trying to shift the CCTV camera with a broom while he stood on a table, but he had to climb on to the roof instead when he realised he could not stretch far enough to reach the camera. A footprint left on the table showed a similar pattern to a pair of Reebok trainers found at Conaghan's home after his arrest.

A fortnight before his death, Francis called Richardson on 71 separate occasions; however, Richardson returned only five of the calls. The frustrated man's attempts came to a head on 11 May 2003 – three days before his death. Mobile phone records also showed that Richardson was in contact with the two hitmen in the lead-up to the killing.

£3 million of the original £26 million from the Brinks Mat robbery is still unnaccounted for.

4

The Kray Brothers

'Who loves you, eh? That's right, Mummy loves you,
you little monsters. Mummy loves you more than
anything - more than all the cakes, more than all the
jewellery, more than all the chocolate in the world.'

VIOLET KRAY TO RONNIE AND REGGIE AGED 3

I met Ronnie Kray at Broadmoor Hospital in 1984,
where he bought me a Diet Coke. Immaculately
dressed in a dark suit, white shirt, black shoes, tie, and
sporting a gold ring with 'RK' set with diamonds, he
chatted to me for an hour at a table in the airy visitors'
room with its view of sweeping grounds leading down to
the high perimeter wall.

It was autumn. While waiting for Ronnie to grant me
an audience, I watched inmates with wheelbarrows,
brooms and rakes sweeping up leaves into neat piles
before a mischievous wind sent them scattering again,
leaving me to ponder just for a moment on Broadmoor's
grim history.

Broadmoor was the country's first purpose-built asylum for the criminally insane. Completed in 1863, it houses about 500 men and 120 women. Lying on the edge of the small town of Crowthorne, in an area of heathland known as Bracknell Forest, it is one of four maximum-security hospitals in the UK.

The 'facility', as our US friends call such places, was built under an Act of Parliament to reform the poor conditions in institutions such as Bethlehem Hospital, the original 'Bedlam'. Its imposing classical Victorian architecture was the work of Major General Joshua Jebb, a military engineer who is said to have based the building on two other hospitals – Wakefield and Turkey's Scutari Hospital, near Istanbul.

Joshua Jebb was no slacker. He participated in the Battle of Plattsburg in Canada during the War of 1812, and surveyed a route between the Ottawa River and Kingston where Lake Ontario flows into Saint Lawrence River.

Around 1876, Jebb was appointed Surveyor-General of Prisons, busying himself with the construction of prisons at Portland, Dartmoor, Pentonville, Chatham, Mountjoy in Dublin, and Portsmouth. He was awarded a KGB for his civil services on 25 March 1859.

Yet, even in retirement, he found time to consider the construction of embankments on the River Thames, and of communications between the embankment at Blackfriars Bridge and the Mansion House, and between Westminster Bridge and Millbank.

One of the most remarkable characters of his time, Jebb married twice and, aged 70, died on 26 June 1863, having enjoyed a passing acquaintance with a gentleman we met earlier, Marriott Ogle Tarbotton, who followed him to the grave in 1887.

On meeting Ronnie Kray, it was extremely difficult for me even to begin to envisage that he was mentally disturbed, even less criminally insane. He didn't provide any obvious outward signs to suggest as much, or talk about the rats and mice that were infesting his cell – as did Paul Beecham, another Broadmoor patient I had previously interviewed. Sentenced to life for slaughtering his parents, and subsequently released as 'cured', Paul went on to murder his wife and then fatally shoot himself. So much for successful reintegration back into the community

Unlike some of his contemporaries at Broadmoor, Ronnie was never regarded in the same demonic way as Peter Sutcliffe, for example, or Kenneth Erskine, 'The Stockwell Strangler', who, circa 1986, murdered 11 elderly people in their south London homes.

Ron was never even in the same league as the cannibalistic murderer Robert Maudsley, either. Dubbed 'the English Hannibal Lecter', in 1974, Maudsley killed a man who picked him up for sex after having been shown pictures of children he had sexually assaulted and abused. Maudsley was arrested and sent to Broadmoor.

In 1977, Maudsley and another inmate took a fellow patient, a paedophile, hostage and locked themselves in a cell with their captive, whom they tortured and killed. When guards eventually smashed their way into the cell, the hostage's skull was found cracked open, a spoon wedged in his brain, and pieces missing. Maudsley claimed he had eaten some of the man's brain, earning him such names as 'Spoons', 'Cannibal', 'Brain-Eater' and 'Jaws' (because of his crooked teeth).

Other patients at Broadmoor who displayed particularly extreme behaviour, way beyond that of Ronnie Kray, was David Copeland, who, in 1999, targeted ethnic minorities with explosive devices in Brixton and the East End, and planted another bomb which targeted the gay community in the Admiral Duncan pub in Soho; Ian Ball attempted to kidnap Princess Anne in 1974; and Graham Frederick Young earned his status as the thallium poisoner.

John Thomas Straffen was committed to Broadmoor in 1951 for killing two little girls. He escaped for a brief period in 1952 and murdered five-year-old Linda Bowyer. Straffen died in November 2007, having earned himself the distinction of becoming the UK's longest-serving inmate.

Ian Brady, of course, was also incarcerated alongside Ronnie, as well as child rapist James Saunders. Nicknamed 'The Wolfman', he escaped for the second time in 1991 after sawing through a 1-inch steel bar in a shower room on the third floor of his wing, and running off, presumably howling into the night.

Meeting Ronnie was my one and only chance to find out why he had been considered suitably 'insane' to earn the maximum-security rating of Broadmoor. Of course, he had, or had had, an anti-social personality disorder of sorts, but even the medical staff at Broadmoor struggled hard to determine exactly what made up this 'disorder'. Fumbling around, they labelled him 'psychotic' and a 'sociopath'. The doctors say that Ronnie Kray had been a threat to society and, despite all the treatment they could offer, they were sure that he would re-offend should he be set free.

However, his conduct, while at Broadmoor, was

exemplary. While he may had some personality defects, there wasn't a blot in his book, and never once did he lose his temper, threaten other patients or members of staff. Indeed, Ronnie Kray was the perfect gent. And it was this perfect gent that I met when he sat down next to me, clicked his fingers to a guard, and ordered that Diet Coke. Just as in a fine restaurant, the response was, 'Certainly, Mr Kray.'

Hoxton was so far down the social scale it was even frowned upon by people from other deprived parts of East London. Traditionally, the only ways of escaping its poverty were either through boxing or crime – and often both.

Reggie and Ronnie Kray were born ten minutes apart late on 24 October 1933, at Stene Street, Hoxton. Their father, 26-year-old Charles David 'Charlie' Kray Sr, was a wardrobe dealer who persuaded people to sell him clothes, silver and gold for resale at a profit. He was a gambler and spendthrift who had little influence on the twins' upbringing. He was a deserter during World War II, and on the run from the police for 12 years, and was therefore rarely at home.

The twins' mother was 23-year-old Violet Lee. The couple already had a six-year-old son, also called Charlie, who was born in 1926. A sister, Violet, born in 1920, had died in infancy; the family's heritage was a combination of Irish, Jewish and Romany descent, a mixed genetic cocktail indeed.

Throughout their childhood, Violet was the dominant figure in the twins' lives. She doted on them, always taking care to treat them with scrupulous equality. She herself had come from a very strict family upbringing. Violet's teetotal father, John Lee, always insisted that his three daughters had to be in by 9.00pm every evening. And so, when she was just 17, she eloped to marry Charlie Kray, whereupon her father disowned her.

After giving birth to Charlie, the twins' elder brother, Violet started to see her parents occasionally. But it was only after the arrival of the twins, who rapidly established themselves as his favourite grandchildren that she was allowed to visit her father's house on a regular basis. The boys first attended Wood Close School and the Daneford Street School and, in 1939, the family moved to 178 Vallance Road, Bethnal Green.

Of the two, Reggie was slightly brighter and more outgoing than his twin brother. Even at an early age, he found it easier than Ronnie to talk to people. Ronnie found ways to compensate, though – either by sulking or screaming to gain attention, or trying to out-do his twin in over-blown displays of love for their mother.

According to their teachers, Reggie and Ronnie were 'salt of the earth, and never the slightest trouble to anyone who knew how to handle them. If there was anything to be done at school, they'd be utterly cooperative... they'd always be the first to help. Nothing was too much trouble.'

Each twin would pay close attention to every move the other made. Fiercely loyal to each other, they were also the greatest of rivals. If one started a fight, the other had to join in. And it was to fighting that both would eventually turn. The influence of their grandfather, John 'Southpaw Cannonball' Lee, led both lads into amateur boxing, which was at that time a popular working-class pursuit for boys in the East End. By 1946, they were feared competitors and are said never to have lost a bout before turning professional at age 28.

Regaling the twins with his tales of bare-knuckle fighting in Hackney's Victoria Park, Grandad Lee was one of the great east London characters of the inter-war years. He fought as a featherweight and had one of the hardest left-handed punches in his class. He also possessed a huge repertoire of showman tricks, which included licking a white-hot poker and walking along a line of bottles balanced upside down on their tops. Even as an old man, he kept himself fit, punching an old mattress hung up in his back yard and, on one occasion, cycling the 42 miles to Southend for a family party at the age of 75. He died aged 98 and, to Ronnie, he was simply 'the most amazing man I've ever met'.

But the twins' big problem was an inability to confine their violence to the ring. Amid the devastation of the Blitz, on the bomb sites and in burned-out buildings, they fought rival gangs of boys, and quickly earned a reputation as the toughest of scrappers. Rapidly they were learning the art of survival, which included outwitting the forces of law and order, and making the most of their passion for fighting.

So, all of the social, physical and psychological ingredients had been put in place for the Kray twins to become hardened villains from the day they were born. They came from an impoverished background; they had an absentee father, and a doting mother who came from a strict household. Her twins became effectively the sons the bare-knuckle fighter had always wanted, yet denied him by the gift of three daughters.

Despite her eventual reconciliation with her father, Violet was determined that her children would be raised in a kind and loving environment, in complete contrast to her father's harsh regime. As a result, and despite the toughness of the area they inhabited, Reggie and Ronnie experienced a comparatively sheltered upbringing during their early years.

There is no doubt that the Kray twins adored their mother, and they continued to show their respect for her until her death in early August 1982, by always stopping off at their Aunt Rose's house next door to clean up before presenting themselves to their mother.

This, I think, says a lot for the Kray twins, and when I met Ronnie in Broadmoor, he'd clearly made an effort with the spit and polish. Not to impress me, but this was how he had been raised to be by his mum; her old-fashioned values had been firmly imprinted on her sons, who would always look after her, and themselves, in any way they could.

The Kray twins' first serious brush with the Old Bill came in 1950, when they beat up a 16-year-old fellow East Ender in a Hackney alleyway. Two witnesses saw the fight and named the Krays as the attackers. Their evidence was supported by the roughed-up victim, and the twins were remanded in custody for trial at the Old Bailey.

Before the trial took place, however, both the witnesses and the victim were threatened, a reminder that giving evidence against the twins was an unwise move. The case was rapidly dismissed for lack of evidence. It was a valuable lesson for Ronnie and Reggie; the power of threats backed up by violence proved how easy it was to escape justice by instilling the fear of God into anyone who crossed them.

A year later, in the summer of 1951, the 18-year-old twins were standing outside a café on the Bethnal Green Road, when a police officer pushed Ronnie in the back and told him to move along. Ronnie turned round and punched the officer in the mouth, knocking him to the pavement. The lads made their escape, but Ronnie was arrested within the hour.

Although Reggie had nothing to do with the original incident, he felt he had let his brother down badly. As a matter of honour, he returned to the Bethnal Green Road in search of the policeman Ronnie had hit. When he found him, he tapped him on the shoulder. As the officer turned around, Reggie slammed his fist into the man's jaw, laying him out for the second time that afternoon. A few days later, the twins appeared before a magistrate. But with a local priest speaking on their behalf, they escaped with nothing more than probation.

In the spring of 1952, the twins received their National Service call-up papers, requiring them to join the Royal Fusiliers at the Tower of London. Post-war National Service had a significant effect on many people, and on society and culture as a whole. Some National Servicemen went on to become celebrities – Bill Wyman of The Rolling Stones played rock 'n' roll while stationed in Germany. Authors Leslie Thomas, David Lodge and David Findlay Clark wrote books based on their experiences – *The Virgin Soldiers*, and *Ginger You're Barmy*, for example. Actor Oliver Reed, comedian Tony Hancock and Hancock's writers Ray Galton and Alan Simpson developed their talents during conscription.

On the other hand, National Service interrupted some men's careers. For example John Clark, a former child actor, was tired of ubiquitous recognition and feared mockery in the armed forces, so he worked in the merchant navy on a Silver Line freighter for over three years. And the Krays reckoned that National Service would interfere with their budding careers, too.

A few hours into their army career, the twins turned and walked towards the door. A corporal asked where they were going. 'Home,' they replied, 'We're going to see our mother.' The corporal caught hold of Ronnie's arm. Ronnie punched him on the jaw, knocking him out, and strolled out, along with his brother.

The following morning, the army came and collected them, and they returned without a struggle to their barracks, where they were sentenced to seven days in the guardroom.

They immediately decided to desert again. In the guardroom, they met Dickie Morgan, a former Borstal boy from Mile End. As soon as their seven days were up, the three of them walked out of the Tower and headed straight for Morgan's home near London's docklands.

If the army couldn't tame the Kray twins, nobody could, and now, for the first time, the twins encountered a world where crime was regarded as a way of life. Through Morgan, they began to drink in clubs and bars frequented by criminals – much like Kenny Noye had done – and by the time the army caught up with them once again, they had opted to forgo the possibilities of boxing for a life of full-time villainy.

From that day on, the army and the law actively aided them. A month in Wormwood Scrubs (for assaulting a policeman) and nine months at the Shepton Mallet Military Prison (for striking an NCO and going absent without leave) only served to introduce them to a wider range of criminals from across the country.

With their sentences completed, the army discharged the twins, leaving them with the problems of earning a living. They spent a large part of the day in the Regal Snooker Hall in Mile End. The place had seen better days – gangs had their fights there, fireworks were thrown at the manager's Alsatian, the baize on the tables was slashed. When the manager resigned, Reggie and Ronnie stepped in with the offer of renting the hall for £5 a week.

Immediately, the trouble stopped. As Reggie later explained, 'It was very simple – the punters, the local tearaways, knew that if there was any trouble, if anything got broken, Ron and I would simply break their bones.'

Apart from maintaining order, it is to their credit that the twins redecorated the hall, moved in 14 second-hand tables and began to earn reasonable money. Their aim, however, was not merely to secure an income. With the Regal, they had found themselves an operating base. One of their first tasks was to see off threats from potential rivals. When a Maltese gang appeared to demand protection money, the twins went after them with knives, and word started to circulate about the newest arrivals in the East End underworld.

With a headquarters and a growing band of regulars who found the twins' patronage useful, the two Krays started to flaunt their violence. In the late evenings, Ronnie would frequently stand up and announce it was time for a raid. Then, accompanied by Reggie and a crowd of followers, he would set off for a pub, dance hall or club to engineer a brawl. At the same time, small-time crooks began to find the Regal a useful place to meet and discuss and plan possible ventures.

The twins also began to operate protection rackets – 'nipping and pensions' as they were known – whereby pubs, cafés, illegal gambling joints and bookies would be obliged to hand over goods or money in return for protection from rival gangs.

But although the income had begun to flow in on a regular basis, the twins were still very much local villains, criminals from the East End who worked the East End. If they were going to break out from their ghetto, they needed an introduction to the wider world of organised crime in the West End.

In 1955, now aged just 22, it appeared as if their break had finally arrived. The joint bosses of the London underworld were two men called Billy Hill and Jack Comer, better known as 'Jack' and 'Spot'. Between them, they had overseen the West End's drinking, gambling, prostitution and protection rackets for more than a decade. But they fell out with each other and, after being badly cut up in a fight, Spot decided he needed some extra muscle. He called on the Krays.

Jack Comer... Jacob Colmore... John Colmore... Jacob Comacho... he was known by a multitude of names. However, 'Jack Spot' was his common title, with him claiming it was because he was always on the spot when trouble needed sorting. More prosaically, it was said to be a childhood alias given for the mole on his cheek.

Born on Friday, 12 April 1912 in Whitechapel's Myrdle Street, Spot was the son of Polish immigrants, his brother a tailor and his sister a dressmaker. But if his siblings took a predictable route for young immigrants, Spot was after better money.

At 15, he became a bookie's runner, then a year later he hooked up with a man running protection rackets on the Sunday morning stalls in Petticoat Lane. Times were tight, and the stallholders' main concern was to prevent new traders moving in and diluting their takings. Quickly showing his aptitude for gangland procedure, Spot managed to fall out with his senior partner, fought him, and took the protection business for himself, emerging as the self-styled 'King of Aldgate'.

He went into partnership with East End bookie Dutch Barney, then took a more direct route, acting as lookout and minder to a successful housebreaker. Arrested and admitting to 40 offences, he was merely bound over. No doubt amazed by his luck, Spot went back to bookmaking.

They say the bookie never loses – Spot made sure he didn't. If he had a bad day at the course, he'd be off before the punters came to collect their winnings, and supplemented his takings with a fairground con called 'Take a Pick', where punters paid sixpence (2.5p) to pull a straw from a cup. Lucky winners (and there were few) won a piece of tat, while Spot pocketed £40 a day. Amazingly, he continued to operate successfully at the racetracks for some time, relying on the never-ending supply of mug punters, backed up by the unspoken threat of violence. Taking his 'Pick' game back to Petticoat Lane, he would make £50 on a good day.

In addition to the reputation he was garnering as a hard-man villain, a major part of the Jack Spot mythology centres on his protection of Jewish shopkeepers from the Blackshirts on their marches down

Brick Lane. His status as friend and protector to East End Jews is certainly partly true – but he did charge the shopkeepers £10 a time. Nonetheless, it did the trick, and stallholders would be queuing up to donate money to Spot's 'Market Traders' Association'; in fact, it was just another protection racket.

After a brief stint of war service in the Royal Artillery, he returned first to the East End and then west, to where the real money was. After a fight in the Edgware Road, and fearing imprisonment, he fled north. He worked as a minder around Leeds and Newcastle, helping up-and-coming gangsters beat or intimidate the old guard out of their nightclubs, gambling dens or racecourse pitches.

Back in London in the late 1940s, Spot ran the Botolph Club in Aldgate, pocketing £3,000 a week from illegal gambling. More romantically, he now saw himself as 'the Robin Hood of the East End', travelling to Leeds, Manchester or Glasgow to beat up villains who threatened Jewish businesses. He even claimed that rabbis would advise their frightened people to call on his services. And he was still making a fortune from the races, meeting anyone who crossed him with instant and savage retribution.

The White family, who had run betting at the major southern courses for years, were harassed, attacked with knives, bottles, machetes and, finally, routed in a fight at Haringey Arena. The date was 9 July 1947. Now in partnership with gangster Billy Hill, all serious opposition had been crushed, but now Billy Hill and Jack Spot had fallen out, and this was an invitation the twins had been waiting for – and immediately they embarked on large-scale preparations for a gang war with Spot's enemies.

They collected weapons, called up their own band of 'Merry Men' and established a base in Vallance Road.

They heard that the opposition was meeting in a pub near Islington. After assembling their army at the Regal, the twins set off for north London. When they arrived, they found the place empty – Billy Hill had got wind of the impending battle and ordered his men to pull out.

What old-timers such as Spot and Billy Hill had long since learned was that power was wielded not through violence itself but by the credible threat of violence. The twins dealt in the real thing. Frustrated by the Islington fiasco, they sought a confrontation elsewhere, and they chose a social club in Clerkenwell Road which was the headquarters of a gang of Italians. 'We were fearless in those days. Fighting was our game. When he got bored we would go to a dance hall or pub, just looking for a bit of bother,' Reggie stated.

Arriving shortly after 10.00pm, Ronnie entered alone and challenged the men inside to a fight. A bottle was thrown at his head, but no one said anything. In response, he pulled out a Mauser and fired three shots into a wall. Still no one reacted, so Ronnie turned around and walked out.

Clearly, he had made his point – the twins meant business. But no one wanted to do business with them. Even Spot tired of their antics and retired to run a furniture business.

Ignoring the twins, however, would not make them go away. Despite their failure to win acceptance, they were no longer East End hoodlums, and it was only a matter of time before a major opening into the London underworld turned up. In the summer of 1956, the owner of a West End drinking club called The Stragglers approached the Krays to help stamp out the fighting that plagued his bar.

The next few years were to be ones of increasing prosperity. Ironically, one of the major reasons for this success was the fact that, on 5 November 1956, Ronnie started a three-year prison sentence for grievous bodily harm. Having installed themselves in The Stragglers, the twins became involved in a dispute between the club's proprietors and a rival Irish gang. Ronnie thought the gang should be taught a lesson and, after raiding the pub where the Irishmen met, participated in beating a man called Terence Martin to near-death.

Although the separation from Ronnie was a great emotional blow to Reggie, it gave him free rein to manage the twins' business interests. Without his brother's continual demands for violent retribution at the faintest hint of an insult or competition, they flourished. One of his first moves was to open a legitimate club of his own – The Double R on the Bow Road – which soon became the East End's premier night spot. At the same time, he moved into minding and protecting the illegal gambling parties held at smart addresses in Mayfair and Belgravia.

Meanwhile, Ronnie appeared to accept his sentence at Wandsworth Prison with equanimity. Armed with his reputation and copious supplies of tobacco from his brother, he had little difficulty ensuring he was treated with due respect by his fellow inmates, many of whom he already knew. But, unexpectedly, because of his good behaviour he was transferred to Camp Hill Prison on the Isle of Wight.

Isolated from both his friends in Wandsworth and his

family, Ronnie's mind began to collapse with amazing speed. He began to hear voices, to imagine that he was surrounded by informers and spies, and he injured several prisoners before being moved to the psychiatric wing of Winchester Prison.

Just after Christmas 1957, now aged 24, his mental breakdown reached a climax following the news that his favourite aunt had died. This may seem ridiculous to some, for the Krays, who spared no feelings for the victims they maimed, retained all the sentimentality of a close-knit Cockney family. After spending the night in a strait-jacket, Ronnie was certified insane the following morning. Two days later, Violet Kray received a prison telegram announcing: 'YOUR SON, RONALD, CERTIFIED INSANE.'

From Winchester, Ronnie was transferred to Long Grove, a psychiatric hospital close to Epsom in Surrey, where his condition rapidly improved. Its former patients included Josef Hassid (a Polish violin prodigy) and former shoemaker George Pelham (a man who survived the sinking of two ships, including the RMS *Titanic*). Understandably, Pelham suffered a nervous breakdown and was admitted to the asylum on 22 January 1935, and died four years later.

For his part, Hassid was first placed in a psychiatric hospital in 1941 after suffering from a nervous breakdown at the age of 18. He was admitted again in 1943 and was diagnosed with acute schizophrenia. He was lobotomised in late 1950 and died at the age of 26.

History tells us that little attention was paid to strict security at Long Grove, and every Sunday visitors could come and see their friends or relatives. Reggie, naturally, was a regular visitor. But while he could see that his brother was on the road to recovery, he knew that if the hospital continued to regard his twin as insane, they could postpone his release date indefinitely. Ronnie had to escape.

The plan was simplicity itself. Reggie entered the hospital wearing a light-coloured overcoat and, while the ward attendant looked elsewhere, Ronnie put on the overcoat and walked through the door to freedom. By the time it was realised that the remaining twin was Reggie, Ronnie was on his way to a caravan in Suffolk.

Although his mind again deteriorated rapidly in the isolation of the countryside, the scheme worked. He remained free long enough for his certification of insanity to expire. Reggie then handed him back to the police, and he completed his sentence in Wandsworth Prison.

Released in the spring of 1958, Ronnie could finally start to enjoy the riches his brother had been accumulating for the previous two years, and he was soon back to his old ways, planning gangland battles and expanding the twins' operations through threats and violence. Then the Krays undertook their biggest and most profitable venture to date – Esmeralda's Barn.

Esmeralda's Barn was a successful casino at 50, Wilton Place, in wealthy Belgravia. One of the most exclusive areas in London, boasting Harrods and Harvey Nichols, two of the premier department stores in the world; just down the road is Buckingham Palace. Tipped off that it was effectively owned by just one man, Stefan de Faye, the twins, accompanied by Ronnie's financial adviser Leslie Payne, paid him a visit in the autumn of 1960. Payne outlined the twins' proposition that de Faye should sell his controlling share in the casino for £1,000. The prospect of falling foul of the Krays was enough to persuade de Faye to accept the offer; thus, overnight, the twins were set up for the Sixties with one of the most lucrative gaming houses in the West End.

With Esmeralda's Barn, the twins gained far more than a West End foothold, with the muscle to back it up. Its gaming tables alone earned them around £1,600 a week, and Reggie was soon busy at work adding protection money from the other clubs and casinos that had proliferated with the legalisation of gambling in 1960. At least ten of them were handing over £150 to the Krays weekly.

At the same time, the twins continued to open their own clubs. In March 1962, the doors were opened to The Kentucky, a larger version of The Double R, in Stepney. Two years later, they bought into another club, The Cambridge Rooms on the Kingston by-pass, and invited the then world heavyweight boxing champion, Sonny Liston, to the opening night party.

Increasingly, Reggie and Ronnie were meeting on social occasions with the rich and famous, who were mostly unaware of their illegal activities. They all seemed to enjoy being photographed with the Krays.

Ronnie and Reggie surrounded themselves with the Sixties glitterati, with showbusiness stars such as Judy Garland, gangster-role actor George Raft, Diana Dors, and her husband, talented and much-loved Alan Lake, and Barbara Windsor, posing with the twins.

Sports personalities, including football manager Malcolm Allison, and the welterweight world boxing champ, Gershon Mendeloff – aka Ted 'Kid' Lewis – were patrons, as were Henry Cooper, Rocky Marciano, and

Victor Spinetti, the Welsh-born comedy actor, comic eccentric, gifted raconteur and close friend of the Beatles. Up-market call-girl Christine Keeler and even soon-to-be disgraced Government minister John Profumo enjoyed VIP status at any of the Kray's clubs, as did numerous minor celebrities and high-ranking police officers, solicitors, barristers and judges.

The Krays has made it to the 'big time', and it seemed that nothing could ever go wrong. But the wheels did indeed come off, and that was mostly down to their failure, during the first half of the decade, an era of expansion, to capitalise fully from either their legitimate or illegal business interests. Largely responsible was the twins' inability to give up the habits that got them where they were, but which also proved a liability.

As fast as the Krays added a new concern to their empire, an old one crumbled away. The Double R had its licence revoked after Reggie refused to give the police information on the whereabouts of one Ronnie Marwood, wanted for the stabbing of a policeman. Marwood was completely innocent of the crime and the Krays believed him, and they certainly were not going to 'grass' him up to the Old Bill.

Esmeralda's Barn, which should have maintained the twins' regular source of legitimate income for years, soon began to run at a loss once Ronnie started handing out credit to gamblers who could not repay their debts. In 1964, the Krays received a tax demand from the Inland Revenue that they were unable to meet. The Barn went out of business.

Strangely, the twins' criminal activities never appeared to be driven by a desire for money – they saw it as a mark of success, naturally, but once they had secured a reasonable return for their efforts, they became bored. Ronnie stated, 'Ron and I never really liked the protection business. It wasn't glamorous enough for us.'

Novelty began to grow more and more important to them. Ronnie, in particular, continually produced one extraordinary scheme after another. Later, in 1964, he plunged into one of the twins' most bizarre ventures.

Ernest Shinwell, homosexual son of the veteran Labour peer, Manny Shinwell, proposed they invest in a project to build a new town and major factory development at Enugu in eastern Nigeria. The twins immediately put in £25,000, later followed by a lot more. The prime motivator was Ronnie, who told me during my visit to Broadmoor that the project was designed to push them further into the international spotlight. The investment yielded no return whatsoever, although the twins did get one or two trips to Nigeria, where they were driven around in a Rolls-Royce, with Ronnie being 'stylishly entertained' by a number of very young Nigerian boys.

One might say that the Kray twins could be taken out of their formative environment, the East End, but one could never take the East End out of the Krays. Born and bred in such an impoverished environment, they would always have reverted back to the socio-mentality, and the living conditions, that their early years had imprinted upon their personalities. They were at home in the East End, and had they stayed there, they might have thrived. Moving into West End business ventures, although successful for a short period, proved to be way above their heads. When they started involving themselves with the son of a peer of the realm, and a half-baked scheme to better the lives of Nigerians, the twins were well out of their depth.

The 'Nigerian Project' had been touted around for quite a while by Ernest Shinwell with no takers. When 'Ernie' visited Esmeralda's, he fell in with the eagle-eyed Leslie Payne – the Krays' business manager – who took up the project and who convinced Ronnie and Reggie that it would be a good investment. Little did the twins know that Payne was on a fat back-hander, by way of a commission, if the Krays put up cash for a consortium deal.

During the negotiations with Shinwell, Ronnie was wined and dined at the Houses of Parliament. And it was here that he was first introduced to Lord Boothby, a bisexual who had declared that he wasn't quite sure if he preferred young boys or young girls.

The twins and their esteemed business associates made several visits to the Nigerian development site. In the beginning, they were treated like royalty and met all the local dignitaries and ministers of the region. On one occasion, Ronnie was given a tour of the local jail and even had his photograph taken with a warder. However, things soon started to go wrong. On another trip to Enugu, Leslie Payne and colleague Freddie Gore were arrested and an associate, Gordon Anderson, and Charlie Kray had their passports confiscated until they could come up with £5,000, said to be the amount of money owed to one of the building contractors involved in the project.

The Krays had met their match with their Nigerian counterparts, who were similarly motivated as the twins as far as underhand dealings went, but were far more street-wise when on their home soil. It was a shakedown in a country where the Krays muscle was worthless. As Ronnie explained to me, 'They had us by the balls.' Charlie had to contact his brothers, who stumped up the £5,000.

As time passed, the project and its funds were slowly disappearing. More investors were needed to keep the project afloat.

If the Krays spent money easily, there appeared to be no shortage of sources of new funds. In 1965, the twins spread their net wider as they began to develop a working relationship with the American Mafia, in an effort to earn big bucks.

Their first chance to prove themselves in the field of international crime came with the theft of $55,000 worth of bonds from a bank in Canada. Too hot to be laundered through North America, some of the bonds were offered to the Krays for sale in Europe. Soon the trade was flourishing.

However, in the same year, the Krays suffered a setback. Hew McCowan, the son of a baronet and owner of a Soho nightclub called Hideaway, told police the Krays were demanding half his profits. Reggie and Ronnie were arrested and, after 56 days in custody, appeared at the Old Bailey charged with demanding money with menaces.

By the time the trial took place, however, they had dug up enough information about McCowan's history as a police informer to throw doubt on the reliability of his evidence. The trial was halted before the summing-up speeches and the twins were released. The very same day, they celebrated their acquittal by buying the Hide-a-Way, renaming it El Morocco and throwing a victory party.

For Reggie, the good times looked set to continue. On 20 April, he married the woman he had courted for three years, 21-year-old Frances Shea. The wedding was celebrated in typical Kray style, with Rolls-Royces, David Bailey as the official photographer, celebrities such as boxer Terry Spinks in attendance and congratulatory telegrams from Judy Garland, Barbara Windsor and many others.

Alas, the marriage didn't last. Frances killed herself in June 1967, at the age of 23, after less than two years of unhappy marriage. The depressing aura the twins had created around themselves was too much for her.

But beneath the veneer of upward mobility, the violence which had been the twins' main asset in getting them to the top began to turn sour on them. Instead of settling down to enjoy the proceeds of their protection rackets, clubs and casinos, Ronnie in particular became obsessed with proving himself to be the unchallenged boss of London's underworld.

Over the years, his suits became slicker, he began to wear ostentatious jewellery, and more and more he regarded himself as a Godfather figure. But while he adopted the appearance of a smart crook, moving with the times and mingling with the jet-set, his mind was slowly disintegrating.

Ronnie's bouts of depression worsened, and he started to regard almost everyone around him with suspicion. His fears would give way to sudden bouts of pathological violence. It didn't take much to set him off. One old friend who tried to borrow £5 was slashed in the face. Another had his cheeks branded after starting a brawl in Esmeralda's Barn.

Ronnie, however, wanted more than random attacks and knifings. Ever since the days of the Regal billiard hall, he took a great pride in his organisational abilities, assembling gangs to beat up rival gangs, and building up an armoury of weapons that included machine-guns. Time after time, however, his dream of releasing his forces on competition worth attacking had been thwarted.

It was only at the emergence of the Richardson brothers and their gang did the Krays look as if they finally had an enemy powerful enough to demand their full attention. The fact that the Mafia was now dealing with the twins added an extra piquancy.

Ronnie found himself in his element. After the meeting when Cornell called him a 'fat poof', he had a double grudge to bear and, when a car ran down a man who resembled Ronnie in Vallance Road, it looked like a gang war was starting. Later, Ronnie recalled, 'I was loving it. Fighting, scrapping, battling... that's what I'd come into it for in the first place.'

Unhappily for Ronnie, the excitement was short-lived. When the two Richardson brothers became involved in a shoot-out with another gang at a pub in Catford, it looked as though they had destroyed themselves without any help from the Krays. Ronnie once again felt he had been cheated of the opportunity to prove himself through violence. And instead of revelling in this stroke of luck that left the twins as the undisputed rulers of London gangland, Ronnie's pathological urge for revenge overpowered him. Within 24 hours, he had murdered George Cornell.

George Cornell

Ronnie Kray famously stated, 'In front of a table full of villains, George Cornell called me a "fat poof". He virtually signed his own death warrant.'

Born George Myers on 9 March 1928, 38-year-old George Cornell was a lifelong criminal who dabbled in pornography and blackmail before moving south of the River Thames to become one of the chief torturers of the Richardson gang. His prison sentences included three years for attacking a woman with a knife.

Business was quiet in the bars of The Blind Beggar pub in the East End of London's Whitechapel Road on the evening of Tuesday, 8 March 1966. It was close to 8.30pm and there was an hour to go before trade was likely to build up. An off-duty police inspector had just finished a snack and left, so, almost as a gesture of confidence, the barmaid put a record on the jukebox – 'The Sun Ain't Gonna Shine Any More' by the Walker Brothers – and its brassy notes created the illusion that the pub was about to come to life. But the pounding beat was no distraction to a dark, pouting customer, George Cornell, absorbed in conversation with his pal Albie Woods in the lounge bar.

Occasionally, the talk between the two was interrupted by short bursts of coarse, tough laughter but, unknown to Cornell, a few hundred yards to the north in The Lion in Tapp Street, Ronnie, Reggie and some members of 'the Firm' were drinking. Someone called them, and told Ronnie that Cornell was just down the road. Taking one of his men, John 'Scotch' Dickson, and with Ian Barrie driving, they made their way down Brady Street, turning into the Whitechapel Road and pulling up outside The Blind Beggar.

Unaware that one of his arch enemies had just arrived outside, Cornell, perched on a bar stool, supped slowly at a glass of light ale. He was relaxed, enjoying his hour or so away from his 'work' as one of London's most vicious gangsters. His glass was almost empty, and ready for a refill that was never to come, when the door to the bar opened and two men stalked in.

Cornell half-turned on his stool and his dark eyes lit with a falsely welcoming smile as he recognised one of the two newcomers, a brooding, boxer-type man with thick eyebrows that almost met on the bridge of his long, flared nose. It was Ronnie Kray.

'Well, just look who's here!' cried Cornell, with mock surprise. Neither man answered him, but Kray's companion, Ian Barrie, a former safe-blower from Scotland, drew a revolver and fired two shots into the ceiling. The barmaid screamed and fled. Cornell and his friend sat frozen, unspeaking. Then with a melodramatic gesture, Ronald Kray pulled a 9mm Mauser automatic from a shoulder holster and pointed it at Cornell's head, pulling the trigger three times.

With blood and brain tissue flying, Cornell bounced back against the pillar and then tumbled to the floor like an abandoned puppet. Barrie fired his gun into the ceiling once more and the remaining few customers dived for cover. A ricocheting bullet hit the juke-box and, as Ronnie and his partner walked out of the bar, it stuck in its track and kept repeating, 'The sun ain't gonna shine any more... any more... any more...' As quickly as they had arrived, Kray and his henchman disappeared. The frightened barmaid ran back to help the wounded man, but he was beyond all hope. He was dead by the time the ambulance arrived.

Within hours, the whole of the East End of London had heard the whispered news that 'Ronnie Kray had "done" a bloke in a pub'. It was a dangerous piece of information, and however swiftly it passed along the grapevines of Whitechapel, Poplar and Bethnal Green, it was not for the ears of outsiders.

When Superintendent Tommy Butler, the outstanding and almost legendary Scotland Yard detective, arrived to begin his investigations, he was met by a wall of silence. Customers in the pub insisted that they had 'not been paying any attention'.

Butler, though, knew the identity of the killer well enough. He and his men had their own 'ears' along the grapevine. But the main problem was one that had prevailed in the East End for so long – no one with first-hand evidence would dare go into court and testify against the 32-year-old Ronnie Kray or his twin brother, Reggie.

In what he was sure would be a fruitless move, but nevertheless one he had to try, Butler put Ronnie into an identification parade at Commercial Street Police Station. The unhappy and worried barmaid from The Blind Beggar went through the motions of walking along the line of men and studying their faces. Eventually, she apologised to Butler, saying that her memory for faces was not good, and she could not swear that she had seen any of the men in the pub at the time of the murder.

The Firm had got away with it again, and it was the glorious draught Ronnie so desperately needed his brother to share. After all, they were inseparable twins. In his frequent rages, he screamed at Reggie, 'I've done my one. When are you going to do yours? Are you too soft?'

The loss of his pretty young wife and Ronnie's ever-growing megalomania served only to thrust Reggie further under Ronnie's dark spell. He drove early one morning to the flat of a former friend whom he suspected of making disdainful comments about his late wife and, in front of the man's terrified wife and children, shot him through the leg.

But no one had a luckier escape from Ronnie's volcanic temper than George Dixon. Once a friend of the twins, he fell out of favour after making remarks about Ronnie's homosexuality. One evening, shortly after the Cornell shooting, he paid a visit to the Regency Club in Stoke Newington. Spotting Ronnie sitting in a corner, he walked straight up to him and demanded to know why the twins had barred him from their clubs.

Instead of replying, Ronnie took out a gun, put it against Dixon's head and pulled the trigger. Miraculously, it failed to fire. Instead of trying again, Ronnie removed the dud bullet and gave it to Dixon as a souvenir.

Frank Mitchell – 'The Mad Axe Man'

All reason now seemed to desert the twins, and one of their most brutal and bizarre escapades involved the Dartmoor prisoner, Frank Mitchell, dubbed 'The Mad Axe Man' for threatening an elderly couple with a woodsman's axe.

On 12 December 1965, the Krays assisted Frank Mitchell in escaping from Dartmoor Prison. Ronnie Kray had befriended Mitchell when they served time together in another prison. Mitchell felt the authorities should review his case for parole, so Ronnie felt he would be doing him a favour by getting him out of Dartmoor, highlighting his case in the media and forcing the authorities to act.

Once Mitchell was out of Dartmoor, the Krays held

him at a friend's flat in Barking Road. To ease the boredom of his days under cover, the Krays provided him with a nightclub hostess, who later declared, 'His virility was greater than any man I have even known!'

But the twins were very soon tired of the burden of being saddled with the great bear of a man who, in physique and childlike character, was reminiscent of Lennie Small in John Steinbeck's novel *Of Mice and Men*. Like Lennie, who needed in his confused way to cling to some other human being, Mitchell complicated the situation by falling in love with the girl who was being paid by the Krays to comfort him.

As a final, desperate solution, the Krays told Mitchell he was being moved to a 'safe' farm in Kent and, for security's sake, the girl would follow within a few hours. So, after dark on Christmas Eve 1966, Mitchell was bundled into the back of a van which sped off down the Barking Road, taking him to an unmarked grave.

Subsequently at the Old Bailey, Albert Donoghue, Mitchell's escort, alleged that, as soon as the van moved off, the two men, waiting inside, poured a fusillade of shots into Mitchell's body. Later, Donaghue telephoned Reggie Kray with the brief message: 'The geezer's gone!'

Freddie Foreman, a former member of the Firm, in his autobiography *Respect*, claimed that Mitchell had been shot and the body disposed of in the sea.

Jack 'The Hat' McVitie

Despite the fact that Mitchell had been murdered on Reggie's orders, he had not actually murdered anyone with his own hands, and this was an issue Ronnie wouldn't let his brother forget. Repeatedly, he pointed out that there was no shortage of people 'taking liberties'. At the top of his list was a squalid, small-time but extremely strong man and once a fearsome, brawling hoodlum named Jack McVitie who, because of his vanity about his baldness, was never seen without a hat and had thereby earned the nickname of 'Jack the Hat'.

Although undeniably a tough man, McVitie also possessed an unpredictable streak of sadism and masochism. On one occasion, a gang smashed up his hands with a crowbar after he was caught playing around with one of their women. Within a few weeks, he was back on the streets eager to fight with anyone. Like George Cornell, he did not restrict his violence to men. One of his most notorious exploits involved throwing a woman from a car travelling at 40mph. Although she broke her back, she was too frightened of the consequences to report McVitie.

Now consumed by drink and drugs, occasionally the Krays offered McVitie a spell of employment. In the summer of 1967, he cheated them of some money. To prove his loyalty, he was told to shoot Leslie Payne, a former business associate of the twins. He was given a gun and an advance of £100, with another £400 to follow on completion of the job. McVitie never did kill Payne, but he kept the Kray's money. When Reggie tried to smooth matters over by lending McVitie another £50, Ronnie taunted his brother that he was turning soft.

Nagged by Ronnie, dispirited by a declining 'business' – Esmeralda's Barn had long since collapsed in debt – Reggie gave in. And, to make matters worse, McVitie got drunk and, armed with a sawn-off shotgun, went to the Regency Club in Hackney claiming he was going to shoot the Krays. His threats soon reached the twins' ears.

On Saturday, 28 October 1967, the twins arranged a party for their mother and friends in a Bethnal Green pub. During the course of the evening, Reggie received word that McVitie was due to turn up at the Regency Club in Stoke Newington later that night. After drinking himself to the point of numbness, Reggie took leave of his guests and arrived at the Regency just before 11.00pm. McVitie was nowhere to be seen. Frustrated, Reggie left his .32 revolver with Tony Barry, one of the two brothers who managed the club, and left to join Ronnie at a party in nearby Cazenove Road.

When Reggie arrived, Ronnie was disappointed – his brother had failed him once again. Resolving on action, Ronnie dispatched his cousin Ronnie Hart to the Regency to retrieve the gun, insisting it had to be delivered by Tony Barry himself. Then he sent out Anthony and Christopher Lambrianou, two half-Greek brothers, to track down Jack McVitie.

Hart returned first. Barry handed over the gun and disappeared into the night. Shortly before midnight, the Lambrianous came back. With them was Jack the Hat. Completely drunk, he walked into the basement room shouting, 'Where's the birds and the booze?' Reggie was waiting for him behind the door. He put his gun against McVitie's head and pulled the trigger. The killing should have been as simple as Ronnie's, but the gun failed to fire. Reggie grabbed McVitie, but he managed to struggle his way free and tried to throw himself through the window. He was hauled back in by his legs, losing his hat in the process. Trembling and pale, he backed away with sweat pouring from his hairless head.

'Be a man, Jack,' shouted Ronnie.

'I'll be a man,' said McVitie, by now in tears, 'but I don't want to fucking die like one... why are you doing this to me?'

His plea and Reggie's oaths were drowned by the hysterical screaming of Ronnie. 'Kill him, Reg! Do him! Don't stop now!'

With McVitie's arms held behind his back by Ronnie, Reggie took a carving knife and plunged it into his face just below his eye. He then stabbed him repeatedly through the chest and stomach until he was dead. The house was cleaned up, and the corpse disposed of. At last, Ronnie could be proud of his brother, who stated later, 'I'm not ashamed of having killed McVitie. I don't believe I had any choice. It was either him or me.'

With no witnesses other than members of the Firm, it was a while before the police got wind of McVitie's disappearance. His wife reported him missing, but with no body, there seemed little reason to suspect foul play. Even when rumours of McVitie's killing reached the police, there was little they could do. For the second time, the twins had killed in cold blood, but sheltered behind the barrier of the East End wall of silence. For the time being, that wall remained impregnable.

What the police needed was a break. It came from the unlikely source of Leslie Payne, the man who had masterminded the acquisition of Esmeralda's Barn and organised many of the 'long firm' frauds, and was triggered by the twins' use of gratuitous violence.

In a belated attempt to test McVitie's loyalty before Reggie stabbed him, Ronnie had dispatched him to murder Payne. Although McVitie bungled the attempt, Payne came to the conclusion that it was either his life or theirs.

He decided to talk to the police and, in December 1967, he spent three weeks in a Marylebone hotel giving a statement that eventually ran to some 200 pages. It contained everything he knew about the twins' activities, from Esmeralda's Barn to their Mafia connections. The task now was to verify Payne's claims, and a deal was struck whereby the statements would never be used unless the twins had first been arrested.

Despite the secrecy of the police operation, the twins' network of sources soon let them know that the Old Bill was on their trail. They were not unduly disturbed – as Reggie later said, 'We didn't think we would go down. We underestimated the cunning of the police.' The brothers contended themselves with buying two pythons and naming them 'Nipper' (after the officer chasing them, Inspector 'Nipper' Read) and Gerrard (after another a detective who had had dealings with the Krays in the past). Ironically, the snakes proved too hard to handle. One escaped and the other was returned to its seller.

At this point, Alan Cooper, a financier, began to play a more important role in the Kray's lives. Cooper had helped the twins dispose of some stolen Canadian bonds. Although Reggie favoured caution until the police hunt had died down, Ronnie was growing obsessed with establishing himself as the Godfather figure of the London underworld. This called for more contact with the Mafia and, in Cooper, he thought he had found the contact who could help him.

Despite the fact that Ronnie had a criminal record, Cooper said he could arrange an American visa for him through Paris and, once in the United States, various meetings could be arranged with the Mafia. Ronnie leapt at the opportunity. Cooper was as good as his word and, in April 1968, the two of them flew into New York for a few days' discussions with a Mafia representative called Frank Ileano.

To Ronnie, it looked like another step up the ladder. After returning to Britain, he warmed to Cooper's suggestion that the Mafia would appreciate the killing of George Caruana, a Maltese club-owner, as a display of the Kray's strength. The two of them decided to put a bomb in his car. Cooper said he knew a man who could supply the explosive. He dispatched an assistant to fly to Glasgow to collect four sticks of dynamite from a contact in the centre of the city.

As he boarded his return flight, the man was arrested. Under questioning, he named Cooper as his boss. Nipper Read hauled Cooper in, only to discover both to his surprise and irritation that Cooper had been operating as an agent of the United States Treasury Department and with the knowledge of Read's superiors at Scotland Yard.

According to Cooper, his task was to implicate the twins in an attempted murder. With the dynamite courier arrested, this now became impossible, so Read decided to use Cooper as bait to get the twins to incriminate themselves. He installed Cooper in a private hospital with a microphone beside his bed. He then got him to invite the twins round.

A certain strangeness in Cooper's manner on the telephone made Ronnie and Reggie suspicious and, instead of going themselves, they sent one of Reggie's friends. He refused to commit himself in front of Cooper and, once again, the twins had escaped Nipper Read.

It seemed that the police had walked into another cul-de-sac. The twins tightened their organisation and opted for a low-profile approach to running their empire. With the Richardsons in jail and the deaths of Cornell and McVitie fading into the past, it looked as if they would weather the storm.

Nonetheless, the strain of endless vigilance had begun to tell. Although the money continued to flow in from the clubs and casinos, with no major deals on the go, life had lost some of its excitement. One evening in early May 1968, Ronnie decided that what the Firm needed was a good knees-up. He told everyone to collect their women and head for Mayfair's Astor Club. Outside, there was the usual gaggle of photographers snapping pictures of everyone who entered. Maybe there were more than usual, and Reggie, visibly irritated, shouted at them to stop. No one noticed that they were never offered the rapidly developing prints as souvenirs later in the evening.

Through the early hours of the morning, the twins carried on drinking, their troubles forgotten. Ronnie was enjoying the company of a young man he had brought along for the evening, and Reggie was enjoying the attentions of a young lady. At 5.00am, they left the Astor and returned to their flat in Braithwaite House, on City Road, Finsbury.

They had barely time to fall asleep when the front door was crashed off its hinges with a sledgehammer. It was 6.00am on Thursday, 9 May 1968, when a specially recruited team of detectives, led by Nipper Read, raided the homes of 24 members of the Firm. Read personally arrested the twins.

But, there is something decidedly odd about the

generally agreed date of their arrest – 9 May – for *The Evening News and Star* ran the following headline on Wednesday, 8 May, a good few hours *before* the Krays were arrested: 'YARD ARREST KRAY TWINS AND BROTHER... 18 men held for questioning after 100 police swoop on London homes.'

The whereabouts of the remains of Frank Mitchell and Jack McVitie have never been established. Theories circulated, some based on court evidence and others on gossip which had worked its way along the grapevine in the East End. No one was found guilty of Mitchell's murder and he remains officially on the run from Dartmoor Prison. But Albert Donaghue, a member of the Firm who turned Queen's evidence, claimed in court that he knew how his body had been disposed of.

He alleged that Freddie Foreman and others had taken it into the country where it had been cut up and burned. He also claimed that Foreman had described Mitchell's brain as tiny and that, when they removed his heart, there were three bullets lodged inside. McVitie's body was variously rumoured to have been buried in the concrete foundations of a City tower block, burned in the furnaces of Bankside power station, and turned into pig food. Another, more likely, theory was that the body was given to an undertaker for secret disposal.

George Cornell is buried at the Camberwell New Cemetery. The grave is situated at the end of the main drive, on the left kerbside, facing the left-hand chapel.

Once behind bars, the twins had time to reflect on what had happened. Reggie said, 'Everyone in London was talking about us. It was getting to the point when either the police had to break us up or we would have broken them. But the party was over, it had been great while it lasted.'

Even locked up in Brixton Prison, the twins were confident they could still escape justice. Every day, their mother brought them lunch, usually cold chicken and a bottle of wine, while friends would drop by with news from the outside world. With their cousin, Ronnie Hart, and Ronnie's minder, Ian Barrie, still at large, most people who knew them thought they could continue to ensure that no one would talk. Even when these two failed to escape Nipper Read's net, the Krays still believed the wall of silence would hold strong – how wrong they were.

Slowly, the first seeds of doubt crept into their minds as the messages reaching them grew more pessimistic. Their fears were confirmed at the preliminary hearings held at Old Street Magistrates Court on 6 July 1968. To generate as much publicity as possible, the twins asked for all press restrictions to be lifted. 'We want the world to see the diabolical liberties the law has been taking,' Reggie said.

Journalists were delighted – the trial would be the biggest they had witnessed for years. The twins were less happy when into the witness box stepped Billy Exley, a former bodyguard of Ronnie's who had been on watch the day of Cornell's killing.

For the first time, Reggie and Ronnie began to look vulnerable. Exley was followed by the Blind Beggar's barmaid, who had suddenly regained her memory for faces.

With the completion of the preliminary hearings, the twins were held in Brixton Prison for another five months. This gave Read the breathing space he needed to convince more members of the Firm to take the witness stand and testify for the Crown.

The trial proper opened at the Old Bailey on Tuesday, 7 January 1969. Reggie and Ronnie were both charged with murder and being an accessory to murder. Public interest was intense. Seats in the public gallery were sold on the black market for £5.00, and celebrities such as Charlton Heston were in attendance. Ronnie recalled, 'Both of us, given the choice, would have preferred to hang.'

The twins' old girlfriend Judy Garland sent them a good-luck telegram, prompting Ronnie to remark to the judge, 'If I wasn't here now, I'd probably be having a drink with Judy Garland.'

It soon became clear that almost all of the twins' Firm had, like rats, deserted them. Ronnie Hart was the principal prosecution witness, proving that there is no honour amongst thieves. Along with John Dickson, the man who had driven Ronnie and Ian Barrie to The Blind Beggar, he turned Queen's evidence in return for freedom from prosecution. Altogether, 28 criminals gave evidence against the Krays.

With the odds weighing so heavily against them, the twins had no chance of escape. They elected, however, to go down fighting. When Ronnie stepped into the witness box, he embarked on a spectacular course of denial. Not only were he and George Cornell friends, but he had never even been to The Blind Beggar on the evening in question.

Reggie, likewise, refused to concede a thing. In their own eyes, they behaved with dignity and integrity throughout the trial, while their former accomplices and friends had betrayed their loyalty.

On only two occasions did the twins lose their composure. Ronnie called the prosecuting counsel, 'You fat slob!' after hearing how the police had confiscated his grandparents' pension books. And when the court was hearing about the circumstances surrounding Frances's death and funeral, Reggie screamed, 'The police are scum.'

In one respect, however, they disappointed the press and public. Many people hoped that there were secrets to reveal about the celebrities and politicians who knew them. But again, according to the twins, this was a matter of honour. Members of the Firm may have grassed them up, but they were not going to stoop to their level. 'We never informed on anyone,' said Ronnie, somewhat hypocritically, adding, 'We believe that two wrongs do not make a right. We believe we are better off than the rats who deserted our ship.'

Only three men remained loyal throughout the trial – Ian Barrie, who received 20 years for his role in the murder of Cornell; the twins' elder brother, Charlie; and a friend of his, Charlie Foreman, who were both sentenced to 10 years for disposing of McVitie's corpse.

After the longest criminal trial in legal history – 61 days in all – the jury retired. They took 6 hours and 54 minutes to find the twins guilty. Just after 7.00pm on 8 March 1969, the judge, Mr Justice Melford Stevenson, finally pronounced sentence, and addressed the twins, saying, 'I am not going to waste words on you. In my view, society has earned a rest from your activities. I sentence you to life imprisonment, which I recommend should not be less than 30 years.'

The Krays had finally been broken. They were both 34. By the time they left jail, they would be almost ready to draw their pensions.

A few other matters remained to be cleared up. The twins were tried for the murder of Frank Mitchell.

Although they pleaded guilty to harbouring him, there was insufficient evidence to convict them of his death. The charges concerning their criminal business activities were left on file – meaning they could be reinstated at any time.

They had lived by the law of the jungle, on the principle that only the fittest had the right to survive. Now the Krays were behind bars, fit only for historical study as one of nature's oddities.

By 1990, Ronnie and Reggie Kray had been in prison more than two decades. Reggie was sent to Parkhurst on the Isle of Wight; Ronnie went to Durham. Their separation lasted three years until 1972 when Ronnie was transferred to Parkhurst, largely due to a sustained campaign by their mother, Violet. Despite their crimes, she continued to adore her twins, and every week without fail would travel up and down the country to visit them both.

Ronnie believed the strain this put her under contributed to her death in 1982. As a tribute to her love for them, the twins were allowed to attend her funeral at Chingford in Essex. But the event was seriously marred for them by journalists who descended en masse to cover the twins' first public appearance in 14 years and because the prison authorities selected two of their tallest warders to mind them – making them look like dwarves, according to Reggie.

Ronnie's reunion with his brother in Parkhurst did not last long. After a series of fights, culminating in him severely beating up another prisoner, he was certified insane for a second time and transferred to Broadmoor where he was heavily sedated for the rest of his life.

Despite his mental problems, Ronnie married a woman

called Elaine who became one of his regular penfriends. As might have been expected, the marriage did not last and, in 1988, she asked for a divorce. A year later, in November 1989, he married again – Kate Howard – in a ceremony at Broadmoor Hospital. On 17 March 1995, Ronnie Kray died of a massive heart-attack in Wexham Park Hospital in Slough, Berkshire. He was 61, and his death was due in no small way to a very bad tobacco habit. He smoked 100 cigarettes a day through most of his adult life. His dying words were supposedly, 'Oh God, mother, help me!'

During his time as a Category A prisoner, Reggie had also been moved several times from jail to jail. In 1968, he was transferred to Wandsworth, then back to Parkhurst, before being taken to Gartree in Leicestershire in 1987. Aged 66, he passed away on 1 October 2000, dying peacefully in his sleep after losing a long battle against bladder cancer in the honeymoon suite at the Beefeater Town House Hotel in Norwich, Norfolk. He had been moved to the Norfolk and Norwich Hospital from Wayland Prison near Watton, Norfolk, ten days earlier. Kray chose the Town House because he wanted to look out over a river. Kray's wife Roberta, 41, who had maintained a bedside vigil since his release, and former gangland friends Freddie Foreman and Jerry Powell, were at his side when he died.

So ended the lives of two of the most notorious – some say iconic – mobsters in British history. Their key to success was an appetite for violence that silenced rivals and bred loyalty through fear. Taken to the extreme of murder, however, their keys to success became the catalysts of their undoing, and eventual downfall.

In judging their 'success', we might ask what net worth the Krays might have had. Although it is impossible to put a precise figure on the twins' earnings – both legal and illegal – there is good reason to suspect that they were not spectacularly successful. They certainly outshone the Gunn brothers, who, by comparison, were as poor as church mice, but the Krays would never be able to match the accumulated wealth that has placed Kenneth Noye in a class of his own.

During their peak in the early 1960s, with Esmeralda's Barn in full swing, protection money from other clubs, the 'long-firm' frauds and their regular East End income, they may have been earning more than £200,000 annually. But the speed with which they had to close the Barn down, faced with Inland Revenue tax demands, the cost of opening their other clubs, and the general unreliability of racketeering as a profession, suggests the actual amounts of cash passing through their hands may have been much lower than that.

On top of this, their outgoings were quite high. Apart from expenditure on the outward trappings of success – cars, clothes and the occasional holiday abroad – they tried to pay members of their Firm around £40 a week and look after the families of anyone who had been locked away.

The fact that Charlie Kray, the twins' elder brother, had to borrow £50 from their mother after leaving jail in 1975, also implies they never salted much away. However, Ronnie has claimed that their remaining business interests, combined with royalties from the Kray Twin merchandise, should have been enough to have supported them had they ever been released from prison.

It is also said by some that they were 'Robin Hoodesque'. They were charitable, and many worthwhile institutions across the East End benefited from their generosity, including Mile End Hospital for Children and various boys' clubs, such as the Bethnal Green Youth Club, which Ronnie Kray visited with the West Indian popular pianist Winifred Atwell and the Mayor of Bethnal Green.

Although there is no reason for thinking that their motives were anything but genuine, this could certainly be seen as a useful PR exercise; undoubtedly, the twins milked their benevolence for publicity purposes. Cameras would be on hand to record donations, followed more often than not by local newspaper reports of their generosity, always identifying Reggie and Ronnie as 'local businessmen'. Indeed, while Reggie was in prison, he carried on this charitable work, donating pictures he had painted to auctions held to raise funds for organisations such as the Addenham Children's Liver Transplant Fund.

While, for a very short period, they enjoyed all the trappings of wealth – the flashy cars, fancy jewellery, smart suits, the patronage of the smart, rich and famous who visited their clubs – they were, at heart, from the lower, uneducated class. Their façade was glitzy, yet underneath both were vicious thugs, and it was perhaps inevitable that they would return to their true selves when the chips were down.

Of course, the twins were inseparable, and that proved to form part of their downfall, too. Of the two men, it was Ronnie – the megalomaniac psychopathic type, the schizophrenic, the eventual madman – who brought about the destruction of his more stable brother, Reggie. Had Ronnie not blasted to death George Cornell, and had he not taunted Reggie into killing Jack McVitie, the Firm may have survived, with Reggie going on to become a truly successful businessman. That was not to be. It was these two murders that ruined them.

Many reasons have been put forward to explain why the Kray twins became violent criminals – the environment they grew up in, the long absences of their father, their rivalry, and so on. But there could have been another factor.

A German study of the 1920s made the startling discovery that if one identical twin had a criminal record, there was more than 75 per cent likelihood that the other twin would also have one. Still more surprising was the fact that this held true whether the twins lived together or not – in some circumstances, brothers separated for years had remarkably similar criminal histories.

The implications of such findings are significant. They suggest that the criminality of the Krays could possibly have had more to do with genetic programming than the poverty and villainy of the East End or the manner in which they were raised. Perhaps a combination of nurture and nature lies at the heart of the twins' rise and fall – what's almost certain is that we're unlikely ever to see again such an iconic and powerful pairing of underworld gang leaders. As brothers, they shared blood; and they shared the blood of their victims, too.

5

The Richardsons

*'It's a conspiracy... It's a tissue of lies.
These people have all ganged up against me.'*

CHARLIE RICHARDSON AT HIS 1967 TRIAL

Public fascination with the Krays has lasted long after the demise of their underworld empire and their deaths, but they were not the only villains of their generation whose names have gone down in criminal legend, for the 1960s produced a large number of characters whose defiance of law and order earned them a recognition that has sometimes bordered on respect and admiration.

Perhaps the single most famous crime of the 'Swinging Sixties' – the era of Carnaby Street, the mini-skirt and the 1961 Morris Mini – was The Great Train Robbery. On 8 August 1963, 15 hooded men stopped the Glasgow-to-London 'Up-Special' overnight mail train at Bridego Bridge, at Ledburn, Buckinghamshire, robbing it of £2.6 million. Up to that time, Britain's most spectacular robberies had yielded only a fraction of that sum and the scale and audacity of the operation appalled the authorities. During the raid, the train driver, Jack Mills, was coshed over the head. Mills never fully recovered and died seven years later. The £2.3 million haul has never been recovered.

John McVicar was once described as 'the most dangerous man in Britain'. His criminal career stretched from the late 1950s through to his final arrest and renunciation of crime in 1970. He was involved in armed robberies, assaults on the police and two escapes. He remained on the run for over two years.

What was most remarkable about McVicar, however, was his transformation from violent crime to study and authorship. In 1974, he published his autobiography and three years later was awarded an Honours degree. After his parole in 1978, he became a journalist and also gave lectures on the subject of crime. In 1980, Roger Daltrey starred in the film *McVicar*, which was based on John's career.

Most people, when they think of English strong-arm rackets, think, often with fondness, of the Kray twins, Reggie and Ronnie, who dominated the British underworld for much of the 1950s and 1960s. There is, however, another lesser known band of brothers who also built a gang to work the protection/extortion racket, and the Richardsons were even more depraved than their more famous counterparts. Compared to the Krays, Charles and Eddie Richardson were almost amateur in their criminal endeavours, but in cruelty and violence they were every bit the Krays' equals.

Alike only in their shared passion for brutal aggression,

Charlie and Eddie Richardson were in all other respects very different from the Krays. Whereas Reggie and Ronnie began from nothing, the Richardsons were primarily dubious businessmen, from a middle-class background, who found brutality a useful supplement to their legitimate activities.

The gang was most famously involved in a mid-1960s turf war with the Krays, which ultimately led to their downfall. Incidents like the murder of Kray associate Richard Hart and the arrest of Richardson gang member Johnny Bradbury in connection with the murder of a businessman in South Africa enabled the police to follow the gang's trail, and a CID squad arrested most of the gang members in 1966.

The trial, which began in April 1967, resulted in the sentencing of Charlie for 25 years, and his brother Eddie for 10 years. Charlie, after escaping from prison in 1980, gave himself up voluntarily and was then released in 1984, while Eddie was sentenced in 1990 for trading in drugs, although he was later released.

Among the accused arraigned for what was dubbed 'The Torture Trial' were Charles William Richardson, aged 32, company director, of Acland Crescent, Denmark Hill; his wife, Mrs Jean Richardson; Roy Hall, aged 25, metal sorter of Rangefield Road, Balham; Derek Brian Mottram, aged 32, caterer, of Somers Road, Balham; Thomas Clarke, aged 33, unemployed, of Fulham Road, Fulham; James Henry Kensitt, aged 51, salesman, of Homer Road, Fulham; James Thomas Fraser, aged 24, porter, of Midwell Street, Walworth; Robert Geoffrey St Leger, aged 44, dealer, of Broomhill Road, Middlesex; and Eddie Richardson, company director, also of Denmark Hill.

The Richardsons' lingering notoriety stems from their treatment of those who fell foul of them, which included beatings, extracting teeth with pliers, and electric shocks from a converted army field telephone placed inside a specially designed brown box, which generated a current when the handle on its side was cranked. They also bought a machine called a 'Spitmatic', a building tool designed to fire nails into concrete. On one occasion, this was used on a victim to pin his foot to the floor, and they often used bolt-cutters to remove toes.

Afterwards, if the victims were too badly injured, they would be sent to an ex-doctor who had been struck off the medical register. This process of trial and torture was known as 'taking a shirt from Charlie', because of Charlie Richardson's habit of giving each victim a clean shirt in which to return home.

The notorious Richardson gang was active during the 1960s. Operating from south London, it was led by Charles 'Charlie' Richardson, his younger brother Edward 'Eddie', and Frances Davidson Fraser, aka 'Mad Frankie', born 13 December 1923. Charlie had turned to a life of crime when the departure of their father left their family penniless, and he invested in scrap metal, while Eddie operated fruit machines. These businesses were, however, merely fronts for underworld activities which included fraud, theft and dealing in stolen goods.

The Richardsons' big scam was buying foreign items like nylon stockings on credit and failing to pay the bill. Charlie was the 'brains' of the outfit that operated on London's south side, in a nightclub they dubbed 'Club Astor'.

In addition to the credit ploy, the Richardsons liked to threaten their way into partnerships with legitimate businessmen who would be intimidated into co-operation by threats of terrible violence.

In the basement of the club, the Richardsons had a torture chamber that rivalled anything from the Inquisition. On one occasion, in 1964, as they sat down to a dinner of scampi, the rest of the gang worked over a businessman who came into the club to collect money Charlie owed him. Derek John Lucien Harris was negotiating the sale of a company, and wanted payment for his services. Richardson greeted him with, 'I like you, Lucien, and I don't want to hurt you.'

'On Richardson's order, they removed my shoes and my toes were wired to the generator,' Harris said during the Torture Trial in 1967. 'Roy Hall turned the handle and the shock caused me to jump out of my chair and I fell to the floor. Afterwards, Richardson screwed his thumbs into my eyes. It was very painful, and I could not see for a few minutes.'

Harris testified that the shock was repeated on other parts of his body. 'After that, I was stripped, except for my shirt, and the shock treatment was repeated. As I rolled on the floor, Richardson said the generator wasn't working very well and orange squash was poured over my feet. Then I was bound and gagged and given further electric shocks to various parts of my body. Finally, Richardson said I was to be taken to the marshes where I gathered I would be killed and dumped under a pile of refuse.'

As Harris was recovering from the treatment and getting dressed, Charlie pinned his left foot to the floor with a knife. In court, Harris removed his shoe to show the two scars on his foot. 'The knife went in there and came out there,' said Harris.

The next ten minutes of court time was devoted to looking at the man's foot. First, the judge inspected it, then the members of the jury filed past it, in pairs. Finally, the foot was surrounded by the barristers on both sides of the trial, Crown and defence – never before, or since, has the foot of a person been the subject of such intense legal scrutiny.

All in all, Harris told the stunned court that his torture lasted for six hours, after which Charlie apologised and gave him the money he had come for – £150 in cash.

While the Krays were willing to murder to maintain order or settle a grudge, the Richardsons seemed to like torture and were never convicted of murder. True, some of their victims did disappear and police were unable to locate them, but no charges were ever brought. 'Edward Richardson punched me in the face,' said petty criminal, Jack Duval, a member of the Richardson gang, who had been pressed into the nylon-importing scam by threats. 'Then, when I fell down, I was beaten with golf clubs. When I asked what I had done to deserve that, I was told, "You just do as Charlie tells you."'

On one occasion, a collector of 'pensions' (protection money from pub landlords and others), who was twice warned by the brothers after he pocketed the money and spent it at Catford dog track, was nailed to the floor of a warehouse near Tower Bridge for nearly two days, during which time gang members frequently urinated on him.

Another notable character in the Richardson gang was James Alfred 'Jimmy' Moody, a gangster and hitman whose career spanned more than four decades and included run-ins with Jack Spot, who is mentioned in the Krays' chapter.

At one time, Moody was the number-one enforcer for the Richardson brothers, did freelance work for the Krays, and he became one of the most feared criminals to emerge from the London underworld – all before he reached the age of 30. In the 1970s, he joined a team of criminals to form 'The Chainsaw Gang', who went on to become that decade's most successful armed robbers.

Moody seemed to live up to his surname very well, for, as soon he fell in with a gang, he fell out, and he changed allegiances at the drop of a hat.

In 1979, he was imprisoned for murder and armed robbery. While in Brixton Prison, his cell mate was Gerard Tuite, a staunch and senior member of the Provos – the provisional IRA. In 1980, during the hunger strike in the winter of that year, the two men escaped and went on the run – the resourceful Moody was never recaptured.

The escape was audacity itself. Tuite, Moody and another inmate tunnelled through walls of their cells in the top-security remand wing, dropped into a yard where they used builders' planks and scaffolding piled up for repairs to scale the 15ft perimeter wall. Today, Gerry, now in his mid-fifties, is a very successful businessman in south Cavan and the north Meath region.

While in hiding, Tuite indoctrinated Moody with stories of brutality and torture inflicted on the Irish by the British and convinced him to join the IRA.

To put a little perspective into the relationship Moody enjoyed with the Richardsons, and the clout they must have had, it is worth noting that Moody didn't mix with just anybody. Gerard Tuite, for example, at 26, had made Irish history in 1982 by becoming the first Irish citizen charged with an offence committed in another country, and he made world headlines. His prosecution in his asylum state, Ireland, for offences committed elsewhere was a landmark in international law governing political crimes.

In 1978, using the *nom de guerre* David Coyne, he had moved into a girlfriend's flat in 144 Trafalgar Road, Greenwich. Before the end of the year, he was found guilty of possession of explosives with intent to endanger life. A sawn-off shotgun and an Armalite rifle were also found in the flat. These and other items, including car keys and voice recordings, linked him to various bombings, as well as the targeting of senior British Conservative and royal figures. It is claimed that he was linked with, or involved, in no less than 18 bombing attacks in five British cities with Patrick Magee, the Brighton Bomber, alone.

Soon, Moody's murderous skills were being put to use as he became the Provo's secret deadly assassin – a man who struck so much fear into Northern Ireland's security services that the Thatcher Government put a three-man SAS hit squad on his tail in the mid-1980s.

By the late 1980s, Moody realised he was in danger of overstaying his welcome in Ireland and, inevitably, the lure of the East End persuaded him to return home. He believed that his reputation as a hired killer would keep him one step ahead of trouble, and the law, but he had lost his edge and the London he returned to was a very different place. Huge drug deals, mainly involving Ecstasy and cocaine, rather than armed robbery, were financing many criminals' lavish lifestyles. The stakes were far higher than 'the old days', and so were the profits.

By the early 1990s, Moody's list of enemies read like a

Who's Who of criminals from both sides of the water. Then there were the police, the Royal Ulster Constabulary and the British security services to deal with, making it only a matter of time before he was murdered in 1993.

Another 'associate' of Moody's and, by extension, the Richardsons and the Krays, was gangster and criminal mastermind William 'Billy' Hill. From a London family, Hill started his career as a burglar in the late 1920s, then graduated to 'smash-and-grab' raids, targeting jewellers and furriers in the 1930s. During World War II, and now in his late twenties, he moved into the black market, specialising in food, diesel and petrol. Another of his specialities was the supply of forged documents to deserting servicemen and, with Jack Spot, running lucrative protection rackets. The two men soon became deadly rivals.

Towards the end of the 1940s, he was charged with burgling a warehouse and fled to South Africa, where he immediately took over illegal activities at several Johannesburg nightclubs. Hill came to the attention of the local police following an assault. He was extradicted to Britain, where he was convicted for the warehouse robbery and served a prison term.

Upon his release, Hill appeared – at least to law-abiding citizens – to have turned over a new leaf. He opened several legitimate nightclubs, which were, in fact, fronts for his expanding criminal activities that included bookmaking and loan sharking. In 1952, he robbed a post office van, netting £250,000, and also ran a cigarette smuggling operation from Morocco.

Towards the end of the 1950s, Hill retired from active

involvement in criminal enterprises, preferring to bankroll other gangsters. With his enforcer, Albert 'Italian Al' Dimes, he continued to run his nightclubs, including one in the fashionable Sunningdale area of Surrey, into the 1970s. He died of natural causes, a very wealthy man in 1984, aged 73.

In 1966, it was Dimes, fronting Hill, who helped arrange a conference between the New York *mafiosi* and the Corsican Francisi brothers regarding investing in London casinos. An associate of Charlie Richardson's, Dimes' formidable presence in Soho delayed the Kray twins from moving into the area for several years.

If anything, the Richardsons were probably 'better connected' to the London underworld than the Krays, and another of their sidekicks was the notorious Frankie Fraser. 'Mad Frankie' first met the Richardsons in the early 1960s. Together, they set up the Atlantic Machines fruit machine enterprise.

In 1966, Fraser was charged with the murder of Richard Hart, an associate of the Krays, while others, including Jimmy Moody, were charged with affray. The only witness to this murder who dared give evidence soon changed his mind. Nevertheless, Fraser served five years for affray.

Fraser was also implicated in the 1967 'Torture Trial'. Fraser himself was accused of pulling out the teeth of victims with a pair of pliers. He was sentenced to ten years' imprisonment; indeed, he spent a total of 42 years behind bars in over 20 different UK prisons. And these sentences were often tainted by violence. He was involved in riots and frequently fought with prison officers and inmates. When the mood took him, he would even take a swing at various prison governors. His richly embroidered criminal CV includes being one of the ringleaders of the Parkhurst Prison Riot in 1969, after which he spent the following six weeks recovering from his injuries in hospital.

An 'old-school' type of villain, when he was released from prison in 1985, he was met by his son in a Rolls-Royce. In 1991, 'Mad Frankie' was shot in the head at almost point-blank range in an apparent murder attempt outside Turnmills Club on the Clerkenwell Road, London. He has always maintained that a policeman was responsible.

At the time of writing, Frankie is well into his eighties. He appears frequently on TV shows such as *Operation Good Guys* and *Brass Eye*. In 1999, he appeared at the Jermyn Street Theatre in a one-man show, *An Evening with Mad Frankie Fraser*, directed by Patrick Newley, which subsequently toured the UK. More recently, he was giving gangland tours around London, where he points out infamous locations, including The Blind Beggar pub where Ronnie Kray shot dead George Cornell.

For those wishing to explore Frankie's life and times even further, his website is well worth a visit: www.madfrankiefraser.co.uk.

It would take a task force of 100 Scotland Yard detectives finally to bring the Richardson brothers to justice, and the leading detective said that the hardest part was finding witnesses willing to talk, but the brothers were not prepared to give up without a fight. During their trial at the Old Bailey, every juror was 'contacted' and threatened with bodily harm if the gang was convicted. Rather than risk a mis-trial, the Yard set up a special telephone number for the jurors to use if they were threatened again, but the judge aggravated the situation by foolishly telling them that it had probably only been a crank who had made the calls since all of the Richardson mob had been locked up for months.

Despite the threats, hopes were high for a conviction, and the tone was set by Mr Sebag Shaw QC for the Crown, who said, 'These men are evil... and I can prove them to be so.'

The weather over central London was changeable for this early April morning. It was rather cloudy with sunny intervals, scattered showers and moderate north-westerly winds. And if the Meteorological Office had decreed that the temperature was a little below normal for the time of year, the police were reaching boiling point until the moment the Richardson gang had finally stepped into the dock... and Charlie Richardson was similarly wound up. For years, he had ensured silence through intimidation and torture, and the criminal empire he had built in the densely-packed tenement and high-rise housing estate areas of London, that stretches south from the Thames, was, he thought, impregnable.

The chubby-faced man, his jet-black hair swept back with Brylcream, had already seen the charge sheet, on which he was described as a 'company director'. And it smarted, for the evidence would show that his 'company' consisted of a motley collection of 'executives' who made their profits from shady deals, and whose 'labour relations' were based upon the theory that dissident employees, or business associates, were best kept in line by facing kangaroo courts and being punished for the smallest infraction by being stripped naked and given electric shock treatment, or worse.

Charlie Richardson considered himself to be a kind of latter-day Al Capone, as he stepped into the dock wearing a £50 suit. He thought of his 'patch' as a scaled-down version of Chicago during the Prohibition era, and his arrogant demeanour was reinforced by the deliberately careless manner in which he bore his stocky, boxerlike frame. When the charges were put to him, he sneered and snapped out, 'Not guilty!'

Rising to his feet, Sebag Shaw QC – the man who had defended Ruth Ellis, the last woman to be hanged in the UK – picked up a document, turned to the jury and, in a measured tone, said, 'Charles Richardson was the dominant leader of a somewhat disreputable business fraternity who operated through a number of phoney companies.'

Richardson glared at his adversary.

'But,' said Sebag Shaw, with a theatrical wave of his arm, 'this case is not about dishonesty or fraud... it is about violence and threats of violence.'

There was a pause. The court room stilled as counsel pulled a spotlessly white handkerchief from his pocket, sniffed, blew his nose, returned the handkerchief to his pocket, and resumed, this time more darkly. 'Not, let me say, casual acts of violence, committed in sudden anger – but vicious and brutal violence systematically inflicted, deliberately and cold-bloodedly and with utter and callous ruthlessness.'

It is often said that advocates are born and not made, and good advocacy depends on good preparation and oral skills. Sebag Shaw was a master of his calling. Later to be knighted, he knew that the hallmark of good preparation and presentation was to know exactly where one is going, what the objective is, and that attention to detail was everything. His preparation for the case had been, as ever, meticulous.

Charlie Richardson was now black with rage. No one had ever insulted him like this upstart wearing a horsehair wig.

Pointing an accusatory finger at the dock, counsel for the Crown continued, 'Beatings and torture of people who upset Richardson, or who were even suspected of jeopardising his business career, ensured that no one ever complained to the authorities about south London gangsterism. Such methods had succeeded for years until, finally, some of the sufferers had told their disgruntled stories to the police.'

The first of the victims called to give evidence was Jack Duval. Born in Russia in 1919, and a one-time French legionnaire, the 48-year-old acknowledged that he had come to the Old Bailey that day from prison, where he was serving a three-year-sentence for an airline tickets fraud.

Duvall, an inveterate gambler at the Astor Club, off Berkeley Square, where the Richardsons had recruited him, was asked to recall a day in 1960, and he did so nervously and in a manner which suggested that the day in question was the unluckiest day of his life.

Very soon after their first meeting, Duvall was serving his 'apprenticeship' as 'European representative' for one of the gang's dodgy companies. The scam was simplicity itself. The well-spoken Duvall would order Italian-made nylon stockings for his London company, have them imported on credit, and not pay the bill. When he failed to perform well, he was summoned back to London and beaten black and blue by his bosses, the Richardsons.

On another occasion, he went to Germany for a few weeks. 'It was about eight weeks, if I recall,' said Duvall wistfully. 'Things did not go as planned and I was recalled... as I entered the Camberwell office, Mr Richardson hit me with his fist, and I still have the mark on the side of my nose from this ring.'

This statement caused everyone in the court to crane their necks to see the scar, but Duval was now so excited he couldn't keep his head still. 'When I came to, I found I had been relieved of my watch, ring and wallet containing $200. Mr Richardson was sitting behind his big desk with chairs all around... like a court.'

But Richardson was also interested in another person in the office, a Mr Alfred Blore, manager of Common Market Merchants. He was, in fact, selecting knives from a canteen of cutlery, and throwing them in Blore's direction – some which were striking him in the arm – with the intention of drawing the terrified man's attention to his business shortcomings and that he did not want Richardson to take over his company.

According to Duval, Richardson kept repeating to Blore, 'I'm the fuckin' boss, and if I tell you what to do, you will do it.'

Blore asked, 'What have I done, Charlie'? Then he screamed, 'Don't do it!'

Other cronies of Richardson's, minor 'executives' of the company, had been lurking on the fringes of the bizarre Camberwell office-cum-court room, and two were ordered to go to Blore's offices in Cannon Street and 'collect the stock and books and make it look as if there had been a robbery'. The reason for that, Duvall drily testified, was that by then Mr Blore 'was covered in blood', and if any questions were asked it would be said that he had been attacked during the supposed robbery.

Mr Geoffrey Crispin, defending Richardson, suggested that it had been Duval, and not Charles Richardson, who had been the real gang leader. Duval admitted that he lived a life of fraud, involving large sums of money. But he denied that in the fraudulent companies run by the gang he was, as Mr Crispin put it, 'the guv'nor'.

Duval sharply turned on the lawyer, saying, 'I have never been the boss. I have worked for Charles Richardson because I had to.'

But, continued Mr Crispin, Duval was hoping to receive a large sum of money by selling his life story to the newspapers.

Duval had a swift answer to that. 'I am,' he said haughtily, 'but at present I am a guest of Her Majesty and cannot indulge in any business activities while I am in prison.'

The next witness to step into the box was 38-year-old Bernard Wajcenberg, a Polish-born businessman, whose dealings with the Richardsons had not been enjoyable. He, it appeared, had sought business 'references' about Charlie Richardson from the police, a move which had met with Charlie's disapproval. At a meeting in the notorious Camberwell office – at which Wajcenberg was 'so paralysed with fear I could not speak' – Richardson told him, 'You have ratted by making enquiries about me to the police. If you don't pay £5,000, you will not get out of this office alive.'

To add weight to his threat, Richardson showed his terrified victim a cupboard stocked with knives, axes and a shotgun. Hoarsely, the witness told the jury of eleven men and one woman, 'Richardson grabbed me by the lapels and said, "When I go berserk, you know what happens."' Wajcenberg did know and took swift steps to borrow £3,000, which Richardson accepted in payment.

Benjamin Coulston also underwent six hours of torture. He was stripped naked, some of his teeth were ripped out with a pair of pliers, lit cigars were stubbed out on his arms and legs, and he was 'toasted' on the face and body by a closely-held electric heater. As an end-piece to the session he was bundled into a tarpaulin sheet, along with two 14lb weights and, from inside the shroud, he heard Richardson say, 'Get rid of him.'

Coulston stared at the jury with sad eyes. 'I thought I was going to be dumped in the river,' he said in an almost inaudible voice. 'And all the time this was happening, Richardson and the others were drinking, laughing, smoking and enjoying the fun.' But lucky for him, Richardson wearied of the episode once the victim's terror had been savoured and ordered his release.

'He gave me a new shirt,' said Coulston, 'and his brother, Edward, drove me home.'

Other victims came to the witness box to recount similar experiences in the firm's office and warehouse. One man, who had been beaten and burned and had his toes broken, heard the screams of another sufferer as he lay in a hole, beneath a trap door, into which he had been thrown when his tormentors had finished with him.

The highlight of the trial came on the morning on which Richardson himself finally entered the witness box to tell his own story. His line was that all of the evidence against him was a pack of lies. Duval's 'story' was an example, and he blandly told the jury, 'It is something out of a storybook and never happened at any time. It is a ridiculous allegation that I should beat him up just to do what I told him to.'

'Have you ever attacked anyone?' he was asked.

Richardson looked around the courtroom with a smile of a man who would endeavour, patiently, to answer all nonsensical questions. Of course he had never attacked anyone. 'Never had a cross word,' he declared. 'There are a lot of clever fraudsters putting these allegations and getting out of their own frauds by blaming me for these incidents.'

On the table in the well of the court stood the electric generator said to have been the principal torture machine. But Richardson eyed it as though it were some totally mysterious piece of equipment. 'That's the only one of those I've ever seen,' he insisted as if butter wouldn't melt in his mouth. 'I've never owned one, and I don't know anyone who has.' He looked at the machine again. 'It's a conspiracy,' he said. 'It's a tissue of lies. These people have ganged up against me.'

One moment of humour came when prosecuting counsel, seeking information about a potential witness whom the police were unable to trace, asked Richardson, 'Is this man alive and well?'

With mock exasperation, the accused man retorted, 'You keep asking me all the time if people are alive and well, and I object to it. It has a very serious inference.'

Richardson was followed into the stand by his henchman Roy Hall, who was alleged to have operated the electric generator. But, like his boss, he firmly declared that he had never before seen such a machine.

Two of Gangland UK's staunchest foes.

Top left: Scotland Yard detective Bert Wickstead, the original gangbuster, who after an exemplary stint solving murders in north London formed his own team to tackle organised crime in the capital.

© PA Photos

Top right: Detective Chief Superintendant Jack Slipper. Before playing a key role in the capture of Great Train Robber Ronnie Biggs, his work on the Shepherd's Bush Murders case, in the nascent Flying Squad and in Britain's first 'supergrass' trial marked him out as one of our greatest policemen.

© REX Features

Bottom: After the fall of the Kray empire, the notorious brothers' reputations guaranteed a huge turnout whenever they appeared in public. Ronnie is pictured (*left*) at the 1982 funeral of beloved mother Violet; Reggie at brother Charlie's funeral in 2000 (*right*).

© REX Features

Top left: Charlie Richardson, who with younger brother Eddie, ran the sadistic 'Torture Gang' throughout the south London of the 1960s.
© *REX Features*

Top right: The Blind Beggar pub in east London's Whitechapel. George Cornell, an associate of the Richardsons, was shot and murdered by Ronnie Kray in March 1966 in the saloon bar.
© *REX Features*

Bottom: 'Mad' Frankie Fraser set up the Atlantic Machines fruit machine enterprise with the Richardsons. Since his release from jail he has given tours around gangland London, and is pictured here inside The Blind Beggar.
© *REX Features*

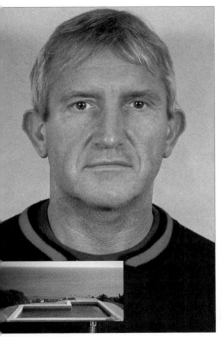

Some members of the gang of Great Train Robbers were able to elude justice for years.

Top left: Ronnie Biggs escaped from Wandsworth Prison in 1965 and eventually settled in Brazil, before his ill health forced him to return to the UK, and incarceration.

Top right: Gang leader Bruce Reynolds went on the run abroad after the heist. His autobiography has become a classic in the true crime genre.

Bottom: Kenny Noye (*left*) ran a smuggling operation which financed a lavish lifestyle, including first-class flights and several luxury villas in Spain (*inset*). Convicted of stabbing David Cameron (*right*) to death at a motorway intersection, he continues to amass a fortune from his financial investments.

A gangland dispute over drugs led to the Essex Boys Murders. Michael Steele (*opposite, top left*) and Jack Whomes (*opposite, top right*) were convicted of the triple killings. Gang member Peter Corey (*opposite, bottom left*) was convicted of conspiring to import cannabis. The bodies of Tony Tucker (*opposite, bottom right*) and Patrick Tate (*right*) were found with that of Craig Rolfe in a deserted farm lane in December 1995. Former gang member Bernard O'Mahoney (*above*) wrote an inside account of one of the most violent and successful gangs of the 1990s. © *REX Features*

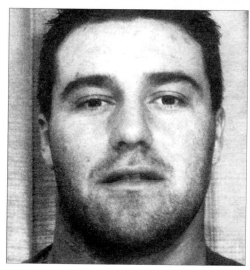

Top left: Nottingham's 'Godfather of Crime', Colin Gunn.

Top right: Patrick Marshall, Colin's odd-job man who fell out with his boss, was shot in the head in a pub car park on the Bestwood Estate. John McSally was convicted of murder; the getaway car contained Colin Gunn's phone bill.

Bottom: Marvyn Bradshaw (*right*) was a friend of Colin Gunn's nephew. In a case of mistaken identity, he was shot by Micheal O'Brian (*left*) in 2003. In revenge, Colin masterminded the killing of Michael's parents, John and Jean Stirland, the following year.

The Securitas heist of February 2006 is Britain's biggest cash robbery.

Top: This still from the depot's CCTV system shows the robbers pointing guns at terrified workers.

Bottom: Metal cages were filled with used notes. They were later abandoned and subsequently inspected by police forensic officers. *Inset left*: Initial press reports gave the impression that John Fowler was the mastermind behind the raid. He was acquitted of all charges. *Inset right*: Michelle Hogg agreed to be a prosecution witness if all charges against her were dropped. She had made the gangs' prosthetic disguises.

Top: Police guard an industrial depot in Bexley, March 2006. Police investigating the Securitas depot robbery recovered several million pounds after a raid on a car workshop there.   © *Getty Images*

Bottom left: The £2 million house that feared crime boss Terry Adams shared with his wife, Ruth (right), in Barnet. During the trial the court was told how Adams made so much money from crime that he was able to retire at just 35.   © *PA Photos*

What was more, he added, 'I have never seen Harris and Coulston in my life before the magistrates' court. I am an innocent, hard-working man. The prosecution witnesses have tried to frame me.'

The jury witnessed a parade of other gang members alleged to have acted as assistants to the chief torturer. One was the man said to have attempted to draw a victim's teeth with pliers, and who succeeded only in tearing the man's gums. Again, he had done nothing, seen nothing, knew nobody. On the day that the loudest screams were being enjoyed by the scampi-eating gang – and the electric generator was pumping out its agonising stream of current – he was busy putting flowers on the grave of his wife's father.

For the Crown, Mr Sebag Shaw summed up this, and similar defence evidence, as 'poppycock produced in the hope of creating a smokescreen through which you, members of the jury, would not be able to see. But this trial is concerned with matters of the gravest import to society. If the charges made out are well founded, it reveals a canker in our midst which, if unchecked, would undermine the civilised society in which we live.' Of Richardson, he said, 'He was the man of power who could get things done and who could succeed by his methods where other methods failed.'

But it was on the 38th day of the trial – the longest trial so far in British criminal history – that an important and significant announcement came from the judge. He had been informed, he said, that threats had been to members of the jury that 'there had better be a disagreement in the Richardson case'. One threat had been hastily whispered to a juror's 75-year-old mother as she waited at a bus stop. Similar 'warnings' had been given to other jurors by telephone.

Mr Justice Lawton, careful to preserve the fair-trial rights of the prisoners, told the jury, 'Whatever has happened must have been done without the co-operation of the defendants, most of whom have been in custody since last July.

'But, unfortunately, whenever there is a trial of this kind, it attracts publicity, and there are busybodies, evil-wishers, misguided acquaintances and friends who will interfere. When they do interfere there is a danger that a jury might take the view that what did happen came about as the result of the intervention of the defendants. Now that I have pointed the position out to you I am confident that no such view will be taken by you.'

All the same, the judge went on, a special police telephone post had been set up with a secret number for jurors to ring immediately, at any hour, if they were approached again. 'A police patrol car will be on the scene within a few minutes,' Mr Justice Lawton said.

The judge repeated his concern over the issue in his detailed summing up of the trial. There was 'not a scrap of evidence', he warned, that Richardson and his fellow defendants had been parties to the jury threats, and the jurors must put the matter out of their minds in reaching their verdicts. He reminded the jury of the importance of reaching a unanimous decision. 'If you cannot agree, there will have to be a new trial,' he told them. 'Just think what that will mean.'

Mr Justice Lawton spent three days on his summing-up – one of the longest addresses ever made from the bench – and, on 7 June, the jurors retired for 9 hours and 26 minutes. As they finally filed back into court, many of them showing signs of fatigue, the eight men in the dock stared anxiously at them. The list of charges was long, and it took time for the foreman to deliver the several verdicts. Richardson and five other gang members were found guilty of some – although not all – of the charges against them.

Richardson, pronounced guilty on nine counts, told the judge, 'I am completely innocent of these charges.' But he and the rest still had to wait before hearing their sentences, and they were stiff. Mr Justice Lawton said he would hand down verdicts the following day. Meanwhile, he discharged the jury 'from your long, wearisome and worrying time', but added, 'You are not concerned with sentencing, but having regard to your long connection with the case you might like to be in court tomorrow.'

As was to be expected, the jury accepted the judge's invitation and were back at the Old Bailey the next morning to hear the sentences. Charles Richardson was handed a 25-year term of imprisonment. Mr Justice Lawton told a still cocky Richardson, 'I have come to the conclusion that no known penal system will cure you by time. The only thing that will cure you is the passing of years.' The judge added, 'I am satisfied that over a period of years you were the leader of a large gang, a disciplined, well led, well-organised gang, and that for purposes of your own material interests, and on occasions for purposes of your criminal desires, you terrorised those who crossed your path, terrorised them in a way that was vicious, sadistic and a disgrace to society. When I remember some of the evidence of your brutality, I am ashamed to think that one lives in a society that contains men like you. It must be clear to all those who set themselves up as gang leaders that they will be struck down by the law as you are struck down.'

Charlie Richardson stared, tight-lipped, at the judge as the sentence was delivered. Then, as three burly police officers formed a guard around him to take him to the cells below the court room, he turned to the jury and snarled, 'Thank you... very much!'

Sentences ranging from eight to ten years were given to the other guilty defendants. Eddie Richardson, Charlie's younger brother, collected one of the ten-year sentences, which was to follow the five years he was currently serving for other offences.

It was the end of the notorious Richardson gang, and it had been achieved through the concentrated efforts of a team of 100 dedicated police officers. As his last duty in the trial, the judge called before him the dozen senior detectives of the team – including young, blonde WPC Gillian Hoptroff. Mr Justice Lawton told the team, 'I want to thank all of you on behalf of the court – and I think I am speaking on behalf of every law-abiding citizen in this country – for the work you have done in breaking up one of the most dangerous gangs I have ever heard of. Well done.'

So how did the Richardson brothers stack up against the Krays and the Gunns? The description of 'a pair of bullying hoodlums' springs to mind, and they were not exactly financially successful in any event. Most certainly, Charlie Richardson was psychopathic, in much the same way as Ronnie Kray. Unlike the Krays, though, they ran their 'empire' from several rundown locations, and could never have aspired to managing a flashy nightclub, or mixing with the rich and famous. In a nutshell, and although they came from a better social background than the Gunns and Krays, the Richardsons, like the Gunns, had no class.

When comparing the particular qualities of the gangs, many would say that the Richardsons clearly left the Gunns in their wake... or did they? It might be fair to say that the Gunns also managed their shady businesses from shady locations – a couple of council houses on an equally rundown estate. The Krays, Gunns and Richardsons ran their gangs using the threat of violence, which they would visit on anyone who crossed them; however, there seems little doubt that the Gunn brothers were financially more successful and, unlike the Richardsons, yet so like the Krays, they were quick to enforce their own particular discipline by the use of firearms. The Richardsons were never charged with murder, although it does seem likely that they may have ordered at least one execution, but this was never proven.

And how has crime literature treated the Richardsons? They have gone down in gangland history wearing the label 'The Torture Gang' hanging around their necks. Apart from that, they are distinguished by little else, except, maybe, that they were arch-enemies of the Kray twins, but at least they are well-known to aficionados of gangland buffs. It is highly unlikely that the Gunns will be afforded such well-publicised infamy, for overshadowing them for all time will be the Krays, and their instantly recognisable 'Firm'.

One area of common ground, one that the three pairs of brothers shared, was criminal empire-building based on shifting sands. The only glue that held them together was the loyalty they expected, and demanded, of their foot soldiers, and this proved to be their undoing. Of course, a chain is only as strong as its weakest link and, as soon as the police targeted the Richardson gang, it was only a matter of time before their house of cards came crashing down. Like the Krays, and the Gunns, informers and victims turned against them and the law took its inevitable course.

6

Thomas 'Tam' McGraw and the Scottish Gangs

'McGraw became one of the most powerful gangsters in Britain, certainly in Glasgow, and he earned a great deal of that power by trading information with the police.'

AUTHOR REG MCKAY

The 'Penny Mobs' was a name used by the press to describe the early street gangs in Glasgow during the early 1870s. Local kids were fined a penny if they stepped out of line, then released back on to the streets. The Penny Mobs, like their New York City counterparts, were among the many gangs which formed following a large-scale migration of Irish immigrants fleeing Ireland during the potato famines of the 1840s and 1850s. One of these gangs, the Ribbon Men, were reported to have blown up a gasometer in Tradeston in 1833.

In Scotland and Ireland, the name Penny Mobs still lived on through to the twentieth century, a period that gave rise to prominent gangs such as the Tongs, the Toils, the Govans, the Powery Gang, the Soo Spiders, the Billy

Boys, the Norman Conks, the Rednecks, the Baltic Fleet, the Black Diamond Gang, the Black Hands, the Nudes, the Ruchill Boys and the Monks.

Glasgow was known as the 'second city of the Empire' and everything was covered in a fine layer of black soot. For their part, the Billy Boys had 800 members at its height during the 1920s and 1930s, then a time when Oswald Mosely's British Facists started a Glasgow branch of the Ku Klux Klan.

Today, the gangs are still around, now populated by Neds, Chavs, Chags, Kevs, Scallies, Spides or White Trash – a very eloquent lot who have their own vernacular that produces some of the 'finest poetry' in the world: 'Ode to me Ma... Slashin' jaws, lickin' baws, punin' jellies, and stabbin' bellies.' Wordsworth, it's not, but there's a certain street dynamism about it that can't be denied.

The Glasgow district of Barlanark was developed in response to the city's post-war housing need – over 2,300 four- and five-apartment tenements characterised by brick balconies, at that time under local council control. And almost from the day the first families moved in, the place became a breeding ground for crime, the area becoming steeped in violence and gang culture.

Perhaps the most infamous of these gangs was the BAR-L Team, made up of members from Barlanark and the surrounding areas, and one of the toughest was Tam 'The Licensee' McGraw. Barlanark was to become part of the bloody Glasgow Ice Cream Wars of the 1980s.

Tam McGraw owned the Caravel public house on Hallhill Road, and it was a well-known meeting place for Glasgow underworld figures. Apart from general revelry, the place that also saw more than its fair share of violence and was subject to drive-by shootings as well as grenades being thrown through the windows. In 1991, the pub was burned to the ground following the alleged retribution murder, in September 1991, of Bobby Glover and Joe 'Bananas' Hanlon, by the crime lord Arthur 'The Godfather' Thompson for the killing of his son, Arthur 'Fat Boy' Thompson Jr.

Paul Ferris was charged with the murder of Fat Boy and later acquitted. He maintained his innocence throughout and said that the murder had been carried out by a hitman known as 'The Apprentice'.

In 1998, Ferris was sentenced to seven years' imprisonment at the Old Bailey for gun-running. He had started out as an enforcer for Arthur Thompson Sr, and he went on to become of the most feared hard men in Glasgow. Aged 38, he was released from Frankland Prison after serving four years and says he wants to use his experiences to write crime fiction books which 'will be more realistic than those currently on offer.'

Thompson Sr was one of the biggest players in Scottish crime history. For years, he had been targeted by the National Crime Intelligence Service, the National Crime Squad and MI5, who knew that he worked with the larger London mobs and sold guns to Loyalist groups in Ireland.

Thomas 'The Licensee' McGraw was born in 1953 in the East End of Glasgow. A product of the ghetto-like housing schemes of Glasgow's inner-city, he took to thieving at an early age like a duck to water. Most of the kids in the area did; how else could deprived 12-year-olds get hold of little luxuries in life like cigarettes or a night at the flicks? They turned their hands to shoplifting, housebreaking and pinching anything that wasn't nailed down to earn a few quid.

As a young man, having spent time in approved schools and Borstals, McGraw moved to London with his young wife. Here, he survived a horrific factory accident and, with the compensation, the couple returned to Glasgow and bought into the lucrative ice cream business. But it wasn't long before the McGraws became involved in the ice cream wars, in which rival firms used guns and violence to seize control of the trade plied among the huge housing schemes.

The ice cream war conflicts were characterised by rival ice cream vendors raiding one another's vans and firing shotguns through windscreens. Superficially, the violence appeared disproportionate and, at times, the situation seemed farcical, with police officers from Strathclyde detailed to follow ice cream vans around on their runs, causing the locals to nickname them 'The Serious Chimes Squad'. But the profits to be had from merely selling ice cream were minimal, as most of the vans also peddled stolen property and drugs behind the cosy, child-friendly 'Mr Whippy' image.

Events culminated in six members of the Doyle family being burned alive in the Ruchazie council housing estate on 16 April 1984 and McGraw was among the suspects arrested. 18-year-old Andrew Doyle, nicknamed Fat Boy, a driver for the Marchetti firm – who owned hundreds of vans throughout the west of Scotland – had resisted being intimidated into distributing drugs on his run, and attempts to take over his route had already led him to be shot a few weeks earlier. Now a further so-called 'frightener' was planned against him.

At 2.00am, a fire was started in the cellar of a flat in Bankend Street, Ruchazie, where Fat Boy lived with his family. The door was doused with petrol and set alight and, with the help of car tyres, it spread quickly. The members of the Doyle family, and three visitors who were staying the night, were asleep at the time. They awoke to a flaming ceiling and dense black smoke on all sides. The resultant blaze killed five people, with a sixth dying later in hospital – James Doyle, 53; his daughter Christina Halleron, 25; her 18-month-old son Mark; and three of Mr Doyle's sons, James, 23, Andrew, 18, and Tony aged 14.

The arson attack caused public outrage in Glasgow, and the Strathclyde Police arrested several people over the following months, eventually charging four of them who were tried and convicted of offences relating to the vendettas. The remaining two, Thomas 'TC' Campbell and Joe Steele, were tried for the murders, convicted and sentenced to life imprisonment, of which they were to serve not less than 20 years according to the judge's recommendation. Campbell was also separately convicted in the involvement of an earlier shotgun attack.

The Crown's case was that Campbell was a man with a record of violence, having already served several years in prison in the 1970s, and having been back behind bars from 1982 to 1983. Upon his release, he had entered the ice cream van business, and had been keen to protect his 'patch' against the rival Marchetti family. Steele was Campbell's henchman, a sidekick recruited to help with the dirty work in his boss's campaign of violence against Marchetti's vans and drivers.

Campbell had been brought up in a cramped flat in Glasgow's Cowcaddens during the 1950s. The youngest of ten children, his father was a safe-breaker. When the family moved to Carntyne, he soon became embroiled in the gang warfare that characterised Glasgow in the 1960s. Like everyone else, he carried a knife and he was never slow in using it. He was first stabbed when he was 13 and, aged 17, he was hit over the head three times by someone wielding a hammer. People who witnessed the attack thought they were watching a murder.

Both men claimed that the police had fitted them up. Campbell said that he had been at home with his wife, Liz, when the fire broke out. There wasn't really any dispute about this, nevertheless the Crown maintained that, in any event, Campbell was the mastermind behind the arson attack. Steele also gave an alibi for the time in question and, in 1989, they tried unsuccessfully to have their conviction overturned.

It was the evidence given by one William Love which was crucial to the case. Love had told police that he had overheard Campbell and Steele, and others, discussing in a bar how they would teach Fat Boy a lesson by setting fire to his house. But Love was no Mr Goody Two-Shoes. He was a known criminal who was facing ten years for armed robbery and who had three times previously perverted the course of justice.

The police also stated that Campbell had made a statement, recorded by no less than four officers, that 'I only wanted the van windows shot up. The fire at Fat Boy's was only meant to be a frightener which went too far.'

The third piece of evidence was a map, allegedly found in Campbell's house, of the Ruchazie district with the Doyle house marked with an 'X'.

In 1992, two journalists, Douglas Skelton and Lisa

Brownlie, wrote a book, *Frightener*, about the conflicts and the trial. They interviewed Love, who later signed affidavits attesting that he had lied under oath 'for my own selfish purposes', and because the police had pressurised him.

As a result, both Campbell and Steele engaged in campaigns of protest to attempt to publicise their cases. Steele escaped from prison several times, in order to make high-profile demonstrations, including a rooftop protest and supergluing himself to the railings at Buckingham Palace. Campbell protested while remaining in Barlinnie Prison, going on hunger strike, refusing to cut his hair and making a documentary.

On Saturday, 27 April 2002, while both men were on bail pending an appeal, Campbell was seriously stabbed while he visited a community centre in Hallhill Road, not far from his home. One of the two assailants was also stabbed with a fish knife during the attack. Campbell was allowed home after treatment at Glasgow's Royal Infirmary.

A week earlier, in what DS Allan McFadyen described as a linked attack, Tam McGraw had been stabbed on Friday, 19 April. He survived because he had been wearing a bullet-proof vest. He received 20 blows, but suffered only minor injuries to his arms and wrists and slightly more serious wounds to his buttocks.

In March 2004, Campbell and Steele's convictions were quashed by the Court of Criminal Appeal in Edinburgh.

Campbell called for a fresh investigation into the murder of the Doyle family, accusing Tam McGraw both of the murders and also of instigating a campaign over 20 years to ensure that Campbell remained in jail and was silenced, with several attempts being made on his life.

While Campbell and Steele were locked away, McGraw continued to sell ice cream by day, while at night he formed and led the infamous Barlanark Team, a gang of robbers who wrought havoc in central Scotland for some fifteen years. Their exploits were both daring and comical, but when police discovered that hash was being hidden in buses taking young footballers and deprived Glasgow families on free holidays abroad, McGraw was put under surveillance for two years.

With his Bar-I gang, McGraw was involved in post office raids all over Scotland. The raids were so successful that the police ran a national campaign trying to catch them. After every job, the proceeds were hidden and collected at a later date, which meant if they were pulled over on their way back from a raid by the cops, none of their haul would be found on them.

The gang were very security conscious, taking a lot of pride in planning the operations with almost military precision, yet, despite all of their meticulous preparations, all of the gang members were arrested and charged at one time or another. In one particular night-time raid on a large social club on the outskirts of Glasgow, things went disastrously wrong. A recce of the club's security system failed to register an important element of the layout; once the outer alarm systems had been dismantled and the pulsar neutralised for entry to the internal system, the entire area surrounding the club would light up with heavy-duty spotlights, illuminating the general surroundings like the stage of a West End theatre. This was an add-on to the particular system the normally efficient gangsters hadn't foreseen.

The job took place as planned. When the spotlights

fired up, instead of abandoning the job, the crew decided to take hurried measures to counteract the lighting system for long enough to get in and out with the goods.

The spotlights on the ground were adjusted to point face down on to the grass, while the ones on the roof were tilted down to focus on the tar and asphalt surface of the roof. With the surroundings now in darkness, the gang continued with the job in hand, relieving the club of all takings, alcohol and cigarettes.

While the team were busy loading up the vans with the swag, a crackling and popping sound could be heard from the roof.

'Fuck's sake... Fire!'

The high-powered spotlights had set fire to the asphalt and the whole roof was ablaze, lighting up the area once again, brighter than before. Everyone ran, just as the blue lights of the fire brigade and police could be seen in the distance. However, despite several of the men shouting at McGraw to run for it, he stayed and kept loading the van.

It was insane. Greed had kept him there, as he tried to get a few more crates of booze on board before the police arrived. But too late. Graw, in the van, smashed straight through a police car, ramming it against an iron fence. He accelerated to about 80mph and hit another police vehicle that had blocked his way back to the street. He then lost control and overturned the van while trying to negotiate a sharp bend. He half-crawled, half-ran from the scene but was soon captured.

This crazy incident throws some light on the reason why McGraw is now suspected by many of Glasgow's underworld fraternity as being a police informer, giving information on fellow crooks in exchange for a green light to operate his own illegal activities almost unhindered by police investigations. He was a very wealthy man, even back then, and he knew that he wouldn't be charged even if caught red-handed, as he indeed was. He should have been charged with conspiracy and organised crime, theft of the van, driving while banned, breaking and entering, and attempted murder of police officers. But he wasn't. The following morning, he walked free without the case ever going to court.

In 1978, McGraw was arrested for the attempted murder of another policeman. Again, he wasn't charged. McGraw himself publicly pointed to the general state of lawlessness in Glasgow at the time, but refused to accept the status that many afforded him – that of being one of Glasgow's foremost gang bosses. 'Glasgow's a town called Malice. Everybody's jealous of everybody else. Nobody likes to see that you are getting on in Glasgow. I'm not one of the controlling influences in the city. I don't think there's anyone capable of running this city. I'm not frightened of anybody, but then they aren't frightened of me.'

In the early 1980s, McGraw started expanding his empire, getting into drugs and buying up pubs and other property. He was now openly bragging to his associates about his connections on the police force and of one of the cops on his payroll. That's how McGraw came by the nickname 'The Licensee', as it seemed to be the case that he had been granted a licence to operate freely by the cops. According to Paul Ferris, another top Glasgow crime figure, and a rival to McGraw at the time, it had been these cop connections that had got him involved in the lucrative heroin trade.

Confiscated drugs were channelled through to McGraw who sold them on. McGraw, at that time, being unfamiliar with the intricacies of the heroin supply business, stupidly sold almost 100 per cent pure heroin directly to the junkies on the streets, who, as a result of over-dosing, were dropping dead like flies.

The drugs trail led from Morocco, through Gibraltar, Spain and Paris to the less salubrious surroundings of a Glasgow garage next to a police depot. The racket netted £40 million, and it was claimed that McGraw was the financier, mastermind and director. But, in 1998, a jury declared him innocent, while other suspects were jailed.

Paul Ferris wrote the book *The Ferris Conspiracy* partly as a way of getting revenge on the City of Glasgow police, whom Ferris claims had waged a war of harassment against him for years and had fitted him up on several occasions. Ferris tells how, in his opinion, the force was full of cops getting envelopes stuffed with cash from a chosen few to turn a blind eye.

Worth an estimated £10 million, Tam McGraw died of a heart-attack at his Mount Vernon home at 3.00pm, Monday, 30 July 2007.

Paul Ferris

Born 1963, Paul John Ferris was raised in the working-class, north-east Glasgow district of Blackhill, which had been developed as a council estate in the 1930s. Most of it was designated 'rehousing', the lowest grade of council housing intended for those families cleared from Glasgow's 19th-century slums at Garngad, a place where a heavy cloud of polluted air perpetually hung over the place from the many heavy industrial works in the area, such as St Rollox Chemical Works and the Tharsis Sulphur & Copper Works.

Garngad became heavily industrialised in the 19th century, with the establishment of flax and cotton mills, iron and chemical and railway works. The tenements that were hurriedly built to house incoming workers were of poor quality, with only outside toilets, leading to overcrowding and insanitary conditions. Diseases such as tuberculosis were rife, and the Garngad slums were regarded as some of the worst in Europe. Crime was rife, and the area was the scene of one of Glasgow Corporation's earliest major slum clearance programmes, beginning in 1933. Many of the residents moved to the new scheme in nearby Blackhill, where the buildings were three-storey, slate-roofed tenements constructed from reclaimed stone, and nearby was a gasworks and a distillery. The fact that Barlinnie Prison was a stone's throw away did not do much to enhance the area at all.

Ferris was the youngest of four children, with one older brother, Billy, and two sisters, Carol and Cath, sired by a Protestant father and a Catholic mother. As a child, Paul Ferris was bullied for several years by members of a local criminal family called the Welshes and, in 1977, Billy stabbed a man to death in a pub fight and was convicted of murder.

Like Tam McGraw, Ferris began his life of crime as a teenager with a series of revenge knife attacks on the Welshes. Aged 17, he was arrested for assault and robbery and sent to Longriggend Remand Centre. He was bailed after several weeks and, while awaiting trial, fled from the police after a car chase, having every good reason to do so – the car contained a shotgun and knives.

After several weeks on the run, he was captured and returned to Longriggend to await his trial, which culminated in him being sentenced to three months in Glenochil Detention Centre at Tullibody.

Upon his release, Ferris returned to court to face charges relating to the car chase, and was sentenced to a year in Glenochil Young Offenders Institution. Shortly after his release, he was again in serious trouble, having been arrested while attempting to rob a jeweller's shop, and returned to Longriggend. But prison did nothing to deter this young man from a life of crime; in fact, if the truth were known, life behind bars merely served to stiffen his resolve. Upon his release, he continued to exact his revenge on the Welsh brothers, which brought him to the attention of the Glasgow gang supremo, Arthur Thompson, aka 'The Godfather'.

According to Ferris, he became involved with Thompson's crime business when aged 19. He collected debts on behalf of the crime lord, and was linked to stabbings, slashings, blindings and knee-cappings.

In 1983, Ferris was arrested following an incident in which shots were fired at one Willie Gibson and three of his relatives while they travelled home from a night in a pub. Gibson's father-in-law sustained a bullet wound to his thigh. The three relatives failed to identify Ferris at an identity parade, but Gibson picked him out as the gunman. He was charged with four counts of attempted murder, and was again remanded to Longriggend. Several months later, he was acquitted of all charges, with the Scottish verdict of 'not proven'.

Now aged 21, Ferris returned to the employment of Thompson, and was soon arrested again and charged with possession of offensive weapons after a pickaxe handle and knives were found in his car. While he awaited his trial, he was involved in a stabbing, and fled to Thompson's holiday home in Rothesay on the Isle of Bute. But the police were hot on his trail. Within a day, he was arrested by armed police and charged with various offences, including attempted murder and possession of heroin with intent to supply. This time, he was remanded to HMP Barlinnie, with a panoramic view over his former Blackhill council estate.

Once again, Lady Luck favoured Paul Ferris. The attempted murder charge was almost immediately dropped, but he did receive a paltry 18-month sentence for possession of offensive weapons.

After being released from prison, it seemed that Ferris might have turned over a new leaf. He stopped working for Thompson and started a company named Cottage Conservatories specialising in double-glazing and conservatories, although he still remained active in the criminal underworld.

On Sunday, 18 August 1991, Thompson's son, Arthur Fat Boy Jr, died after being shot outside his home. Ferris was arrested and charged with murder. On the day of Fat Boy's funeral, the cortège passed a car containing the bodies of two friends of Ferris's – Robert Glover and Joe 'Bananas' Hanlon, who were also suspected of involvement in his death, and had been killed by gunshots to the head.

Ferris stood trial in 1992. The charges against him were: the murder of Arthur Thompson Jr, with the help of Glover and Hanlon; the attempted murder of Arthur Thompson Sr by repeatedly driving a car at him in May

1990; threatening to murder William Gillen, and shooting him in the legs; conspiracy to assault John 'Jonah' Mackenzie on 26 Mar 1991; illegal possession of a firearm; supplying heroin, cocaine and Ecstasy; and the trivial breach of bail.

With over 300 witnesses, the trial lasted 54 days and cost £4 million, at the time the longest and most expensive trial in Scottish legal history. Ferris was acquitted of all charges.

According to Paul Ferris's book, he returned to Glasgow and set up a car dealership named Jagger Autos. He also became a consultant for a security firm called Premier Security, which had a reported turnover of £6.2 million. Still he maintained his contacts with the underworld, including Paul Massey and Rab Carruthers in Salford in the north of England.

Salford was once the fiefdom of Paul Massey, also known as Salford's 'Mr Big', whose security company once held a monopoly on the doors of Manchester's biggest and best-known clubs. He was jailed for 14 years in April 1999, for stabbing a man outside a nightclub. Rab Carruthers was a ruthless Glasgow-born drug-dealer who ran a crime empire in Manchester.

In 1963, Ferris's brother, Billy, escaped from a prison escort van after being allowed temporary release to visit his sick father, becoming one of the six most wanted men in Britain until being recaptured in Blackpool. In August 1994, Ferris received a £250 fine for possession of crack cocaine, and thereafter it appears he was frequently in trouble.

In 1997, Ferris was arrested in London following a two-year surveillance operation by MI5 and Special

Branch. At his trial at the Old Bailey in July 1998, he was sentenced to ten years' imprisonment after being convicted of conspiracy to sell or transfer prohibited weapons, conspiracy to deal in firearms and possessing explosives. In May 1999, the sentence was later reduced to seven years at the Court of Appeal in London.

While in prison, Ferris co-authored his biography *The Ferris Conspiracy* with Reg McKay, a widely-published investigative journalist and regular crime columnist for the *Daily Record*. The book sold 20,000 copies.

Ferris was released from Frankland Prison, County Durham, in January 2002, pledging to give up his life of crime, and released another book with McKay; this time a novel called *Deadly Divisions*, in April 2002. However, in May of the same year, he was sent back to prison for breaching the terms of his parole. He had been in a knife fight with Tam McGraw, and there was an alleged connection with a £900,000 shipment of cannabis. Ferris was released again in June 2002, and returned to Scotland, where he started a new security company named Frontline Security.

In December 2003, his brother, Billy, was convicted for a second time. He had been released in 1999 after serving 22 years of a life sentence but he was convicted of the February 2003 murder of a 15-year-old boy, after mistaking him for the older boy's brother who had assaulted Billy's wife.

In 2004, Frontline Security was criticised when it was revealed the company was guarding the Rosepark Nursing Home, Uddingston, near Glasgow, where ten pensioners had died in a fire, and several more suffered from smoke inhalation, three of them critically, which started on Saturday, 31 January. Relatives demanded to know how it was that a company linked to Ferris had been awarded the security contract.

Throughout his life, Paul has never been far from controversy and, months after the nursing home fire, he became embroiled in more adverse publicity when it emerged that Frontline Security had won a contract to protect speed cameras on the M8, the busiest motorway in Scotland linking Glasgow to Edinburgh. A police source stated, 'That this firm has been awarded this speed camera contract is just plain ridiculous,' but not half as ridiculous when it became known that Ferris's company had been paid a lot of taxpayer's money to protect a building all too familiar to the former gangster – Dumbarton Sheriff Court. A court spokesman commented, 'When we found this out, we decided not to use the company again.'

Nevertheless, in terms of managing his public image and maximising his earning opportunities, we are obliged to give this Glasgow-born hard man some credit. He has been filmed by Channel Five for a 'fly-on-the-wall' documentary, and TV bosses were accused of glamourising his life of crime, moving one senior detective to say, 'Now we have Ferris the TV star – it makes you sick,' adding somewhat spitefully, 'He can try to become a Z-list celebrity all he wants, but he is a career criminal and no matter how many times he tries to re-invent himself, we will always know the truth.'

In April 2005, Edinburgh police began investigating Ferris over concerns that he was attempting to invest in the city's taxi trade and, in May of the same year, details of a planned film about his life came to light, starring actor Robert Carlyle, and Oasis singer Liam Gallagher. He released his third book *Vendetta* in October 2005, and followed that with an appearance at the Festival of Scottish Writing in Edinburgh in May 2006. This was, in turn, followed by the release of his fourth book, *Villains*, in October 2006.

In 2007, the then Scottish Minister for Justice, Cathy Jamieson MSP, announced a planned initiative to prevent convicted criminals from profiting from the publication of their memoirs – a precedent that would have certainly put a stop to the likes of Jeffrey Archer, and pretty well most of the politicians alive today.

Walter Norval

Walter Norval was another man marked by destiny to be a career criminal in one of Britain's hardest cities. As a boy, he grew up in a world of illegal betting, violent, canal-bank, pitch-and-toss schools, sleazy dance halls, brothels and bars where the denizens of the slums on the north side of Glasgow slaked gargantuan thirsts and plotted murder and mayhem. Before he reached his teens, close relatives had died as blood was spilled in the streets.

As a youngster, Norval ran messages for the toughest gangsters in the city and stood guard over pots of cash in illegal gambling schools. It was a remarkable apprenticeship, dangerous and often deadly. It honed a latent toughness and a talent for lawbreaking that saw him emerge in the 1970s as the first of a succession of Glasgow godfathers. Dressed immaculately in pinstripe suits, he controlled his foot soldiers with fearsome fists and he planned robberies with the attention to detail of a military general. He organised various Glasgow fighting factions into a single gang, which pulled off a spectacular series of robberies. But, unlike his successors, he abhorred drugs and drug-dealing. And, in a remarkable twist, he joined the anti-drug campaign later in life.

Back in the Sixties, Walter Norval's XYY Gang had terrorised almost every bank, warehouse and factory on wages day up and down the country and, when he and his sidekicks were eventually arrested, those still at liberty blew up the High Court in an effort to destroy all of the case paperwork. They were deemed so dangerous that the judges – four in all, as the gang were to face separate trials – top police officers and the jury were placed under armed guard. The trial, due to start in 1977, had to be delayed, and a leading prosecution witness in prison at the time was provided with a constant police escort and kept in solitary confinement. In spite of these precautions, he was scalded with boiling water.

The crew was called the XYY Gang, not by the mobsters themselves but by the police; for years, the cops didn't know who they were chasing so they referred to them by the radio code, which was determined by how dangerous an unknown suspect or culprit was – the more dangerous, the further through the alphabet the code would be.

Norval's daughter, Rita Gunn (no relation to the Gunn brothers from Nottinghamshire), was charged with conspiring to damage the famous North Court but was acquitted. Her husband, William Gunn, wasn't so lucky, getting a five-year prison term for threatening to murder one of the leading witnesses.

For a while, it looked as if Norval and his crew were going to beat the rap. Eventually, six were acquitted and seven found guilty of the armed robbery of a bank and a hospital payroll. Out of all of the major robberies, the Crown could only make two of the jobs stick. The police were livid, and they became even angrier when Norval received a mere 14 years.

While their cronies served their time, the remaining members of the gang went on to commit more robberies, many becoming major players in Scottish organised crime. Meanwhile, Norval served his sentence quietly. A popular man in prison, he often organised concerts for the cons' entertainment and was never slow to get up on the stage himself.

The world had all but forgotten about Walter Norval until June 1999, when a 71-year-old man limped into the dock at Glasgow's Sheriff Court and pleaded 'not guilty' to possessing cannabis. Norval's lawyer said the old man used it relieve the pain of arthritis – the Crown believed him and dismissed the case.

7

The Essex Boys

*'Whilst I live and breathe and represent
Michael Steele, I will fight to ensure that he does not
die in prison for offences he did not commit.'*

CHRIS BOWEN, STEELE'S SOLICITOR

One of the most horrific gangland killings of recent years took place along a remote farm track on Whitehouse Farm, Rettendon, Essex, during the early evening of Wednesday, 6 December 1995. Around 8.00am the following morning, farmer Peter Theobald and a colleague had driven down the snowy track in their Land Rover and found a metallic blue Range Rover, index number F424 NPE, blocking a gate which led into a field. Upon closer inspection, the two men saw three bodies inside. The interior of the vehicle was splattered with blood and brain material, so they dialled 999 and waited for the police.

The dead men were 38-year-old Anthony Tucker, Patrick 'The Enforcer' Tate, 37, and Craig Rolfe, 26.

Rolfe, the crew's gopher, had been blasted to death at point-blank range as he sat in the driver's seat. Tucker was in the front passenger seat, while Tate was slumped over on the nearside rear passenger seat. The murder weapon was a 12-gauge shotgun. All three were well known to Essex Police as drug-dealers and extremely violent individuals – wholly admirable characters they were not.

Prior to the murders, business had been especially hectic. In August, Darren Kerr, a friend of Tucker's, had been abducted and then had had acid thrown in his face, blinding him in one eye and completely disfiguring him to the extent that he had to wear a plastic mask, such as those worn by ice-hockey goalkeepers. While in Billericay Hospital, he was shot by a man disguised as a clown with a huge wig, red nose, Dracula teeth, and carrying a bunch of flowers. The shotgun wound was so extensive, a doctor said, that it looked as if an artillery shell had caused the almost fatal injury.

The once handsome 26-year-old, with a wife and young son, later remarked, 'Even in the criminal fraternity, there are certain rules. What happened to me broke all those rules. Throwing acid into my face was a horrible, evil thing to do.'

Police soon learned that a few days before his death, Tate, a 6ft body-builder –a reputed gentle giant – had smashed up a pizza parlour in what was called a 'trivial dispute'. It was claimed that his girlfriend had called the London Pizza Company in Basildon and had ordered from the young manager a pizza with different toppings on each quarter. Roger Ryall explained that this was an order he couldn't complete, then Tate, high on cocaine,

THE ESSEX BOYS

grabbed the phone. 'You will deliver the pizza I want or I'll come over there and rip your fucking head off!'

'I wasn't going to take that', Ryall said later, 'So I said to him, "Get rid of the bolshy attitude and I'll send you a pizza."'

Tate then demanded his name and drove straight to the pizza parlour. He stormed into the pizzeria, shouting, 'Which one of you is Roger Ryall?' When Ryall put his hand up, Tate picked up the cash register and threw it at him. Ryall quickly backed up and pushed the panic button as Tate vaulted the counter and rushed towards him. 'He punched me in the face and then smashed my head up and down on the glass plate on the draining board,' said Ryall. 'The man was insane.'

Tate warned him not to call the police or he would return to beat up all his staff and torch the place, but it was too late – the panic button brought police officers to the scene and Tate was traced to his home. A badly concussed Ryall was determined to have Tate arrested but, as friends told him more about Tate's reputation, his resolve softened. By the following morning, he had withdrawn his complaint and decided not to press charges.

Tate controlled a club in Southend. A one-time physical trainer for Kenneth Noye, prior to this incident he had served six years and, in December 1998, had escaped from Billericay Magistrates' Court when he leapt from the dock and disappeared on a conveniently parked motorcycle. Within days, he was in Spain, where he remained until he foolishly went to Gibraltar for the day and was arrested.

The beating up of Roger Ryall was an incident that swiftly spread around gangland Essex. For his followers, it was a testimony to Tate's increasing arrogance and influence that he could commit such a public crime and get away with it. However, other local villains saw him as a man who had once been an asset to their illegal trade but was now a major liability.

Anthony Tucker was no shrinking violet either. During the 1980s, he had served prison time with his now dead colleagues. Together with Michael Steele, Jack Whomes and a Darren Nicholls, they formed a close bond and started a 'firm' together when they were released.

Tucker, from the quiet village of Fobbing, Essex, had acted as a minder for boxer Nigel Benn, leading him into the ring before bouts. However, more importantly, he controlled the doormen of no less than 16 nightclubs from Southend to East London. As James Morton says in his book *East End Gangland*, 'Control of nightclub doors is essential in the drug-dealing world. Only those favoured by the management or the bouncers are let in, and rival organisations have their salesmen excluded.' So Tucker was a very powerful man, ideally placed and who, without doubt, had connections with south London criminals and probably with the Triads and Yardies.

Mick John Steele owned a specially adapted fast motor launch and was an expert at smuggling drugs from Holland, Belgium and France to remote areas of the Kent, Sussex and Essex coastlines. He was also a pilot, highly-skilled at flying aircraft loaded with drugs in and out of small landing strips. Because of his criminal antecedents, HM Revenue & Customs were well acquainted with Steele and his activities, but were rarely able to nab him. He had been imprisoned for dealing in cannabis and handling counterfeit money and eventually proved to be a pivotal character in the events that would follow.

For his part, Craig Rolfe was a small, bit-part player who had been born on the wrong side of the tracks – in Holloway Prison to be precise. His mother, Lorraine, was serving an 18-month term for impeding the arrest of John Kennedy, who received life for murdering her husband, Brian, on Christmas Eve 1968. In this case, the murder weapon had been a ten-pin bowling skittle. The body had been driven to the A31, near Vange, Basildon, where the death was made to look like a botched robbery.

The fifth person in the unfolding drama was fitness fanatic Jack Arthur Whomes, another gopher, or 'Joey', who was totally dedicated to working for Michael Steele. Describing himself as a 'commercial engineer', he ran a small business at Unit 3, Haulage Yard, Norwich Road, Barham.

It transpired that while the brains of the outfit, Steele, handled the smuggling operations, Tate, Rolfe and Tucker managed the distribution of cannabis, cocaine and Ecstasy pills. Tucker ran a company that provided bouncers and bodyguards for celebrities. The company enabled Tucker and Rolfe to control all drug-dealing activities in the clubs, and outsiders who wanted to sell the drugs to youngsters had to pay them a hefty fee in cash. Anyone who bucked the system was beaten up by the Tate gang, which comprised of well-suited hard men who believed that their fists could always be relied on to resolve any disagreement.

As might well be imagined, things went well for the firm for quite a while. Money poured in and Steele and Tucker grew rich from the profits. They bought large houses, drove expensive cars, enjoyed exotic holidays abroad and dressed their women in designer clothes and jewellery. Yet, as experience has shown time and again, it would only be a matter of time before the individuals became over-greedy. A falling-out was inevitable.

At the trial of Steele and Whomes, the Prosecution claimed that a consignment of bad cannabis had been supplied to Tate by Steele who had brought in the consignment along with Whomes and a Peter Thomas Corry. One of the cargoes in November 1995 had been of such poor quality that refunds were demanded and paid.

It was Tucker, though, who was the front man in the sales chain, so it was Tucker who would be seen to be the rip-off merchant. It was his reputation as a good supplier that was at stake.

The Prosecution also had it that Tucker, whom they claimed was mentally unstable, had a number of heated arguments with Steele, who, in turn, blamed his suppliers in Belgium. Muscle prevailed over Steele, who ordered a Darren Nicholls to dump the narcotics into a lake near his Braintree home. Thereafter, Steele tried to recoup his losses from his supplier abroad. He was partially successful, receiving some of his cash back before the dealer went into hiding.

The 'crunch time' came on 16 November 1995. Just a few days before her 18th birthday, Leah Betts, the daughter of a former Essex police officer, was found dead, allegedly from an overdose of Ecstasy. There are various reports that she had been to Raquel's nightclub in Basildon, a place renowned for its potential for violence, and a growing list of discontented customers who had been buying dodgy drugs through Tucker and Rolfe Inc.

The fact is that she died during her 18th birthday party at her home in Latchington. Leah's father, Paul, and her mother, Janet, ensured that Leah's death received maximum publicity.

Essex Police clamped down. It became increasingly difficult to sell drugs in any of the clubs to which Tucker and his crew governed security and the illegal substances. Steele was now very worried about the heat that Leah's death was bringing down, and several unsubstantiated reports that the pill the young woman swallowed came from a batch of much stronger tablets that Tucker had purchased from a new supplier, and without the knowledge of Steele.

In the event, it has since been proven that Leah did not die as the result of Ecstasy ingestion. An inquest determined that her death was actually not directly due to Ecstasy consumption at all, but rather the large quantity of water she had consumed, apparently while observing the advice commonly given to ravers to drink water to avoid dehydration resulting from the exertion of dancing continuously for hours. Leah had been at home with friends and had not been dancing, yet consumed about 7 litres in less than 90 minutes, resulting in water intoxication and hyponatremia (low sodium levels; in this case due to the dilution of blood), which in turn led to serious swelling of the brain (cerebral edema), irreparably damaging it. However, SIADH – a condition in which a hormone is released, causing water retention – may have been directly related to the Ecstasy Leah had taken, leaving her unable to urinate, which would have allowed expulsion of the excess water and prevented hyponatremia. At the inquest it was stated, 'If Leah had taken the drug alone, she might well have survived. If she had drunk the amount of water alone, she would have survived.'

However, it is inconceivable that Leah obtained her Ecstasy pill from anywhere else than a batch from Messrs Tucker and Steele, so both men had every cause for concern. They had every reason to become paranoid, especially as Tucker, like Tate, was now consumed by drug addiction.

Around this time, Steele more or less fuelled the fire, telling his partner that he had just closed a deal – and it was a big one. For an outlay of £30,000, he was to fly 30kg of top-grade Colombian coke from Holland to a remote field in Essex. The load had a street value of £1 million… it was the deal of the century. Or would have been, had the two crooks trusted each other.

It would be right to say that Tate was excited about the offer. He and his side of the firm couldn't pull this deal off on their own – they relied totally on Steele – and Tate reasoned that Steele and his guys should be cut out of the enterprise once the aircraft had landed. In 1994, Tate and Rolfe had killed a small-time dealer named Kevin Whittaker who had ripped them off, so they were quite prepared to kill again should it prove expedient.

Steele was no mug either. He knew the risks. In fact, there was no 'big deal' and no shipment of Colombian cocaine. What he was planning was a classic double-cross. He asked Tate, Rolfe and Tucker to meet him in the Halfway House pub near Rettendon during the evening of 6 December, and they would drive in Rolfe's Range Rover to the field where he planned to land the aircraft a few days later. He would instruct them to light fires to aid his landing. After fully discussing the plan, they would then drive back to the pub.

At 6.30pm on 6 December, Darren Nicholls drove Steele and Jack Whomes close to the rendezvous point. Steele left them and walked to Craig Rolfe's Range Rover parked in the pub's car park. Nicholls then drove Whomes back down the A130 and dropped him at the entrance to Workhouse Lane, which led down a slope, where it met a junction, then turned right to a field, barred by a gate.

Whomes told Nicholls to drive half-a-mile further on and wait until he received a call on his mobile phone to return and pick up Steele and himself. Nicholls noticed that Whomes carried a large holdall as he stepped out of the car. Steele, now sitting in the back of the Range Rover alongside Pat Tate, stealthily pulled on a pair of surgical gloves as Rolfe drove them to the soon-to-be-murder scene.

As the Range Rover turned into Workhouse Lane, Tate received a phone call from his girlfriend, Sarah Saunders. Had Tate mentioned to her that he was with Mick and the boys, the plot would have been scuttled there and then. Tate effectively sealed his own fate by saying nothing of importance at all – Steele breathed a deep sigh of relief.

When they reached the end of the lane, they found the so-called landing field barred by a gate. It was dark, a clear sky and stars illuminated the narrow, rutted track, bordered by thick hedgerow, all blanketed in snow. Steele climbed out and allegedly said, 'You boys stay in the warm.' He walked a few yards from the vehicle and was met by Whomes, who handed him a sawn-off, double-barrelled shotgun.

Rolfe was the first to die. As soon as the rear passenger door had opened and Steele was clear, Jack Wholmes leaned in with a pump-action shotgun. He pressed the barrel against the back of the driver's headrest and pulled the trigger. The shot ripped through the fabric and straight through Rolfe's skull, leaving him dead where he sat. When his body was found, both hands were on the steering wheel, his foot on the brake.

Tucker was next. With the blast ringing in the ears from just a split-second earlier, he had no time to react. Whomes moved the gun and pumped in another round and shot him in the back of the head. Steele then appeared by the side of Whomes and trained his weapon on Tate, who was the only one given time to know that he was about to die. He screamed and pushed himself back into the corner of the vehicle in a futile bid to escape. Steele fired both barrels into his stomach. Then Whomes finished him off with a shot to the face and another to the stomach.

There was no doubt that the three men were dead but this was more than an execution. Whomes pumped his weapon again and opened the front door of the car. He placed the barrel up against what was left of Tucker's head and fired again. Then Whomes went round to Rolfe and did the same. Meanwhile, Steele reloaded both barrels and shot Tate's corpse in the face. This time, his gun fell apart as the stock came away from the barrels and trigger guard. Both men burst out laughing as Steele scrambled around on the floor of the car to retrieve the parts of his broken gun.

Just after 7.00pm, Whomes called Nicholls on his mobile phone and told him to collect them. Nicholls drove back to Workhouse Lane and then Whomes climbed in.

'Where's Mick?' asked Nicholls.

'He won't be long,' said Whomes. 'He's dropped something… doesn't want to leave it there.'

The case was handled by DS Ivan Dibley of the Essex Police. He was a veteran cop from the old school and regarded any gangland slaying on his patch as a personal challenge – having solved 23 of the 25 homicides during 31 years in the force. But the triple Rettendon murders was a tough nut to crack; fingerprints found in the vehicle belonged only to the three victims, and an overnight frost had distorted footprints, making them unreliable as evidence. In fact, the forensic evidence amounted to just seven expended cartridge cases on the floor of the Range Rover.

Mick Steel was swiftly identified as a suspect, but there was not a shred of evidence to convict him. Dibley even worked out how the hit was played out – by two men, one of whom had been a passenger in the Range Rover. A third man must have driven the killers and, if the police could find him, he was the best bet for a first-hand witness to the crime. Cellular telephone network records indicated that the mobile phones belonging to the victims, plus Steele, Whomes and Nicholls, had all logged on to the satellite relay beacon nearest Workhouse Lane from 6.45pm to 7.10pm on 6 December. This placed them all close to the crime scene when the triple murder was committed. But with no firm evidence, the police investigation was stalled.

Then, in January, Nicholls had become very scared when Whomes threatened him. 'What happened to Pat could easily happen to you, my old son. You can be replaced.'

For months following the murder, the hunt for the execution-style killers led nowhere… that was until May 1996, when Corry and Nicholls were arrested in possession of 10kg of cannabis. DS Ivan Dibley was to be proved correct. He coughed all he knew when he was charged as accessory to the murders.

With a £500,000 price on his head, and now facing a long sentence, Nicholls turned supergrass. He was placed in the Witness Protection Programme. He and his wife Sandra were installed in a safe house in February 1997, with the trial due to commence at the Old Bailey on 1 September, during which time he was kept in jail where he was put in a cell, and had, at his disposal, a multi-gym as well as a colour television. He also enjoyed takeaway meals.

The evidence later given by Nicholls was crucial to the Prosecution at the trial of Whomes and Steele. Identified as 'Bloggs 19', Nicholls related, 'Jack made this really weird sound, like a series of quiet little snorts. I could just make out his silhouette in the rear-view mirror and his big shoulders were bobbing up and down. It took me a while to work out what was going on. Jack was giggling.

'I was still looking at Jack,' he said, 'when Mick Steele appeared and opened the front passenger door. The interior light came on and that's when I saw his hands. He was wearing surgical gloves and they had been splashed with streaks of blood. I then realised what they had done. I felt like someone had sucked all the air out of me and I could not speak. Mick told me to get going and I drove to Basildon on autopilot.'

As he drove, Nicholls listened with mounting horror as Whomes and Steele, still on an adrenalin high, discussed the triple murder. They told him that Pate Tate, the self-styled 'hard man' had 'squealed like a baby' just before he was shot.

During the five-month trial, the defence lawyers for Steele and Whomes challenged the grim story told by Nicholls in the witness box. However, the carefully prepared alibis provided by the accused men began to unravel under intense cross-examination, with Steele doing himself no favours by boasting of his previous convictions, mostly for drug offences, despite the advice of his lawyers.

The 'star witness' for the defence team was a William 'Billy' George Jasper. But the Crown proved that he was a 'Walter Mitty', a habitual confessor to major crimes. Jasper was a heroin addict who simply loved all the publicity.

The story concocted by Whomes, Steele and Jasper was that the gangsters had been killed by members of the Canning Town Cartel. Jasper had himself been arrested in January 1996 and had given police a yarn that he had met Jesse Gale, another East End heavy, then, with another man, they had gone to a Mexican restaurant to discuss the future of Tate, Tucker and Rolfe. In a nutshell, Jasper claimed that the deceased men had planned to take delivery of a haul of drugs and not pay for them. Jasper explained that Tate and Tucker had ripped off Gale and another man for some £20,000. He added that it had been him, and not Nicholls, who had driven a grey Fiat Uno and, for a fee of £500, had driven a man to Workhouse Lane to collect 4kg of cocaine – but his story was not believed.

The trial, which cost the taxpayer £1.5 million, concluded on 20 January 1998 when Whomes and Steele were jailed for life with a minimum serving tariff of at least 15 years. 'There is no other sentence I can pass on you for these horrifying murders of which you been convicted than that of life imprisonment,' Mr Justice Hidden told the pair in the dock. 'You are both extremely dangerous men and you have not the slightest compunction for resorting to extreme violence.'

But was Nicholls to be believed? His testimony was riddled with holes, although he did earn himself the distinction of becoming the most famous supergrass in British criminal history since Bertie Smalls, who is the subject of some scrutiny in the next chapter. Nicholls was given a new name, a new passport and completely new identity and is now living a long way from Essex. He is quoted as saying, 'I have this terrible guilt. I feel like I've been a right bastard, grassing up my mates. I know I shouldn't feel guilty, but I just can't help it. It's going to be a long time before I can feel good about myself again.'

Whomes and Steele continue to protest their innocence for the triple Rettenden murders. Their appeals have been rejected by the Court of Appeal and they have now applied for relief from the European Court. It might be obvious to say that, with a life sentence in front of them, any chance of being freed is one to be taken seriously, however long the odds.

8

The Adams Family

'It is suggested that Terrence Adams was one of the
country's most feared and revered organised criminals.
He comes with a pedigree, as one of a family whose
name had a currency all of its own in the underworld.'

ANDREW MITCHELL QC, PROSECUTING COUNSEL

Most certainly not to be confused with the American
Addams Family, the creation of American cartoonist
Charles Addams that appears in print cartoons, television
shows, movies and video games. The Adams family ruled
through intimidation and violence and are rumoured to
have been involved in 30 murders.

They had links to Colombian cocaine cartels and the
Russian Mafia, loan sharking, protection rackets and
money laundering through the Hatton Garden gem
district in central London. They are said to have flooded
nightclubs with Ecstasy in the 1990s, and are believed to
have invented the 'bike hit', where two killers shoot their
target from a motorcycle. Their terrifying reputation

struck fear into the hearts of rival gangsters, while police, lawyers, and even judges, learnt to tread extremely carefully when they dealt with them – with one judge given around-the-clock armed police protection before the later trial of brother Tommy, who faced a million-pound cannabis smuggling charge.

In the early days, detectives were no match for the brothers' sophisticated techniques and ability to corrupt. Scotland Yard failed again and again to nail them. Once henchman was sent a pig's trotter through the post – a grim warning of worse to come, should he step out of line. He reported it to the Old Bill, who advised him to 'forget it...what's the point?'

Ordering brutal and sadistic punishments – and he often carried them out personally – the head of the family enterprise, Terrence 'Terry' Adams, was the brains behind their criminal operations. He looked like an ageing dandy, a cross between Liberace and Peter Stringfellow, but he was at the top of his profession and controlled his empire with such ruthless efficiency that he could have run BP or ICI. Yet Terry, who made Tony Soprano look like a pussycat, was the godfather of the nearest underworld network Britain had to the Mafia. He was the Capone of his time and, like Alphonse Capone, it was the taxman who finally nailed him.

One has to give Terry respect. He was ever the dapper gent in his velvet-collared overcoats. He lived in a £2 million house in north London crammed with stolen antiques; it was a far cry from his upbringing on the rough Barnsbury council estate in Islington. His family and close associates were reputably worth about £200 million, and they were feared far more than the Krays ever were.

THE ADAMS FAMILY

Sean Adams – aka Tommy – handled the financial side of the firm, which was known as the A-Team, or the Clerkenwell Crime Syndicate. Patrick provided the muscle. Terry was the most level-headed of this wild bunch; Tommy was wild, and the other brother, Patrick or 'Patsy', could be wild *and* crazy. As a former associate of the Adams has remarked, 'A lot of people involved in this kind of business don't have a lot going on up top. But Terry and his brothers were different. They were a real class act. Terry was always well dressed and in charge of whatever was going on. When he walked into a room, everyone stood up. He was like royalty.'

Terry was the oldest of 11 children, born on 18 October 1954 to a law-abiding, working-class, Irish Catholic family. He was raised in Islington, north London, and he was closest to his younger brothers Patrick, born 1955, and Sean, born 1958, with whom he entered a life of crime – a career of extorting money from traders and stallholders at street markets close to their home, in the Clerkenwell area, before graduating to armed robberies. For the record, Patrick served seven years in prison for armed robbery in the 1970s.

By the 1980s, the Adams family had moved into the lucrative drugs trade. They built up links with Yardie firms and the Colombian cocaine cartels. The money they made was laundered through various corrupt financiers, accountants, lawyers and other professionals; they subsequently invested in property and other legitimate businesses that left the Krays, the Richardsons and all of the Scottish mobsters put together, in the shade. And if anyone crossed them, revenge was swift and brutal.

In 1989, a 39-year-old pub accountant, Terry

Gooderham, who skimmed £250,000 of drug money from the brothers, was found dead, alongside his girlfriend, Maxine, in a Mercedes. The killing ground was that most favourite body-dumping ground of east London mobsters – Epping Forest. According to underworld folklore, Gooderham begged, 'You can't kill me in front of my girlfriend.' The executioner turned to Maxine, levelled a gun to her head, and shot her dead, saying, 'You're not with her now,' and squeezed the trigger again.

32-year-old Irishman, Tommy Roche, was shot through the heart by a motorcycle hitman while working for a road repair team near Heathrow Airport in 1993. To alleviate his financial shortcomings, Roche had offered to act as a go-between for a cocaine syndicate, but he was suspected by the Adamses as being a scammer and a grass. He paid a heavy price.

Terry Adams suspected the former 32-year-old British high-jump champion, Claude Moseley, of trying to short-change him over a drugs deal. He sent enforcer Gilbert Wynter to 'talk it over with him' in 1994. Moseley was literally sliced in two with a Samurai sword. Wynter went on trial for murder, but the case was dropped when the key prosecution witness refused to give evidence. The hitman later disappeared, possibly concreted into the foundations of the Millennium Dome!

In the 1980s, the gang's reputation for violence was pushed even further. The decade produced a shoot-out with a rival Irish family, the Reillys, who challenged the Adamses' dominance of Islington. Patrick Adams and an associate went to a pub controlled by the Reillys and insulted one of them. The Reillys left the bar to arm themselves and returned. It was an ambush. Their BMW was fired on repeatedly by members of the Adamses' gang. Remarkably, no one was killed, but the message sent out was crystal clear – 'the Adamses *run* Islington.'

In 1991, 'Mad' Frankie Fraser, a gangland veteran, was shot in the head outside a London club in another attack attributed to the Adams gang.

David McKenzie, a Mayfair financier, paid a high price for losing £1.5 million for Adams. He was summoned to 'The Godfather's' house to explain. 'Everyone stood up when he walked in. He looked like a star; he was immaculately dressed in a long black coat and white frilly shirt. He was totally in command,' McKenzie said. Several days later, McKenzie was savagely beaten. The man accused of the attack stood his trial at the Old Bailey in 1999. However, the jury accepted his version that he had broken up a fight between McKenzie and another man.

By now, the Adams brothers were gaining a Teflon reputation – no accusation would stick. Tommy was acquitted in 1985 of acting as a courier, moving gold bullion stolen in the £26 million Brinks Mat robbery out of London. Patsy, who had been jailed for armed robbery, was acquitted of importing three tons of cannabis.

By the late 1990s, the heat was on. In 1996, the Inland Revenue caught up with Terry Adams. He offered to settle with them for £95,000 in cash.

In 1998, Sean 'Tommy' Adams was convicted of organising an £8 million hashish smuggling operation, and was sentenced to seven years' imprisonment. When a judge ordered that he surrender some of his profits or face a further five years, his wife turned up twice to the court, carrying £500,000 in cash inside a briefcase on each occasion.

In May 2003, Terry Adams was arrested and charged with money laundering, tax evasion and handling stolen goods... and only with the full co-operation of MI5 was a solid case built. But the cost was colossal, and what was surprising was that Terry Adams's boastfulness eventually turned out to be his undoing – he was caught on tape crowing about his crimes, battering his enemies with iron bars and kneecapping debtors.

In July 1997, Terry Adams was overheard talking to 41-year-old Saul 'Solly' Solomon Nahome, about a rival gangster who owed him £250,000. He said, 'Then you let Simon give the geezer a hiding, right? I don't give a fuck about the geezer... the geezer's gonna be stamped on. He's using the family name, the geezer's using the family name... And, he's gotta be hurt, this fella. We ain't gonna be no one's cunt, Sol.'

On 27 November 1998, financial adviser and diamond merchant Saul Nahome was shot dead outside his home in Arden Road, Finchley. Nahome was said to have arranged for £25 million to be hidden in property deals and offshore accounts. He was ambushed by a gunman who pumped four bullets into him and escaped on a motorcycle. Married to Joanna, with an 11-month-old daughter, it had been Nahome who had helped the Adams family melt down gold bars, and they believed he had squirrelled away some £25 million and transferred the cash away into offshore accounts.

Police also claimed that the family tortured a businessman so badly his ears and nose were left hanging by slivers of skin.

In another conversation, Adams tells a mobster, 'He's got to be spoke to and a slap... a right-hander in his face. You'll have to tell Jimmy from me, I want the geezer livened up. I want them hurt double, double, double bad.'

He tells his notorious enforcer, Gilbert Wynter, how to deal with someone who has not 'come up with the goods' – repaid the money he owes. 'I want to grab him, that's it. That's what I want, Gil. Gil, you do that for me, I'll love for that, mate… I mean it, Gil. You've got to liven him up, put the fear of God into him, mate, and he knows it's only down to you that he's walking about and breathing fresh air.' Wynter assured Adams he'd 'open him up like a bag of crisps'.

The MI5 tapes would later prove crucial evidence against Terry Adams. He later told Wynter that when he catches up with another associate he is going to 'knock him out, put him on his arse.' In another recording, in September 1997, while watching the TV show *Blind Date* with a friend named Dan, he says, 'Anyone who has it with a grass, is a grass. On my daughter's life, I'll do what I'll do… on my baby's life, I'm gonna butt him. I'm gonna smash him in the face with an iron bar.'

His associate replied, 'You are mad!'

Adams laughed, adding, 'I'll do it in front of his kids. I'm gonna do them. I'm gonna fuckin' do them. When I hit someone, I do them damage.'

Other tapes recorded Terry Adams boasting about his history of violence to a man who owed him £100,000. 'On my baby's life Dan, his kneecap come right out there, all white Dan, all bone. If I have to fight, I cut them with my knuckles.'

Adams also talked to his wife Ruth about collecting money from debtors in July 1998. 'Tell 'em, they get hurt if they don't pay. It's like that, Ruth. They have that word by an Adams.'

The tapes also document Adams's anger with his own brother Tommy, jailed in 1998 for a cannabis smuggling plot. 'When you have got your so-called brother having it off with a fuckin' Paki... Informers getting us in the fuckin' papers and with the fuckin' Old Bill... When you have got a so-called brother who is trying to get us all done in so that he secures his freedom... he's worse than a fuckin' grass because he's had it with a grass.'

Terry Adams finally came undone after a specialist police team spent 21 months bugging his £2 million mansion. It was a joint enterprise between the National Crime Squad, MI5 and HM Revenue & Customs – the latter two agencies being among the most powerful law enforcement agencies in the world. Stacked up against him, the odds were overwhelming, and the investigation would cost the taxpayer £50 million.

In May 2003, his home was raided. Police found £50,000 worth of stolen antiques and £60,000 in cash was discovered hidden in the attic. And despite using his fortune to fly first-class around the world, stay at the best hotels, splash out on expensive jewellery and send his daughter to a private school, Adams claimed, tongue-in-cheek, that he was merely a marketing consultant earning £200 a week. He was granted legal aid and released on £1 million bail. He now claimed that his IQ was so low he didn't even understand the charges, and demanded the surveillance tapes be transcribed before the trial.

In February 2007, 52-year-old Terry Adams pleaded guilty to conspiracy to launder £1.1 million. Of the defendant standing before him, His Honour Judge

Timothy Pontius said, 'Your [guilty] plea demonstrates that you have a fertile, cunning and imaginative mind capable of sophisticated, complex and dishonest financial manipulation.'

On 9 March, he was sentenced to seven years in prison. He was ordered to pay back all his defence costs and £750,000 compensation or face another four years behind bars. His Honour Judge Pontius remarked that Adams had delayed the case for four years and had changed his legal team three times. It was said that prosecution costs were about £4 million. Costs still have not been fully assessed and another hearing will decide if Adams would be forced to contribute. Further charges of mortgage and tax deception against Adams were allowed to lie on the file.

Charges against his wife, Ruth, were not proceeded with. A third defendant, 38-year-old Johanna Barnes (formerly the wife of Solly Nahome), admitted one charge of forgery involving a £15,000 loan agreement. She was fined £5,000 and ordered to pay £2,500 in costs. The judge told her, 'You foolishly but deliberately and I think callously decided to forge your late husband's signature within weeks of his murder for the purposes of subterfuge for the benefit of Terry Adams.'

Terry Adams was the British crime godfather who built up a £200 million empire because he was feared more than death itself. After more than a decade of investigation by police, the Revenue and MI5, Adams's millions are still hidden. He is known to have a yacht, a house in Hendon Wood Lane, Mill Hill, London, worth at least £750,000, and an interest in a villa in Cyprus. The gang also owned clubs and discos in north London, were silent partners in clubs in the West End and Soho, ran protection rackets and reportedly commissioned armed robberies from which they took a cut. At one stage, the brothers tried to invest in the London Arena and Tottenham Hotspur, although they are said to be Arsenal fans. Indeed, such was the gang's power and fearsome reputation, it even ran a franchise operation, allowing other gangs to use its name at a cost of £250,000 per operation. The condition – 'pay within a week, or else'.

Patrick, a married father of four, still has a home near the family's traditional Islington base, but is now living in Spain. Sean – aka Tommy – was cleared of involvement in the laundering of gold bullion from the Brinks Mat job in 1985. He is suspected of establishing connections to other criminal organisations as well as gaining an $80 million credit line from Colombian drug cartels. In 2001, the *Independent* stated that Sean 'was living in exile in Spain in a walled villa bristling with security cameras a few miles south of Torremolinos'.

Family member Michael Adams, born in 1965, was convicted of possessing a firearm in the mid-1980s. And brother Robert (deceased), a relative, was imprisoned for his part in a huge attempted robbery at the Millennium Dome, London, on 7 November 2000.

Among other associates of the Adamses' were Billy Isaacs, who was convicted of passing secret files to the Adams family. Christopher McCormick, who was alleged at a 1999 trial to be an enforcer for the family. He was cleared of causing grievous bodily harm to a businessman who failed to repay £1.4 million to Terry Adams. Anthony Passmore, a conman jailed in 1999 for six years over a multi-million-pound fraud who escaped from Ford Open Prison two months after his trial and has not been seen since. Anthony Jones, 42, and David Tucker, 62, who were suspected, in 2005, by authorities in Florida, of trying to smuggle cocaine worth $8 million on behalf of the Adams family.

Pat 'Pat the Rat' McCadden, millionaire Scottish gangster, is another of the Adamses' associates. McCadden and his family lived in a stunning mansion in the upmarket Costa del Sol resort of Marbella, after fleeing a £1 million tax bill in Scotland.

His shoe importation firm, Genoa Footwear, seemed to be a huge success and gave McCadden a life of luxury, including three Rolls-Royces. But despite slick TV advertisements, Genoa went bust amid claims it was selling counterfeits of expensive Italian shoes. Pat was bankrupted in 1985 and, in the same year was jailed for ten years over a £600,000 heroin haul.

In 1998, the former playboy was back in the public eye. Now aged 44, the *Mail on Sunday* revealed that McCadden, then living in upmarket Bearsden, near Glasgow, was linked to a security firm, which was fronted by his second wife, Louise, and daughter, Jane, from his first marriage. Elite Security (Scotland) Ltd later went bust.

In 2001, Inland Revenue investigators and police launched a probe into the tax affairs of Elite and McCadden. It was calculated that he owed £1 million and, just as the investigation was coming to a head, 'Pat the Rat' sold up and hot-footed it to Spain.

On 1 December 2003, a Guardia Civil cop was hit following a robbery at a telephone shop in Marbella. The store's British owner was shot in both legs. The police started chasing an Opel Astra, which matched the description of the two so-called thieves' getaway car, when the police officer suffered serious gunshot wounds to his stomach, lungs and liver.

Insisting that it was a case of mistaken identity, McCadden was picked out by the cop at an identity parade, and he was arrested by Spain's national police, the Cuerpo Nacional de Policia on 8 February 2006.

Terry Adams could be a free man in 2009.

9

The Wembley Mob

'There is no doubt that "grasses" such as
Bertie Smalls and other filth like him deserve to
be shot like the sick dogs they are.'

'MAD' FRANKIE FRASER ON SUPERGRASS BERTIE SMALLS

By 1972, the 'Wembley Mob' was one of the most prolific crews in London. They lived like lords in big houses and drove fast cars, although there seems to be some dispute as to who their leader was. Various accounts identify the boss to be the reclusive Mickey Green, described by an old friend as 'a good old-fashioned London villain'. Other sources point a finger at Derek Creighton 'Bertie' Smalls, who is considered by many as Britain's first supergrass, moving 'Mad' Frankie Fraser to demand that people like him should be shot 'like the sick dogs they are'.

By all accounts, the two men couldn't have been more different. One was a straight-up London gangster, the other a rotund, prematurely balding man with a drooping moustache... and a supergrass. But they shared one common aim – they loved robbing banks. And even by today's standards, they were rich men. For his part in a robbery on a savings bank in Brighton, Smalls was paid £10,000 – about £200,000 in today's money.

Bertie Smalls was born in the East End of London. While still under police protection, he died in February 2008 at his Victorian semi in Croydon at the age of 72. There had once been a £1 million price on his head during the late 1970s, with signatories including the Kray twins.

Mickey Green was born in 1942. A convicted armed robber, he has allegedly been one of Britain's leading drug-dealers for many years. His worth is estimated at £75 million, and he currently lives on the Costa del Sol.

The gang had been at large throughout the 'Swinging Sixties', and during the summer of 1972, the Metropolitan Police were feeling the heat more than usual. The armed robbers were tearing apart the banks and building societies of the capital with daylight smash-and-grab raids that had netted an estimated £1.3 million (some £8 million at today's rate). The law seemed powerless. Newspapers published a photograph of a police officer removing a baby's pram from the firing line in one raid on Barclays Bank in Harlesden, north-west London, and looking on powerlessly while the Wembley Mob completed the job.

It was a PR disaster. The crooks were making monkeys out of the Met. The spree culminated on Thursday, 10 August 1972, when the audacious and slick gang took just 90 seconds to raid a branch of Barclays Bank in Wembley, north London. Known as The Ilford Job, it carried all the trademarks of the gang's meticulous methods. Through inside information, they learned that the bank received large deposits consisting of the takings of a Tesco supermarket and that, when these large amounts arrived, the security van was preceded by a red Mini, presumed to be sent to inform the manager. This enabled the robbers to pick the appropriate day to secure the largest amount of cash.

After 'recruiting' two employees of the security van company, Smalls sent one of the robbers into the bank dressed as a City worker, complete with pin-stripe suit and an umbrella, to write a cheque to distract bank staff while the van approached. The raid went as smooth as silk, with the corrupt security guards handing over the money and the robbers escaped.

The haul was over £237,000 – a record at the time and, by 15 August, the entire crew had fled England via various routes with the police soon to be hot on their tails. For his part, Smalls travelled by ferry from Newhaven to Dieppe, by train to Paris, and then flew to Torremolinos, for the Costa del Sol – aka the Costa del Crime –where the gang met up and read the British newspapers for updates on the hunt for them.

Indeed, they were certainly audacious, this Wembley Mob; apart from terrorising bank staff and members of the public, and scaring them out of their wits, no one was ever shot, although a few hairs turned grey in the process.

The 1970s was also a record decade for armed robberies in the capital. This was partly because the culture was rife with bribe-taking. Cops were sharing in the proceeds of crime and 'verballing', or fabricating evidence against suspects. In fact, Sir Robert Mark,

Commissioner of the Metropolitan Police, went on TV at one point, claiming that many of his own officers were 'so bent they couldn't lay straight in bed', and he was anxious to remind his detectives which side of the law they were supposed to be on. 'A good police force is one that catches more criminals than it employs.'

Not since the 1920s had a British police force faced such criticism. During those early years, most of the Liverpool City Police were committing robberies by night and investigating their own handiwork the following day. And at the centre of Sir Robert's focus was the CID, and its élite Flying Squad. Chief Superintendent Ken Drury, commander of the Flying Squad, and one of his inspectors, Alistair Ingram, later went to prison for corruption.

Indeed, the 1970s was a dark period for the Flying Squad. An internal police investigation, Operation Countryman, revealed an extensive and tangled web of corruption. Bribery was endemic, especially between officers and Soho pornographers. In a scandal which still resonates today, Ken Drury was jailed along with 12 other Scotland Yard detectives for accepting bribes and, if the truth were known, the Wembley Mob must have had a few bent cops on its own payroll.

An early break in the investigation was made, when luck unearthed a nark who provided the names of every member of the gang. The police case then cooled until the robbers returned to Britain.

Bertie Smalls was tracked down and then arrested in a suburb of Northampton in late November 1972. He sweated Christmas out in jail, then, on 2 January 1973, he started to cough. In exchange for a 25-year prison term, he offered to name and incriminate the entire gang, not only those in the Barclays Bank heist, but to spill the details on every single piece of criminal activity he had ever been involved in. 'I can give you every robber in London,' Smalls was reputed to have said; to the police at the time, this was gold dust.

A deal was struck between Smalls and Sir Norman Skelhorn, then Director of Public Prosecutions. Between February 1974 and April 1975, his 'assistance' secured the imprisonment of 28 of his former colleagues for a total of 414 years, with sentences ranging from 5–18 years.

The trial relating to the Barclays job commenced in Court 2, The Old Bailey, on 11 February 1974. As Smalls concluded his evidence during one of the committal hearings, the ad hoc choir in the dock sang a rendition of the blues ballad 'Whispering Grass', then pointing their fingers into the shape of guns, they sang the Vera Lynn song, *'We'll meet again, don't know where, don't know when...'*

The trial finished on 20 May. The jury returned guilty verdicts on all defendants on 22 May. In total, the judge handed down sentences totalling 106 years for the Barclays job alone. Smalls' old partner, Mickey Green, got 18 years. During the following months, a further 21 associates of Smalls were convicted with sentences totalling 308 years. But all was not bad news for his fellow cons, particularly one who was already being detained at Her Majesty's Pleasure – Jimmy Saunders.

Saunders had been arrested by the incorruptible DCI Albert 'Bert' Wickstead for his part in the 1970 Ilford Barclays robbery. It was claimed that Wickstead, known as 'The Old Grey Fox' and 'Gangbuster Wickstead', had verballed Saunders up. Smalls gave evidence that Saunders had not been on that particular crew, and was cleared.

As part of his never-to-be-repeated deal, which the Law Lords later described as 'unholy', Smalls received a new identity. Within a few years, though, he had returned to his old London haunts, drinking openly in the pubs around Hornsey and often boasting that he was paid £25 per week by police for his betrayal. Bobby King, one of the robbers his evidence convicted, once spotted Smalls in Crouch End. He saw it as a test of his own rehabilitation that he didn't 'whack' Smalls.

But the trials and convictions of the Wembley Mob didn't see the end of a grim period in police history, in which the authorities were compromised and often outwitted by what many misguidedly considered to be the swashbuckling and daring masterminds of eye-catching, set-piece bank robberies. The Flying Squad saw the number of raids in London rocket from 380 in 1972 to 734 by 1978. The total reached 1,772 by 1982. Nevertheless, the testimony of Smalls showed how much damage could be inflicted by a high-level informer, 'snout' or 'stoolie'. The number of robberies in the area of London where the Wembley Mob had been active plummeted from 65 to 26 in the year after their arrest and subsequent imprisonment.

After his release from prison, Mickey Green – at one time the main suspect in the murders of Gilbert Wynter and Solly Nahome – has been wanted by police in several countries for suspected drug smuggling. His ability to evade arrest has led to him being nicknamed 'The Pimpernel'. He is said to have first become involved with drugs during the early 1980s. It is alleged that he has a number of bent cops on his payroll, and he is well acquainted with the Adams brothers. He was named Europe's most wanted drugs baron and his other nickname is 'The Octopus' for the tentacles of his ever-expanding criminal network wrap themselves around the globe.

He owns pubs and other property in Wembley, West Hampstead, Dublin (he holds Irish nationality), and for than 20 years he has operated in Morocco, France and the United States, where he co-operated with organised crime figures running cocaine in from Colombia until his arrest by the FBI. He was caught while lounging by a pool, drink in hand, living in a Beverly Hills mansion formerly owned by Rod Stewart. He was later released without charge.

Apart from his prison sentence for the Ilford job – and it is fair to say he wouldn't have been caught for that if Smalls had kept his mouth shut – Green has always stayed one step ahead of the law, leaving behind speedboats, yachts, Rolls-Royces, a Porsche, a Ferrari, gold bullion, cash and cocaine in his haste to get away.

More recently he was implicated in a £150 million cocaine-smuggling ring based in Britain and was seized by Spanish police while staying at the Ritz in Barcelona. Following the arrest of British drug-trafficker Michael Michael during Operation Draft, Green was one of 60 others implicated in the £150 million enterprise.

He spent months in custody before Customs decided to drop the charges. He is now free again and it is alleged that he is back in his Spanish villa on the Costa del Sol. However, his options for travel are severely limited. He is wanted in France, where he was sentenced to 17 years in his absence; he is wanted in Holland; he also faces arrest if he returns to Ireland, over allegations that he 'fixed witnesses' at an inquest. In the UK, he is wanted for questioning about alleged links to corrupt allegations involving a Scotland Yard élite unit.

'Mickey Green is the original gold medallion man with a taste for the booze and birds,' a former buddy told the *Independent* newspaper.

As an ironic footnote to the life and crimes of Mickey Green, DCI Tony Lundy, named the 'Supergrass Master', who raised the efficiency of the supergrass system to new heights, running it from a police station in Finchley, retired aged 49 to the Costa del Sol, where Mr Green was, or still is, one of his neighbours.

10

Bert Wickstead – Gangbuster

'I look for three main qualities in my officers – honesty, integrity and professional capacity.'

COMMANDER BERT WICKSTEAD

Born Monday, 23 April 1923, in Plaistow, the son of a railway foreman, Albert 'Bert' Wickstead was the UK's answer to Eliot Ness. He was educated at Burke senior school, and then took up factory work. His chosen career would have been as a West Ham footballer, but two broken legs put paid to any possibility of him kicking a ball around a pitch; he did, however, go on to kick a large number of criminals into touch.

During World War II, he served with the SAS, and was stationed in India, Burma and Ceylon. He joined the police after being demobbed, encouraged by his uncle, also a police officer.

As a young inspector at Stoke Newington, north London, he solved 19 murders in two years – a record that has never been equalled. In 1965, he investigated a series of arson attacks on synagogues by the neo-fascists of the National Socialist Movement. The perpetrators were jailed. He was dubbed 'The Old Grey Fox', and was renowned for jumping up and disappearing almost as quickly. He was affectionately known as 'Gangbuster Wickstead', one of the last of the high-profile Scotland Yard detectives, part of an era when men in belted raincoats and trilbies would stand on the steps of the Old Bailey after a trial and pronounce on the latest twist or a successful verdict in underworld-related trials.

Unlike many of his contemporaries at the Yard, Wickstead was an honest cop and a man never to take a bribe. In fact, when the chance arose, he pursued the Met's bent policemen with as much relish as he chased the villains.

Bert was promoted to the rank of commander to run what was then 'J' Division, in London's East End. In 1970, he headed the investigation into what was then Britain's biggest bank robbery, committed by the Wembley Mob. A year later, he was given a free hand to form his own team, the Serious Crimes Squad, to tackle major professional crime in the capital. The group was the first of the specialist units set up by the Metropolitan Police in the 1970s.

Perhaps Wickstead's most controversial case was the torso murder investigation of 1976–77, at the end of which Reg Dudley and Bob Maynard were both jailed for life for the murders of Billy Moseley and Micky Cornwall. At 135 days, it was the longest murder trial in British history, and both men furiously protested their innocence from the dock. Between them, they would go on to serve more than 40 years behind bars.

The thrust of the case was that Moseley had been having an affair with another criminal's wife and had also accused Dudley of being a police informer. For this, he had supposedly been murdered in September 1974, and his body had been chopped up and dumped in the Thames – hence, 'The Torso Murder'.

According to the prosecution, when Moseley's friend, Cornwall (a character known as 'The Laughing Bank Robber' because he was always smiling) was later released from prison, he went hunting for the killers. He, in turn, was murdered. He was shot in the head and dumped in a shallow grave in Hertfordshire in September 1975.

Dozens of people fell under suspicion for the murders before the police charged the seven who appeared at the Old Bailey. The prosecution evidence came primarily from two sources – the alleged confessions made to the police by Dudley and Maynard, who worked at the illegal end of the jewellery business, and their so-called admissions to a fellow inmate, a young bank robber called Tony Wild, while they were awaiting trial in Brixton Prison.

According to police, Dudley had, during a journey in a police car, said, 'The cunt [Moseley] had it coming. He tried to fuck me so I fucked him good and proper.' Later, Dudley was said to have told the police questioning him about Cornwall, 'You can take it from me it is not on my conscience... He deserved what he got and that's it.' For his part, Maynard had supposedly told the police after his arrest, 'It's about time you came for me.'

The police investigation was led by Bert Wickstead, and although he was not a man to accept a bribe, it was a well-known fact that he *was* prepared to do what was necessary to ensure that those whom he believed to be guilty were brought to justice.

The trial, in front of Mr Justice Swanwick, seemed everlasting. Maynard and Dudley ran a criminal empire which was named the 'Legal & General' – a nickname the two men had been given after walking into a pub dressed like two characters from a Legal & General television commercial. In reality, there was no gang.

The dramatic high point in the trial came when Wild – a prison snitch – walked into the witness box. A handsome figure, he gave evidence that he had met the two accused men in prison. He said that Dudley had boasted about killing Cornwall, who had apparently said, 'He went up in the fucking air, didn't he, boys?' Wild also claimed that Maynard had said, 'I didn't know guys would squeal like a pig.' All in all, Wild made for a compelling witness, although later events would prove it all to be something less than the truth.

To put no finer point on it, the evidence was, at best, slim – anorexic would be a more suitable term. Of the seven accused with varying degrees of responsibility for the murder, three were acquitted, including the man whose wife had been having an affair with Moseley. When Maynard was sentenced, he shouted to the judge, 'I am still innocent, sir.'

Dudley then let loose against Wickstead. 'Are you happy? You have fitted us all up, but don't worry – you'll be fitted up in the end by your own kind.'

In the years to come, Wild finally came clean and told the press that he had stitched up the two men in return for a lighter prison sentence, and that Wickstead was in on the deal. There followed a campaign to free the men and, after a three-year examination of the evidence, the Criminal Cases Review Commission recommended that the matter should go to the Court of Appeal. Dudley was paroled in 1997, and Maynard was released on bail in November 2000.

Wickstead also played a leading part in the investigation of Soho pornographers Bernie Silver and Jimmy Humphreys, whose revelations led to the jailing of thirteen corrupt members of the Met's Obscene Publications Squad.

On 25 June 1956, a Tommy Smithson was found dying in the gutter outside a house in Carlton Vale. His last words were said to be, 'Good morning… I'm dying.'
A handsome man, who, in his chequered and largely unsuccessful career, suffered at just about everybody's hands, was an ex-fairground fighter with a liking for silk shirts and underwear. He was a man, as James Morton described in his book *East End Gangland*, 'of immense courage and little stability or ability and was known as Mr Loser'.

It was some years before Bert Wickstead got to the bottom of the matter, and he set his sights on Bernie Silver, a club and brothel owner, whose operations could be traced back to the 1950s. In a nutshell, Silver lived off immoral earnings as part of a highly lucrative business venture. Prostitutes were worked liked slaves, and charged for the privilege of doing so. Bert Wickstead had been called in to investigate the Soho vice syndicates, and he was immensely successful. Two Maltese criminals were eventually charged with Smithson's murder, although both were cleared after a key witness mysteriously disappeared.

Thereafter, Wickstead became known as one of the country's finest detectives, a man who would also investigate the case of the prostitute, Norma Levy, which was to lead to the downfall of the Conservative minister, Antony Claud Frederick Lord Lambton, 6th Earl of Durham.

During his three years with the Serious Crimes Squad, Wickstead was often in the newspapers for his gang-busting exploits. His critics query whether the gangs, who were supposedly trying to fill the vacuum left by the Kray twins, were quite as mighty as he claimed. And, if the truth were known now, and as we have seen in previous chapters, the Krays were not on a par with many of their modern-day contemporaries as far as their ill-gotten gains were concerned. Consider wheelers and dealers such as the Adams family, for example.

It would be fair to say, however, that some of these firms were just extended families back then – people with violent tempers. But among those he jailed as career criminals were the Tibbs, the Dixons, and Philip Jacobs – standing just 5ft 2in, he was known as 'Little Caesar'.

The Dixon family had grown up at the end of the war in Limehouse where, in time, they controlled the local pubs and clubs. In the borough of Tower Hamlets, Limehouse is on the northern bank of the River Thames opposite Rotherhithe and between Shadwell to the west and the Isle of Dogs to the east. Primarily 'debt collectors', they had worked as freelancers for the Krays and, until his marriage broke up, and drink and drugs consumed him, Alan Dixon had been a 'running-mate' with Jack 'The Hat' McVitie. Although the Dixons had known the Krays for some time, it hadn't stopped Ronnie

Kray from attempting to shoot George Dixon one night in a mock trial held at the Green Dragon Club in Aldgate over some alleged misdemeanour. As described earlier, Ronnie had pushed the gun barrel into his mouth and the gun misfired. Ron gave him the cartridge, telling him to wear it as a souvenir on his watch-chain. He did. For a fuller account of the Dixons and the Tibbs, James Morton's book, *East End Gangland,* is a must-read.

Unimpressed by the trappings of wealth which dazzled many of his less-than-honest colleagues, Wickstead lived for many years in a council flat in Plaistow, east London, with his wife and three sons. His squad – whom he liked to call the 'Incorruptibles' – was devoted to him, as he was to them, sending flowers to sick wives and showing great concern for their welfare.

He was to become one of Britain's best-known and most active thief-takers. As a former colleague later remarked, 'He didn't take money and, if you're a policeman, you have to deal with scumbags every day. You have to go down to their level to achieve results, so I understand why he did what he did.'

Bert Wickstead retired from the police to become a security adviser to what was then News Group Newspapers, which serialised his memoirs in the *Sun*. He later became seriously ill with emphysema, but he remained, to the end, one of the Yard's legendary figures.

Bert was far removed from today's insistence on performance figures, civilian officer managers, budget restraints, and the need to satisfy the stringent requirements of the CPS, who will not prosecute unless there is a 99 per cent chance of a conviction. He was admired and often hated by his colleagues, and abhord by the villains, yet they always called him 'Mr Wickstead' out of old gangland respect; it was the way he would have wanted it.

Bert Wickstead died on Monday, 19 March, 2001. He was survived by his second wife, Jean, their two sons, and a son from his first marriage.

11

The Securitas Crew

'It was a horrific experience... it was the worst
night of my family's life. I was angered beyond belief.
It was brutal and traumatic.'

COLIN DIXON

£50 million is an awful lot of money, and an awful
amount to spend, and that's what Kent's newly-
appointed Assistant Chief Constable Andrew 'Andy'
Leppard pondered upon when between 1.00am and
2.15am on Wednesday, 22 February 2006, a gang of men
robbed the Securitas Cash Management Ltd, Vale Road,
Tonbridge, Kent, of precisely £53,116,70 in used
banknotes. It was an audacious operation that netted the
crooks the largest amount of folding money in British
crime history. At least six of the crew had abducted and
threatened the family of the manager, tied up fourteen
staff members and escaped with their haul into the night.

As nuts go, the Securitas depot was a tough one to
crack. The holding company, Securitas AB, is Swedish-

based, and the largest provider of security services in the world with over 230,000 employees. The firm specialises in uniformed security officers, consulting and investigations and cash-in-transit. Their cash handling division, the one that was robbed, oversee the transport, packaging, counting and storage of cash and precious metals.

On paper, at least, there are few companies as experienced at handling extraordinarily valuable cargo as Securitas. But they have had a few misfortunes. Shortly after the depot snatch, a Securitas van was rammed by criminals in a stolen tractor who subsequently hot-footed it with hundreds of thousands of pounds. The heist, which took place in Warrington, Cheshire, on Wednesday, 8 March 2006, also involved a low-loader lorry which had forced the security van to stop at the junction of Hardwick Grange and Kingsland Grange, in the Woolston area of the town at 8.15pm. Two men in balaclavas and carrying crowbars attacked the windows of the van and set it alight. The two guards were uninjured, but police acknowledged that ambushes on cash transit vans were on the increase – there had been scores of attacks in 2005 alone – and this one was less than a mile away from a Securitas facility. A Volvo V40 had been the getaway vehicle, and was found dumped less than a mile away.

In 2006, an armed gang robbed a Securitas van as it unloaded money at Gothenburg's Landvetter Airport in Sweden.

Another incident occurred on Thursday, 4 October 2007, when two armoured truck guards were shot dead, execution style, with a 9mm automatic in north-east

Philadelphia. Another man was critically wounded. The guards, retired police officers, died at the scene. Hit once in the chest, William Widmaier, 65, married with grown-up children, and Joseph Alullo, aged 54, with three daughters, shot three times in the chest and abdomen, were not wearing bullet-proof vests. The third guard was hit by glass as a shot slammed into the windscreen.

The fatal robbery seemed ill-planned. The FBI believe that 36-year-old Mustafa Ali, aka Shawn Steele, simply followed the truck on the spur of the moment and murdered the guards as they serviced an ATM machine. Ali would have got away with the robbery had it not been for several tip-offs to the police. A dark-coloured Acura saloon was recorded leaving the area on CCTV, and Ali owned the same type of car.

In 1993, Steele, then 21, had been convicted of stealing $25,000 in eight Philadelphia robberies during 1992.

Then, on Friday morning, 19 October 2007, the cash-strapped company, now renamed 'Loomis', was hit again – on Highway 70, just south of Hedemora, Sweden. This time, however, two robbers, both aged 25, were unlucky. They were arrested as they fled the scene in a car. Less than an hour later, two teenagers were also arrested.

In the aftermath of the extraordinary heist perpetrated on the Securitas facility in Kent, ACC Andy Leppard knew very little of the crime on his patch, but what he did know was that the robbers would have had to have used a lorry, or a large van, to carry such a large amount of money, and they would need a discreet location where they could park up and distribute the haul. The gang would have had to dump any sequentially-numbered or traceable notes, and plan to launder the rest in sizeable chunks, around £1 million at a time. The cop reasoned that if he could find the vehicle, he could trace the crooks; unless, of course, an informer gave the police a tip.

One option of disposing of the money was to buy JCBs, diggers and earth-movers which can cost hundreds of thousands of pounds. Many of these nearly-new models are traded at auctions for cash. Another option was diamonds. One of the few industries left in the world where cash is the preferred method of payment, diamonds also have the advantage of being small and easily smuggled. Stones can be bought in one country, taken elsewhere, repolished to remove distinguishing marks and resold.

A third option, one that Leppard considered, was the setting up of 'legitimate' bureaux de change. The money could then be fed through the accounts alongside the takings.

And yet a forth option is 'Hawala' (also known as 'hundi'), an informal value transfer system based on performance and honour and, for £50 million, Leppard knew the gang would need a huge network which would have to be primarily located in the Middle East, Africa or Asia. Successfully robbing a Securitas depot was one thing; laundering the loot was a different problem altogether. Perhaps a Kenny Noye might be able to pull it off, but the Securitas boys, maybe not.

An ancient Indian system increasingly used by gangs, the cash is deposited at an office in one country and can be collected in local currency in another – like a type of illegal Western Union network. In the most basic variant, money is transferred via a network of hawala brokers, or hawaldars. The money is deposited with the hawala, who, in turn, calls another hawala broker in the recipient's city, gives disposition instructions (usually minus a small commission), and promises to settle the debt later.

The unique feature of hawala is the total absence of a paper or electronic trail. In addition to commissions, hawala brokers often earn their profits through bypassing official, and often extortionate, exchange rates. Most governments do not favour the system, and accusations have been made in recent years that terrorist funding often changes hands through hawala networks.

The Securitas depot robbery was planned with military precision. It started when manager Colin Dixon was abducted at about 6.00pm on 21 February 2006, in a tactic known as 'tiger kidnapping', due to the way a beast follows its prey before it strikes. Coerced, often at gunpoint, the employee takes the robbers through the coded alarm systems, in the knowledge that one false move could mean the end of his or her loved ones. Although it's a method commonly associated with paramilitary groups such as the IRA breaking into banks in Northern Ireland, a similar heist on the British mainland sent shockwaves through the security industry as long ago as 1972.

The manager of the NatWest bank in Sunbury, Middlesex, was kidnapped and held hostage with his family overnight in Surbiton. He was brought to the bank in the morning, when staff arriving at work were bundled inside while the vaults were cleared. And there have been plenty of other examples in the intervening decades, concerning banks and building societies, culminating in the Northern Bank raid in Belfast in 2004, which netted the perpetrators £26 million.

Dixon was driving his silver Nissan Almera to his home in Herne Bay, and was pulled over on the A249, just outside Stockbury, a village north-east of Maidstone, by what appeared to be an unmarked Volvo S60 police car. It had flashing blue lights behind the front grill, and the two cars stopped in a lay-by close to the Three Squirrels pub.

A man, wearing high-visibility clothing and a police-style cap, approached Dixon, and asked him to get into the 'police car', which Dixon did. He was then handcuffed by other men in the car and driven west on the M20 motorway to the West Malling bypass, where he was bound more securely, transferred into a Parcelforce van and driven to a farm in Staplehurst, Kent. Here, he was threatened at gunpoint, being told that, if he didn't co-operate, his family would be killed.

While all this was going on, at about 6.30pm, two other gang members, also posing as police, went to Mr Dixon's home and told his wife Lynn and eight-year-old son Craig that Colin had been involved in an accident. They were taken from their home and driven around for six hours, before being taken to the same farm in Kent.

After a short discussion, during which Colin Dixon was again threatened with a gun, he, his wife and son were driven in the truck to the Securitas depot where they arrived around 1.00am. Threatening the employees with a Skorpion machine pistol, a pump-action shotgun, a handgun and an AK47 assault rifle, fourteen employees were bound and held at gunpoint by the crew wearing balaclavas, and the crooks left with their haul in a 7.5 tonne Renault Midlum truck at about 2.45am. They left behind a further £154,833,29 because there was no more room in their truck.

The staff and Dixon family had been locked into the cash cages, although eight-year-old Craig was small enough, and brave enough, to be able to squeeze through the bars and free the others. The alarm was then raised.

The Bank of England, to whom most of the money belonged, was reimbursed to the tune of £25 million by Securitas the same day, with a promise that the rest would follow once an audit had been completed. The robbery proved to be the firm's undoing; in July 2007, Securitas announced that it intended to leave the cash management market, and withdraw from the joint venture which gave them business from Barclays and HSBC.

With the money being virtually untraceable, the task facing ACC Leppard was to become career-defining. Described as a broad-shouldered, square-jawed police veteran of 22 years, he cuts an imposing figure. He made his mark in 2000 after leading an investigation which resulted in three people being jailed at the Old Bailey for a contract killing. He hoped that a £2 million reward might now help him solve the country's largest cash heist, and he didn't have to wait long for a break. The thieves, so methodical in the planning and execution of the robbery, bungled everything from then on in a manner that defies belief.

On Thursday, 23 February 2006, a Parcelforce van thought to have been used in the abduction of Dixon and his family was found abandoned at the Hook and Hatchet pub in the village of Hucking, near Maidstone. The same day, a Volvo S60 and a red Vauxhall Vectra – also thought to have been used and made to look like a police car for the abductions – were found in the village of Leeds Castle. The Volvo had been set on fire. On the same day, police arrested a 29-year-old man and a women, aged 31, in Forest Hill, south London. A 41-year-old woman was also arrested by the Metropolitan Police at the Portman Building Society in Bromley, south London. She was dressed as a Salvation Army nurse and drew attention to herself by trying to pay in £6,000 in notes in tape marked 'Tonbridge'. Hours later, Dixon's Nissan Almera was also found in the car park of the Cock Horse pub in Detling.

On Friday, 24 February, Kent Police recovered a white Ford Transit van from the car park of the Ashford International Hotel. It was found following a tip-off from a member of the public. The vehicle contained two suitcases and a holdall containing £1,370,500, along with guns, balaclavas and body armour. Again, on the same day, metal cages and packaging material that had been used to transport the money were found in a field near Detling and, on the evening of Saturday 25 February, armed police also raided a house in Southborough, near Tunbridge Wells.

On the afternoon of 26 February, Kent Police challenged two men who sped off in a blue BMW 3 Series coupé on Marine Parade in Tankerton, near Whitstable. Police marksmen shot at the car's tyres – other accounts say a Stinger was used – and two men were arrested. Then, on 27 February, two men were arrested by armed officers in the Greenwich area of London.

The following day, 28 February, the white 7.5 tonne Renault Midlum truck was discovered. Again, that same day, Kent Police raided Elderden Farm, off Forge Lane, in the Staplehurst area and conducted extensive forensic searches of the surrounding land and buildings, and conducted further searches they found £105,600 under a tree in an orchard.

Late on 1 March 2006, police confirmed that they had arrested a car dealer, John Fowler, and that he had been charged with conspiracy to rob Securitas; they also referred to three other charges of kidnapping Colin, Lynn and Craig Dixon. A Stuart Royle had been charged with similar offences and Kim Shackleton had been charged with handling stolen goods.

They appeared at Maidstone Magistrates' Court on 2 March, and were remanded in custody until 13 March, when they appeared at Maidstone Crown Court.

During a police raid on an industrial depot run by Roger Coutts on 2 March, a substantial amount of cash was discovered. Twelve holdalls containing £9,655,040 were found at ENR Cars. A Jetmir Bucpapa was charged with conspiracy to commit robbery, as was Lea John Rusha the following day. A further arrest was made in Bexley on Saturday, 4 March, and a man was subsequently released on bail. John Lupton was not seen again.

On 5 March, detectives found another £8,601,990 in a lock-up in Southborough. So, as of 6 March, police had recovered £11 million – stashed somewhere was a further £39 million in used banknotes.

A further development occurred on 7 March when two employees of a firm that had been contracted from a local employment agency by Securitas were arrested, strengthening suspicions that it had been an 'inside job'. In fact, it was a story that couldn't possibly have been made up – an illegal immigrant called Ermir Hysenaj, and Anthony Black, the brother-in-law of a London gangster and veteran robber, worked at the place.

Two days later, the police recovered a further £8.7 million. The investigation now moved to Morocco, where, on 25 June, in a joint operation with local police, four men were arrested in a shopping centre in the Souissi district of the capital Rabat. Among the men taken into custody was a 26-year-old Sidcup man, Lee Murray. He was arrested with a man known as Paul 'The Enforcer' Allen. Police now confirmed that a total of 30 people had been arrested in connection with the robbery and, because of the costs of the operation, Kent Police requested a top-up of £6 million from the Home Office to help them out. Chief Constable Mike Fuller said, 'Our own view is this is unique as far as robberies and armed robberies go. We hope the Home Office will support us in paying some of the costs.'

The trial began at the Old Bailey on Tuesday, 26 June 2007, amid tight security. Prosecuting counsel, Sir John Nutting, told the jury, 'They [the accused] were inspired by the lure of luxury, ease and idleness, and were prepared to target the innocent and vulnerable to achieve it.'

Presided over by Mr Justice Penry-Davey, the first few weeks focused on the role of the manager Colin Dixon, with the defence cross-examination highlighting the 'coincidences' in his conduct which might be interpreted as suggesting that he could have been the inside man.

However, on 28 January 2008, the jury returned guilty verdicts on Stuart Royle, Jetmir Bucpapa, Roger Coutts, Lea Rusha and Ermir Hysenaj. £8 million had been found in a lock-up near Rusha's home, and his fingerprints were all over the loot.

John Fowler, 59, of Chart Hill Road, Staplehurst, and Keith Borer, 54, of Hempstead Lane, Maidstone, were cleared of all charges. Fowler had told police of the location of £105,600 under a tree on his farm. He had found the cash in a vehicle which he had loaned out and had been returned to him. A 32-year-old hairdresser, and former Harvey Nichols sales girl, Michelle Hogg, agreed to be a prosecution witness if all charges against her were dropped. She had made the gangs' prosthetic disguises, normally worn by actors. For his part, Keith Borer received £1,350 for spraying a van, but he claimed that he had had no idea that the money had come from the robbery.

Later in 2006, a further £1 million was found in the boot of a car, but more details cannot be disclosed for legal reasons.

On 29 January 2008, Hysenaj, 28, of New Road, Crowborough, East Sussex, was sentenced to 20 years in prison with an order that he serve a minimum of 10 years. Royle, Rusha, Bucpapa and Coutts were all given life sentences with an order that they serve a minimum of 15 years.

Rusha was one of the two men dressed as police officers who first kidnapped Colin Dixon, while Hysenaj was a Securitas employee who had filmed inside the Securitas depot using a hi-tech video camera the size of a 50p coin that was fitted to his belt.

Speaking after the jury returned their verdicts, Roger Coe-Salazar, the Chief Crown Prosecutor for Kent, said, 'When you have a case of this magnitude, it's easy for it to be romanticised like *Ocean's 12*, as a victimless crime. There is nothing romantic about a child being held at gunpoint by a masked man. This was a callous and highly dangerous crime.'

A total of £21 million was finally recovered. The outstanding sum is thought to be in Morocco and northern Cyprus, a testament to the ingenuity of those who sought to launder their share of the proceeds quietly and efficiently.

Under the 2002 Proceeds of Crime Act, estate agents, solicitors, accountants, bankers, even casinos face prosecution if they knowingly – or negligently – allow crime proceeds to be laundered. This can carry a jail term of up to five years and a heavy fine. Any deposit over £10,000 will automatically trigger red flags with a bank. At one time, prior to this Act, it was not unknown for crooks to wander into an HM Revenue office and ask for a large sum of cash to be paid into their account in lieu of paying their returns. This deposit – and it could amount to several million pounds with no questions asked – would then be banked locally and then electronically transferred to the Revenue's accounts office centre at either Cumbernauld or Shipley.

When the audit was completed, the payee would be notified of overpayment and receive his money back, via a cheque, in the post. One could then bank the cheque with no suspicion at all – the money had come from the government after all! Today, however, HM Revenue & Customs is not allowed to accept cash.

In attempting to launder the massive proceeds of the robbery, the Securitas Crew would have certainly looked abroad and, during the trial, much was heard about money being laundered in Turkish-controlled northern Cyprus, which has no extradition treaty with Britain, and is not covered by the European Union rules on money laundering. It is a haven for money launderers because no one is going to be alert to its origins – the minute you pay it into a bank, it stops being paper money and just becomes figures on a piece of paper. 'It becomes part of the bank's sterling reserves,' says Nick Kochan, author of a book on laundering called *The Washing Machine*.

Brinks Mat forensic lawyer, Bob McCunn, who spent 20 years pursuing a number of people through the civil courts both in Britain and abroad, and who has recovered £27 million, said, 'If I was planning a big robbery like the Securitas job, the first think I would do is set up a good way of money laundering.'

The Securitas trial also heard suggestions that Sean Lupton, who jumped bail in December 2006, may have been involved in laundering the money. Indeed, Coutts, in his defence, sought to point an accusatory finger at two brothers, who, he said, were in northern Cyprus. This moved Turkish Cypriot diplomat, Ms Serap Destegur, to stress, 'Money laundering and the black market are looked at very seriously in our country and I'm sure my government would be happy to co-operate if the British police asked for our help.'

Coutt's lawyer, Graham Blower, said Hussein and Mustafa Basar – who were both of Turkish-Cypriot origin – had left the UK shortly after the robbery. He said that Hussein worked for a 'Mr X', the robbery's alleged mastermind, who could not be named for legal reasons.

The trial heard that some of the Securitas money had been invested in property. The Old Bailey also heard that Coutts had visited Cyprus only a month before the raid to look at potential properties, leaving Bob McCunn to speculate, 'They might have bought property as an investment or they might just have bought property and then sold it again to launder the money through the banking system.'

Over the decades, northern Cyprus has gained itself something of a reputation as a haven for fugitives from British justice. Tycoon Asil Nadir, who fled while awaiting trial for offences of dishonesty in connection with the collapse of his Polly Peck trading empire, has lived in northern Cyprus since 1993.

In 2007, Brian Wright was jailed for 30 years for running a multi-million pound ring smuggling drugs into Britain from South America. He was discovered living in the region by a BBC film crew in 2002. He remained in his home in the village of Lapta until 2005 when he was arrested after travelling to Spain. Customs officials said the network was 'probably the most sophisticated and successful global cocaine trafficking organisation to ever target the UK'. There were 19 convictions worldwide.

Wright was one of the richest criminals ever punished. The 60-year-old, who also had a home in Chelsea, was jailed for 30 years, and he'll probably die in prison as Mr Justice Moss told him, 'I accept that you will be a very much older man when you are entitled to be released. I accept, too, the possibility that you may not live that long.' The judge added, 'Your activities caused unqualifiable misery to tens of thousands of victims. Those who import and distribute it [drugs] call upon themselves lengthy terms of imprisonment... you played for the very highest stakes and won, for a number of years, a luxury lifestyle. You knew the consequences of detection and conviction.'

Wright's gang used luxury yachts to import the drugs from Venezuela, via the Caribbean, to the UK, and when he was asked for any mitigating circumstances, he replied, 'There is no mitigation, Your Honour.'

THE SECURITAS CREW

The Wright probe was sparked in September 1996 when a yacht named *Sea Mist* was discovered off course in Cork, in the Irish Republic. It was carrying 599kg (1,320lb) of cocaine with a street value of £80 million hidden in a dumb waiter.

Over the next two years, four further boatloads of cocaine were smuggled ashore under the control of the Wright organisation. In February 1999, officers seized 472kg (1,040lb) of cocaine from a lock-up garage in Leigh-on-Sea, Essex, and from a farm in Laleham, Surrey. Mega-rich, well-known in horse racing circles, rubbing shoulders with the rich and famous, including comedian Jim Davidson – who was called to testify at his trial – it was also learned that Wright had previously been involved in serious incidents that defrauded the betting public.

If the Securitas Crew had managed to launder their money, they would have had to accept making a huge loss on the £32 million to turn it into 'clean money'. They would lose around 20 per cent, and there was always the inherent risk of being ripped off. In fact, several people believed to have been handling money from the Brinks Mat job ended up dead, with the suspicion being that they were killed while trying to embezzle money from the heist.

With five of the Securitas robbers now locked away, there is still one important suspect on the run – the second phoney cop who pulled over Colin Dixon is thought to be Keyinde Patterson, who was captured wearing a high-visibility jacket and police cap on the depot's CCTV. Originally from Jamaica, and now thought to be somewhere in the Caribbean, he has an identical twin called Taiwo, whom police traced and interviewed during the inquiry. The Patterson twins ended up in Croydon and it is thought that Keyinde may have been the 'Mr X', the mastermind of the robbery through a south London underworld connection.

Ironically, Keyinde Patterson might not have been free if it had not been for the CPS, who dropped charges of conspiracy to murder against him on 18 October 2005. He had been accused of being part of a gang who were responsible for a horrific night of violence on 2 October 2004. He and two other men were accused of shooting dead Rufus Edwards and Mark Warmington at the Spotlight Club in Croydon. Just over an hour later, the same gang fired a hail of bullets at a car in Bristol, hitting two beautiful women, Asha Jama and Donna Small, who had taken a lift from a nightclub with Curtis Brooks, whom police believed was the actual target. Brooks and another male passenger were uninjured in the shooting, but Donna was left permanently disabled and Asha blinded in her left eye after being hit by flying glass. And in another sickening twist of fate, Patterson's co-accused were eventually acquitted of all charges, but not until July 2006 – five months after the Securitas robbery. So detectives have accepted they do not have a prima facie case against the fugitive, so even if they could trace him, they would not have sufficient grounds to extradite him.

For a very short time, the Securitas Crew were the richest criminals in British history. Their plan to execute the raid was flawless, and it relied on an inside man for the venture to succeed. Detectives know from experience there will always be an 'inside man' in armed robberies of this magnitude, and the Securitas job was no exception.

In 1975, £8 million was stolen from a Bank of America

branch in London's Mayfair. Stuart Buckley, an electrician who gave the robbers codes to the vaults, was later jailed for seven years.

1982 witnessed £26 million in gold stolen from the Brinks Mat warehouse at Heathrow. Security guard, Anthony Black, who gave evidence against the robbers, was jailed for six years.

In September 1997, $18.9 million was stolen from Dunbar Armored Depot in Los Angeles. The company's regional safety inspector, Allen Pace, was later given 24 years in jail.

In October 1997, $17.3 million was taken from the Loomis Fargo (part of the Securitas group) depot in Charlotte, North Carolina. Vault supervisor, David Scott Ghantt, was later imprisoned for seven years.

'On all big jobs, there will always be someone "opening doors",' says John O'Connor, former head of the Flying Squad. 'When there isn't one, it usually becomes a complete disaster, like the Millennium Dome robbery, which was just a glorified ram-raid. Sometimes people [who work in a bank or cash depot] start fantasising about what it would be like, and then they start talking and soon they come to the attention of a gang and, before they know it, they are in on it and they can't back out because they are frightened of them. It's rare for an inside man to come out and look for a team. Usually it's the other way round. A team of robbers will learn about someone who works in such a place.'

The temptation when dealing with millions of pounds in cash is obvious, and the irony is that most people working in such depots are on very low wages. This was most certainly the case with Ermir Hysenaj; he was an illegal immigrant who had been deported back to Albania, only to be allowed back into the country by the Home Office on a two-year visa because he had married an Englishwoman. He had signed up with a Kent recruitment agency, Beacon, and, in December 2005 – only two months before the robbery – they sent him for an interview at the Securitas depot. He handed in his CV, had a ten-minute interview and was offered a job. He was paid just £5.50 an hour, from which Securitas would even deduct his lunch hour.

In hindsight, it was all a recipe for robbery for he was soon in the cash deposit processing area, sorting money and handling tens of thousands of pounds every day. And once detectives discovered that Anthony Black was the brother-in-law of veteran south London robber, Brian Robinson, and that Black had also been in on the Brinks Mat raid, they brought him in for questioning. Hysenaj soon cracked and confessed, giving key information about Robinson and other members of the gang.

Of course, the real victims of this robbery were the innocent employees of the Securitas firm and the Dixon family, who, it is fair to say, were terrorised for hours at gunpoint.

At the trial, however, there were suggestions by some defence lawyers that the inside man was, in fact, Colin Dixon. Added to Colin's trauma was the fact that one of the officers who looked after Mr Dixon in the wake of the robbery had harboured suspicions about him and had emailed her boss. Victim liaison officer PC Lorraine Brown said she believed he was intentionally deceiving the police over a camera and photographs of the inside of the high-security depot that were found in his desk.

Former police officer Graham Huckerby also knows what it is like to be wrongly suspected of being the 'inside man'. He was driving a Securicor van on 3 July 1995 when it was ambushed by armed robbers near the Midland Bank clearing centre in Salford, Manchester. The gang made off with 29 cash bags containing £6.6 million, making it the biggest cash-in-transit robbery in British criminal history. None of the robbers was ever caught but, four years after the raid, Greater Manchester Police decided that Mr Huckerby's actions on the day had been suspicious and, in 2002, he was convicted of conspiracy to rob and jailed for 14 years.

His girlfriend, Luci Roper, fought a long campaign to clear Graham's name and, in December 2004, three Court of Appeal judges quashed his conviction, saying, 'We are not satisfied as to the safety of the conviction.' Huckerby – who had been the victim of a robbery seven months before – was suffering from 'post-traumatic stress disorder' at the time of the Midland Bank cash-in-transit robbery, which was why he did what the robbers told him when they pointed a gun at his head, instead of following company policy – which was, one might suppose, to duck!

The entire saga has since ruined Graham Huckerby's life. His girlfriend has since left him, he lives in someone else's back room, and he'll probably never get a decent job again.

And what about compensation? According to Luci, who sold her house to help pay for his appeal, he has been offered nothing.

12

The Great Train Robbers

'Jack, the wires are cut.'
CO-DRIVER DAVID WHITBY TO THE TRAIN DRIVER,
JACK MILLS

It must be said that the Great Train Robbery was brilliantly planned and executed. Apart from the attack on the train driver, Jack Mills, it was non-violent and no firearms were used. The raiders managed to steal much more money than they had planned – they even left several bags of notes behind because they had run out of time – and perhaps it was the greed in sharing all the money out which led to them being careless and leaving so many fingerprints behind, sealing their own fate.

It was a crime which, for its magnitude and sheer audacity, made the exploits of train robbers in the past, such as the legendary Jesse James in America's Wild West, appear almost child's play. Indeed, one American newspaper, the *New York Herald Tribune*, printed an account of the opening of the trial on its front page and devoted six columns to the story under the headline: 'HISTORY'S GREATEST ROBBERY – THERE'LL ALWAYS BE AN ENGLAND.'

The trial opened on the bitterly cold Monday of 20 January 1964 in the courtroom at Aylesbury Assizes in Buckinghamshire. Amid what the press like to call 'tight security', seventeen men and three women were seated in the dock with its spiked-topped mahogany surround. As soon as the presiding judge, portly Mr Justice Edmund Davies, had taken his seat on the bench, and before the jury was sworn, the decision was taken to 'put down' seven of the accused – including the three women – who were charged with the lesser offence of receiving stolen property.

Of the remaining thirteen, 41-year-old florist shop owner Roger Cordrey, of East Molesey, Surrey, had pleaded guilty to conspiracy to rob and also to two charges of receiving. He had a serious gambling habit, and was of a neurotic temperament, and had 'helped' the police by leading them to the recovery of £141,000 of the stolen money. The Crown accepted his plea and he, too, was removed from the dock.

The remaining twelve defendants included William Boal, 50, a small, red-faced man with defective eyesight. Married with three children, he lived in Fulham and was just working up a nice little business in aircraft components and precision work when he became involved with criminal types outside his class. He was later sentenced to 24 years, reduced to fouteen on appeal. He eventually went on to serve only seven years in prison before he died. All he got out of his participation in the robbery was a short-lived spending spree.

Charles Frederick Wilson, 31, was a dark, good-looking and amiable bookmaker, who also ran a greengrocery business and came from Clapham. He was married to a pretty young wife and, like Boal, had three children – all daughters. He was sent down for 30 years.

Thomas William Wisbey, 34 – another jovial character, married with children, also ran a betting shop in London. A former private in the Royal Army Service Corps, discharged with a good character. Wisbey would be sentenced to 30 years.

James Hussey, 31 – a painter and decorator, he was a bachelor and looked rather stupid which was said to be the result of nervousness. He was reputed to be good company and popular among his friends. Hussey was also given 30 years' imprisonment.

Leonard Dennis Field, 31, was sentenced to 24 years, later reduced to 5 years on appeal. He was also a florist, and one-time shoreside waiter with the merchant navy.

Douglas Gordon Goody, 34, was a hairdresser from Putney. Always immaculately dressed, he was about to marry a pretty redhead named Patricia Cooper, who lodged in his house.

Sitting in the back row of the dock was the one and only defendant with a public school and university education. John Denby Wheater, 42, a London solicitor, with a dark, heavy, impassive face and a moustache, he lived in a prosperous commuter belt in Surrey with a wife and two young daughters. Like Wisbey, he had a good wartime record and had been awarded the Member of the British Empire medal for 'personal courage of a very high order' while serving as an officer with his regiment in Italy. He would receive three years' imprisonment.

Brian Arthur Field, 29, was no relation to Leonard

Field. He was Wheater's managing clerk who lived in Oxfordshire with his second wife Karin, who was German. He was sentenced to 24 years.

Robert Alfred Welch – a 35-year-old club proprietor, he was pale and tense and was said to look more like a research student than a criminal. He got 30 years.

Indeed, none of the men in the dock looked at all like criminals and this applied to 28-year-old Roy John James. A silversmith by profession, unmarried but very attractive to women, he was much addicted to motor racing and was nicknamed 'The Weasel'. He also got 30 years.

Ronald 'Ronnie' Arthur Biggs, a 34-year-old carpenter from Redhill, Surrey. Tall, dark and mild-mannered, he was a kindly husband and father to his wife and two children. He had previously served in the RAF and, prior to the trial, was working up a lucrative business in the building trade. His sentence was 30 years.

Finally, there was John Thomas Daly. A 32-year-old Irish antique dealer and skilled craftsman, his wife, Frances, was the sister of another antique dealer in London, Bruce Reynolds, a Michael Caine lookalike and the acknowledged leader of the gang, whom the police only managed to arrest four years after the robbery. John Daly was discharged.

Altogether, 40 barristers were engaged in the case. Leader of the prosecution was Mr Arthur James QC, who took ten hours to open the case for the Crown. The trial lasted 48 working days, six of which the judge took to sum up the evidence, after which the jury were kept in seclusion for three days and three nights.

Prior to 1963, the 'Great Train Robbery' referred to

the theft of gold bullion from a train travelling between London and Paris in 1855. However, the events of Wednesday, 7 August 1963 displaced this as being one of the most audacious robberies in the UK.

The narrative revolves round the TPO (Travelling Post Office) night train which travelled nightly between Glasgow and London, making scheduled stops en route to pick up additional mail. On the night of the robbery, it comprised a diesel engine and 12 coaches, which were exclusively concerned with the carriage and sorting of mail. The coach second from the engine was known as the HVP (high-value package coach) where registered mail was sorted. On this occasion, it also contained 128 mail bags filled with banknotes, most of them in denominations of £5 and £1, which were being sent by banks, mainly in Scotland, to their branches or head offices in London. The total on the day of the robbery was £2.3 million (the equivalent of about £30 million today).

On the footplate was the 58-year-old train driver Jack Mills, and the fireman David Whitby, 26. They both boarded the train at Crewe where they lived. The man in charge of the high-value package coach was a postal employee named Frank Dewhurst, a taciturn, 49-year-old Londoner, who had other colleagues helping him to sort the mail in that and the other coaches. The reason for there being such a large amount of money on board that day was because it was just after the Bank Holiday spending spree.

The two co-drivers had just finished their last cup of tea and the train, travelling at 76 mph, had just passed Leighton Buzzard at about 2.30am the following day. Just after Leighton Buzzard there was a dwarf signal known as the 'distant signal'. If this showed green, it meant that the driver could proceed at full speed, but if it showed amber, it meant that he must slow down, since he must expect that the next signal, known as the 'home signal', would be red.

A minute or two later, Jack Mills saw a red signal ahead at a place called Sears Crossing. He did not realise that the red light was false – a glove was obscuring the correct signal and the red light was activated by attaching it to a 6-volt battery.

When he stopped, David Whitby climbed out of the diesel engine in order to ring the signalman to ascertain the problem. He discovered that the cables from the line-side phone had been cut and, as he turned to return to his train, he was attacked and thrown down the steep railway embankment where he was overpowered by two men. One of them put a hand over Whitby's mouth and hissed, 'If you shout, I'll kill you.'

'All right, mate,' the terrified man answered when he had recovered his breath, 'I'm on your side.'

At the same time, a masked man climbed into the train cab. Mills fought back and was struck around the head with possibly a cosh, some say an iron bar, others claim an axe handle, rendering him unconscious. Meanwhile, other robbers were uncoupling the rest of the carriages, leaving the engine and the first two carriages containing the high-value property.

Whitby was then taken back to the train, where he saw Mills in the driver's cab on his knees bleeding heavily from the head. He also saw that the cab was full of men in boiler suits and balaclavas. Then, because the diesel was a new type with which the gang's railway expert was unfamiliar, and which he was consequently unable to operate, Mills was forced to drive the engine a distance of about half-a-mile to Bridego Bridge, where the track crossed a road. Mills and Whitby were handcuffed together and the windows of the HVP were smashed with coshes and an axe.

Frightened post office staff were pushed to one end by some of the 15-strong gang – but in the remaining ten carriages (left at Sears Crossing), staff did not even realise anything had happened.

At Bridego Bridge, a human chain of robbers removed 120 sacks containing 2½ tons of money. The robbery was well organised and swift. Before leaving, one of the gang threatened the post office staff to stay still for 30 minutes before contacting the police, then the gang drove off to their hideout at Leatherslade Farm, which was about 20 miles away. The alarm was raised and both drivers were rushed to the Royal Buckinghamshire Hospital in Aylesbury, where Mills was treated for a black eye and facial bruising. They had to wait for a police officer to arrive before the handcuffs could be removed.

Leatherslade Farm at Oakley had been rented and, during the next few days, the jubilant gang shared out the proceeds of the heist. They even played Monopoly using real money, while a huge police investigation was launched, run by the Flying Squad at Scotland Yard and senior detectives from the Buckinghamshire force. The officer in overall command was Detective Chief Superintendent Jack Slipper – or 'Slipper of the Yard'.

Born Sunday, 20 April 1924, the high-water mark of Slipper's career was the Great Train Robbery, and he became so involved with its aftermath that he continued in retirement to hunt down many of the robbers who managed to escape. He worked as an electrician's apprentice until 1941, when he enlisted in the Royal Air Force, joining the Metropolitan Police in 1950.

He was also involved in several other cases, including the 1966 Massacre of Braybrook Street. Also known as The Shepherd's Bush Murders, three police officers were shot dead in what was then the worst police killing in British criminal history.

Slipper also set up the Robbery Squad, which later merged into the Flying Squad. He was also responsible for Britain's first 'supergrass' trial in 1973, in which bank robber Bertie Smalls testified against his former associates in exchange for his own freedom. In the 1980s and 1990s, Slipper worked in security for IBM UK, working out of their Greenford, Middlesex, offices. His local pub was the Black Horse, in Harrow Road, Wembley. He died after a long illness on 24 August 2005, aged 81.

Meanwhile, back at the farm, the gang were becoming spooked by low-flying RAF aircraft, which they took to be police spotter planes. Actually, the aircraft were merely on training flights had nothing to do with the manhunt that had now been established. However, a nearby resident, a herdsman named Maris, saw vehicles coming to the farm on various dates between 29 July and 11 August. A Mrs Mappin had also become suspicious of the comings and goings at the farm and had contacted the police. She was able to give some useful particulars of the movements of the vehicles on the night of the robbery. Then, another neighbour, Mr Wyatt, had noticed dirty curtains being put up at the farm to cover the windows and had chatted with several of the occupants who described themselves as 'decorators'. Finally, there was Mrs Brooke, who had delivered the keys of the farm to its new owners.

The police arrived in the form of PC John Wooley, although by now the robbers had fled. They had split the money up, with Biggs receiving £147,000, and had gone to ground. A thorough scene-of-crime examination found several fingerprints, including some on the Monopoly board and others on a ketchup bottle. There was a miscellaneous collection of other clues, including a can of paint and two Land Rovers with the same number plate. The fingerprints and other enquiries led to the perpetrators and, one by one, they were arrested.

The first two arrests – that of Cordrey and Boal – came about when two men turned up in Bournemouth in an Austin A35 van, and spoke to Mrs Ethel Clark, a policeman's widow, about renting her lock-up garage in Tweedale Road. There was no thought in her mind that the two had anything to do with the train robbery, but when they offered to pay three months' rent in advance and pulled out a large wad of 10-shilling notes to do so, her suspicions were aroused. Mrs Clarke phoned the police and, in a matter of minutes, two plain-clothes detectives turned up.

During the initial questioning, one of the robbers made a dash for it and was brought down by a rugby tackle. The other also tried to escape, but was quickly captured.

While Cordrey and Boal were 'helping police with their enquiries' at the nearby police station, their van was subjected to a thorough search. It revealed notes to the value of £141,000. A further sum of £300 was discovered at Boal's house in Fulham.

At about the same time, a young couple were walking through Redlands Wood, a beauty spot near Dorking, Surrey, and spotted two holdalls and a briefcase lying just off a pathway. There was nothing inside any of the abandoned articles to identify the owner, but the contents consisted of thousands of banknotes. Rightly convinced that they had stumbled on some of the loot of the robbery, the couple immediately telephoned the police, who arrived on the scene with tracker dogs, which sniffed out another case filled with money. The total recovered was £101,000, now leaving the police to believe that the robbers had panicked when they realised the heat was on, and that they had stashed the money away in various hiding places to be retrieved later.

Further arrests were made quickly, with Brian Field, Leonard Field, Goody, and Daly following Wilson into custody. The solicitor, John Wheater, was charged with conspiracy, and harbouring Leonard Field; the conspiracy charge being concerned with negotiations leading up to the sale of Leatherslade Farm. Finally, Roy 'The Weasel' James, who disguised himself by growing a beard, was arrested after a dramatic roof-top chase in St John's Wood, where he had been living in a flat with Bruce Reynolds, who had fled much earlier. A further £12,000 in notes was recovered, but it would be another four years before the mastermind behind the heist was arrested and sentenced to 25 years in jail.

As there were over 200 Crown witnesses, the evidence took over three weeks to present. Most unforgettable was the unfortunate driver of the train, Jack Mills, unsteady on his feet, sometimes inaudible in his speech, gripping the top of the witness stand and plainly showing the traces of the terrible beating he had received and from which he never recovered; indeed, he never returned to work. The total compensation he received from British Railways was a meagre £25. Due to the balaclavas the robbers had worn, he was unable to identify any of the men. In 1970, he died of leukaemia, which an inquest confirmed, perhaps unsurprisingly, to be unrelated to his injuries. As an innocent victim in such an infamous crime, he is very often mentioned when the subject is raised in the press, sometimes in the erroneous belief that his death was caused by his injuries from the robbery.

Most of the defendants then took the stand and testified in their own defence, although Wilson and James did not do so. It was difficult, if not impossible, to give any convincing answer to the Crown's circumstantial evidence – for example, Hussey's palm print on the lorry in the yard at the farm; Wisbey's fingerprints on a bathroom rail; Welch's palm print on a beer can; Wilson's on the window sill; and James's on a cat's dish. Only Daly was lucky – his fingerprints had been found at the farm on a box of cards and tokens for playing Monopoly. But when his counsel submitted that there was no evidence to show when and where the prints got on the items – or, for that matter, where the set was at the time the impression was made – the judge accepted the submission and Daly was discharged and did not 'Go to Jail'.

Another of the defendants, Ronald Biggs, had already been discharged by now – but only on a technicality which involved his being tried separately at a later date.

The verdict was delivered by the foreman at 10.30am on 26 March 1964, and public reaction to the sentences was, to some extent, shocked astonishment. Journalist

James Cameron, writing for the *Daily Herald*, pointed out that the gang would have been much more lightly punished if they had been convicted of second-degree murder, blackmail, and breaking a baby's leg.

The story of the Great Train Robbery did not end with the trial, however. Two years later, in 1966, another member of the gang, James White, was sentenced to 18 years' imprisonment. That same year, Buster Edwards was also arrested and given 15 years. Bruce Reynolds had only £6,500 left when he was arrested in 1969 – and he went down for 25 years.

Bruce Reynolds was a career criminal, an accomplished housebreaker and jewel thief, who liked the high life and drove an Aston Martin. After the heist, he went on the run, living under several aliases abroad, and spending considerable time in South America before returning to Britain. Since his release in 1979, he has enjoyed a moderately high profile as a media 'former criminal' celebrity and his book, *The Autobiography of a Thief*, was generally well received. Reynold's son, Nick, is a member of the group Alabama 3.

Charlie Wilson escaped from prison and stayed on the run for just over three years before being recaptured. On 12 August 1964 – just four months into his 30-year sentence – Wilson, then 32, was freed by a gang of three men who broke into Winson Green Prison in the early hours of the morning. They had stolen a ladder from a nearby builder's yard to break into the grounds of a mental hospital next to the prison, and then used a rope ladder to scale the 20ft-high prison wall. They coshed one of the two patrolling warders on duty and tied him up, before opening Wilson's cell door.

He took up residence outside Montreal, Canada, on Rigaud Mountain. In the upper-middle-class neighbourhood, where the large, secluded properties are surrounded by trees, Wilson was considered to be just another resident who enjoyed his privacy. It was only when he invited his cousin over from the UK to meet him, that Scotland Yard was able to track him down and recapture him on 24 January 1968.

Perhaps the best-known Great Train Robber, Ronald 'Ronnie' Biggs also escaped and lived with a beautiful young girlfriend in Brazil. Born in Lambeth, at the age of 18 he joined the RAF but was dishonestly discharged in 1949 for desertion and served two years in a military prison. In 1960, he married Charmian Brent, with whom he had three sons. He escaped from Wandsworth Prison in 1965 by scaling the wall with a rope ladder. He fled to Paris, where he acquired new identity papers and underwent plastic surgery. In 1970, he quietly moved to Adelaide, South Australia, where he worked in set construction for Channel 10. When a reporter recognised him, he fled to Blackburn North, Melbourne, staying for some time before again fleeing to Brazil in the same year. His wife and sons stayed behind in Australia.

In 1974, he was tracked down by British police in Rio de Janeiro, but could not be extradicted because the United Kingdom did not benefit from reciprocity of extradiction to Brazil. Additionally, Biggs' then girlfriend, Raimunda de Castro, a nightclub dancer and prostitute, was pregnant; Brazilian law would not allow the parent of a Brazilian child to be extradicted. Therefore, he was able to live quite openly in Brazil, completely untouchable by the British authorities.

Despite evading justice for so long, however, Biggs admitted that life in Brazilian exile was not necessarily idyllic. 'My only wish is to walk into a pub a British man and have a pint of bitter,' he said wistfully. He spent the next three decades of his life as a fugitive and became something of a celebrity, despite having played a rather minor role in the actual robbery.

Eventually, just about broke and unable to meet mounting medical costs due to failing health, Biggs expressed a desire to return to his native country, fully aware that he would be arrested upon his arrival in England. He returned voluntarily on 7 May 2001, and was immediately arrested and re-imprisoned. The trip, on a private jet, was paid for by the *Sun*, which reportedly paid his son, Michael, £20,000, plus other expenses in return for exclusive rights on the news story. He still had 28 years of his sentence to serve.

Since then, Biggs has made several attempts at being released on compassionate grounds, and failed. In December 2007, he issued a further appeal from Norwich Prison. 'I am an old man and often wonder if I truly deserve the extent of my punishment. I have accepted it and only want freedom to die with my family and not in jail. I hope Mr Straw (the then Home Secretary) decides to allow me to do that. I have been in jail a long time and I want to die a free man. I am sorry for what has happened. It has not been an easy ride over the years. Even in Brazil, I was a prisoner of my own making.'

Today, almost 45 years after the heist, it is still not certain how many people were involved in it or its organisation. No one knows who hit Jack Mills over the head and, if they do, they are not grassing anyone up.

Only some £400,000 of the total haul has been recovered. Even so, just like the Securitas job, the Great Train Robbery was a disaster for most of those involved in the daringly conceived but finally unsuccessful 'big job'.

Train enthusiasts might be interested to note that one of the post office carriages involved in the robbery is now preserved at the Nene Valley Railway, near Peterborough, and has been restored to operational condition. The English Electric 2,000 hp Co-Co 1 Type c(4) designated D326 was cut up at Doncaster yet seemed to carry a curse. On 4 August 1965 it was stabled in a siding near Winson Green with no crew when it careered off in the direction of Birmingham New Street. At Monument Lane it crashed into a permanent way train and was derailed; to be towed away to Crewe on 17 August for major repairs.

As a result of this robbery, the British Railways rule book was amended. If stopped by a red signal, drivers had previously been instructed to contact the signaller by telephone – requiring them to leave the driving cab. After the change, drivers of mail trains were no longer allowed to leave the cab at any red signals and were always to keep their cab doors locked. These rules remained in force until the retirement of mail trains in the UK.

13

Street Gangs UK

'I noticed it because I saw a gun outside on the
passenger side. I saw the gun. I heard gunshots.
It was like a machine gun. I fell to the floor
and got up an started running.'

CHERYL SHAW – SHOT BIRMINGHAM, NEW YEAR'S EVE 2003

Street gangs, now more than ever in the UK, are
developing strangleholds on their local communities
to an unprecedented extent. And our current Home
Secretary, Jacqui Smith, proposes to slash British
police manpower by 12,000 officers, and replace them
with a police 'Dad's Army' using the Neighbourhood
Watch scheme.

And far from being a phenomenon limited to the
capital, writer Paul Lashmar notes, 'London is far from
the only city infested by gun gangs.'

Teenagers Letisha Shakespeare, 17, and Charlene Ellis,
18, died on Thursday, 2 January 2003 when they were
caught in the drive-by, gang-related crossfire of a violent

feud between Birmingham rivals, the Burger Bar Boys and the Johnson Crew. Charlene's twin, Sophia, and their cousin, Cheryl Shaw, 17, were badly injured. The legal term to describe what happened is 'transferred malice'. This means those responsible can still be charged with murder – even if they had meant to kill a member of a rival gang instead.

Gun crime is at an all-time high across the Midlands. In Nottingham, police declared themselves 'astounded at the bravado' of openly armed drug-dealers. Manchester has been nicknamed 'Gunchester' because of the gang shootouts in Moss Side, Longsight and Hulme. And the St Paul's area of Bristol has become a battleground for the Aggi Crew and their rivals – the Hype Crew, the Mountain View Posse, the Back to Back Gang and the Gucci.

The events that led up to the drive-by shooting deaths of Letisha and Charlene began on Friday, 6 December 2002, when 24-year-old Yohanne Martin was shot dead as he sat in his Mercedes in West Bromwich High Street. Yohanne – whose street name was '13' was a 'shot-caller' (a key member) of the Burger Bar Boys, whose territory included nearby Smethwick and Handsworth. The Johnson Crew were based in Aston and Lozells, the latter a loosely-defined area in the West of Birmingham. It is centred on Lozells Road, and is known for its multi-racial population.

Later, in 2005, Lozells Road was the scene of violent riots on the night of 22 October, which left two men dead and a police officer shot and wounded. The riots were started by a rumour about a girl being raped, which had been broadcast on a pirate radio station.

Yohanne's brother Nathan Martin, 26 – whose street

name was '23' – believed the Johnson Crew were behind the killing, and particularly a man who was at the time known as 'Mr X'. Martin began plotting his revenge, and later commented in the injustice that he perceived in the way the media was reporting the gangland feuds. 'The shooting of the girls was in the headlines for weeks and weeks, but my brother's death had been in the headlines for a day.'

Soon, Martin found a willing recruit in Michael Gregory, 23, whose sister Leona had been Yohanne's girlfriend and had had a child with him. He also recruited 24-year-old Marcus Ellis, another gang member known as 'E-Man', who was coincidentally the half-brother of Charlene Ellis. Known as 'Chunk' because of his size, Gregory was given the job of co-ordinating the hit, and he bought a pay-as-you-go mobile phone and used it to negotiate the purchase of the getaway car, a red Ford Mondeo, from a dealer in Northampton. It was the use of this mobile phone that brought about their downfall.

On the afternoon of New Year's Eve 2002, the car was brought back to Birmingham and the windows were tinted because the gang did not want witnesses to get a good look at them – a motive the specialist tinter was unaware of. All the gang needed now was an opportunity, and it arrived in the early hours of 2 January 2003.

Rodrigo 'Sonny' Simms, 20, another member of the Burger Bar Gang, was at a party at the Uniseven salon, a hairdressers in Aston, which his cousin owned. He spotted several members of the Johnson Crew there and guided the killers into position just after 4.00am. Earlier that night, Jermaine Carty had been 'bigging it up' in

Rosie O'Brien's nightclub in Solihull, taunting the Burger Bar Boys. Carty was later named in court by witnesses as being in the rival Johnson Crew, something he denied. Nevertheless, Carty was said to be one of the principal targets when the shooting started outside to the rear of the Uniseven salon.

Dressed in their favourite party clothes and 'shades', four teenage girls were on top form when they were dropped off by one of their mothers at the start of the new year's night out. They posed for a photo in front of a Christmas tree, giggling and teasing each other, before heading off to a club. They began their evening on 1 January at RB's club in Solihull, near Birmingham. From there, they moved on to an after-party at the Uniseven salon, in Aston, a few miles from Birmingham city centre on the A34. The A34 road acts as a boundary between the Burger Bar Boys and the Johnson Crew, both vying for control of the crack cocaine trade in central Birmingham.

Just after 4.00am, the girls joined a crowd seeking relief from the pounding music in the alley behind the salon. Jermaine Carty, who was regarded as having links to the Johnson Crew, had also appeared and was standing ominously nearby.

While the friends gossiped, the red Mondeo, its windows tinted, headlights off, cruised slowly by. 'I noticed it because I saw a gun outside on the passenger side,' Cheryl Shaw was later to tell the jury. 'I saw the gun. I heard gunshots. It was like a machine-gun. I fell to the floor and got up and started running.'

The men in the Mondeo were armed with three weapons, including a Mac-10 submachine-gun (Military Armament Corporation Model 10), which can unleash a six-second burst of fire. Nicknamed the 'spray and pray' because its fierce recoil makes it almost impossible to aim accurately, about 40 .45 ACP bullets were fired, in what was described as a 'fusillade of shots'. This weapon is the most popular of its kind used by street gangsters in the US today.

After completing their bungled attack, they crew drove off and, a few hours later, the getaway car was found burned out; it was some time before Martin, Ellis and Simms were arrested and charged with murder.

As a chilly dawn broke on 2 January, residents were already blaming the shooting on the two gangster crews. Over the past ten years, the gangs had grown rich on drug profits. Young black males, often poorly educated with few prospects, had become powerful and feared. But many had been killed. If a gangster was murdered, a rival was hunted down and taken out. If passers by were caught in the crossfire – too bad.

While police quickly dismissed any rumours that the victims had been involved with the gangs, or drugs, they did initially focus upon the killing of Christopher Clarke in March 2000. Yohanne Martin had been charged with Clarke's murder but the case was dropped. Detectives believed that after Martin's death, the Burger Bar gang put together a team and 'killing kit' – mobile phone, car and weapons – and waited until they heard that Carty was at the Uniseven party and targeted him.

Establishing a motive was one thing; identifying those responsible was quite another. The pressure for a result was huge. The mothers of the girls claimed the authorities were failing to tackle the gangs, and the then Prime Minister, Tony Blair, said he would not rest until the killers were found. But police hit a brick wall when they looked for witnesses. They identified 75 people they believed could have provided valuable evidence and, as might be expected, all refused to testify.

Eventually, officers started looking at Yohanne Martin's associates, particularly at those who were closest to him at the critical times. Largely through analysis of telephone records, they established that, around a month before the shooting, his younger brother Nathan had visited a car dealer in Northampton with a friend, Michael Gregory – whose sister was mother to Yohanne's child. The pair sent two stooges to buy the car – the red Mondeo, a vehicle identical to the one used in the murders and identical to the car found burned out shortly afterwards. This was a solid lead.

Further telephone traffic analysis showed that, as they arrived back in Birmingham, Nathan made a further call to a Marcus Ellis. The net was tightening on the gang, and police intelligence confirmed that Ellis was a shot-caller for the Burger Bar Gang.

Yet more probing led detectives to what they believed was a 'team phone', bought to co-ordinate the attack. Gregory had been in charge of that phone, and police and police liaison officers with the mobile phone company soon plotted a time/call graph, and focused on calls between the phone and a man called Rodrigo Simms, who was at the Uniseven party. Simms received a string of calls just before and after the shooting. He had been the 'spotter' who had guided the 'gun car' in.

In the weeks after the shootings, there was a lull in the violence but it soon began again. One of the most shocking killings came at the end of 2003 when another teenager, 19-year-old Daniel Bogle, was 'blown away' by masked gunmen in Smethwick, between Aston and West Bromwich. Tumbi 'Muscles' Beckford, 21, and his accomplices were found guilty and sentenced to 18 years in prison.

When the double murder case came to trial, Nathan Martin admitted playing a part in buying the Mondeo but he said he didn't know what the car was intended for. He also denied being a member of the Burger Bar Gang and having anything to do with the shooting, claiming that old favourite alibi, 'I was at home in bed with my girlfriend when it happened.'

When asked why he had failed to mention this 'alibi' beforehand, he said, 'It's bad what happened to them girls, but I didn't want to get involved. My brother had been murdered, my mum was having a very bad time, I was the only thing my family had left. I lied to protect myself and my family.'

None of this, of course, washed with prosecuting counsel, Timothy Ragget QC, who snapped, 'Your brother *was* a gangster and you *are* a gangster. You committed crimes together... you were inseparable.'

Martin, who made every effort to look like butter wouldn't melt, replied meekly, 'No. We were close, he was my only brother but he was trying to reform... to put behind him, to make something of his life.'

During the trial, another man, Tafarwa Beckford – half-brother of pop star Jamelia – was acquitted of murder on the judge's directions because the only evidence against him came from a witness, a jailbird known by the secret name of 'Mark Brown', whom the judge had concluded had been lying in an effort to have a current prison sentence reduced. Another sibling, Kairo Beckford, 21, was later convicted of shooting Daniel Bogle three times in the head. Beckford and his co-defendants – Josiah Faure, 23, David Perry, 27, and Anslow, 22 – will each serve a minimum of 18 years.

DS David Mirfield, who led the double murder inquiry, admitted that the gang still saw themselves as 'untouchables', but today hopes the murders of the young girls – and the convictions of the killers – will lead to change. 'Four young, innocent girls were shot and two were killed,' he has said. 'If that does not wake up a community and a nation, then nothing can.'

Another large gang rivalling the Burger Bar Boys in the Midlands is the Muslim Birmingham Panthers, which was formed in the early 1990s. The members are mostly Pakistani Pashtuns and Mirpuri/Kashmiris, and there are also other Muslims of other ethnic groups such as black Africans, Bangladeshis, Indians, black Caribbeans and Afghans. The Panthers operate in Lozells, Handsworth, Alum Rock, Sparkhill, Sparkbrook, Aston and Small Heath. It was formed to protect the Muslim community of Birmingham from white power skinheads and black gangs such as the Burger Bar Boys and the Johnson Gang. Membership of the Panthers is around 1,000, and they also have many members from Niazi and Durrani clans.

*

London, being the nation's capital, is today the centre of street warfare. Ladbroke Grove is run by a variety of Jamaican and black British drug gangs, none of which has overall control.

Harlesdon is mainly run by the Jamaican Lock City Crew, who see themselves as the real Yardies, while the Much Love Crew are mostly local homeboys. Three deaths and 45 other attempted murders or non-fatal shootings took place on this patch in the first half of 2003 and the numbers are rising.

Southall is the home turf for Asian gangs with such names as Holy Smokes and Tooti Nung, and the up-and-coming rivals, the Bhatts and Kanaks.

Camden is crewed by the Drummond Street Boys, who are a much smaller set-up than their rivals but very keen to recruit and expand their territory.

Not surprisingly, Soho and Chinatown are run by the Triads who specialise in gambling, drugs, extortion and people trafficking.

King's Cross is where the Albanian gangs rule and traffic girls to feed prostitution rings in all of Britain's major sex districts, and they are running an increasing number of 'saunas'. The Metropolitan Police estimates they control up to 80 per cent of off-street prostitution in London, as well as smuggling immigrants from the Balkans. Well armed, they are challenged by the Turks for control of heroin supplies.

Islington is the home turf of the white, 'working-class' A-team which still holds sway in this part of inner-city north London, despite intense police operations over the past 15 years.

Finsbury Park is dominated by Turkish gangs who run heroin rackets, despite frequent armed police raids and arrests among many of the main families. Politicised Kurdish gangs also run drugs through a network of clubs like the Turks, and with them control an estimated 70 per cent of the 30 tonnes of heroin imported into Britain every year.

Tottenham hosts two major black gangs – the Spanglers and the Fireblades – who take their name from the Honda Fireblade 2 motorcycles ridden by gang members.

Bangladeshi and other Asian gangs proliferate around Brick Lane, and are widening their power base beyond local drugs sales and petty crime. Second-generation teenagers give themselves names such as the Brick Lane Massive and the Stepney Posse. Lesser groups include the Bengal Tigers, Cannon Street Posse, the Shadwell Crew, and the East Boys of Bethnal Green.

In the late 1970s, vigilante gangs of second-generation Asians took to the streets to help protect the Asian communities from white racist groups such as the National Front in east London. The Asian Gangs formed to protect their community and local businesses and they mark their territorial boundaries with graffiti. They are predominantly Bangladeshi, while those of the West End are Indian and Pakistani.

Gang violence between groups such as the Holy Smokes and Tooti Nungs back in the 1980s was organised by the Asian mafia to take police attention away from its organised activities. Newer Asian gangs, such as the Bhatts, are more 'street gang' orientated, fighting violent battles over the heroin distribution in their area. However, many of the Asian gangs are still influenced by Asian families owning reputable businesses within London.

Good old Hackney is where the black gang, the Kingsland Crew, battle the Hackney Posse for dominance, while in Bow and Canning Town, the Hunts – a white, working-class crime family – have gained ascendancy in drugs, extortion and, until relatively recently, the theft of upmarket cars. They have also moved into Soho and are thought to 'go very big' very soon.

Bermondsey and Rotherhithe is traditionally the base for largely white crime gangs with big interests in drugs. The Brindle family and the Arifs have fought turf wars here for over a decade.

To some, the name 'Arif' might conjure up a string of kebab outlets, those of the type that teem with late-night boozers and produce vomit-stained pavements, but nothing could be further from reality. Indeed, the Arifs are a south London-based Cypriot-Turkish criminal organisation heavily into armed robbery, contract killing, drug trafficking and just about any other racketeering-related activity one can think of. They have been part of London's seedy underworld since the late 1960s, and they command respect among their underworld colleagues.

To begin with, following the downfall of the Kray empire, the Arifs were one of several criminal organisations who took control of the London underworld, including the Clerkenwell crime syndicate and the Brindle family, with whom they were engaged in a highly publicised gangland war during the 1990s.

The Arifs themselves were considered the leading crime family in the London area throughout the late 1980s, before the arrest and conviction of its leadership, including most of the Arif family members, for armed robbery and drug-related offences in the early 1990s. In 2004, the *Irish Daily Mirror* called the Arifs 'Britain's number-one crime family'. Considering that the newspaper had the IRA on its doorstep, this was praise indeed!

Led by brothers Dennis, Mehmet and Dogan Arif, the organisation had been involved in a decade-long gang war between the Daley and Brindle gangs which has resulted in eight deaths since 1990. In November 1990, Dennis and Mehmet, wearing Ronald Reagan masks and wielding shotguns, were arrested in Reigate Street as they attempted to rob a Securicor van. By the new millennium, Dogan Arif was ranked seventh in the *Sunday Times* 'Criminal Rich List'. Clearly, these guys were seriously big players, with considerable staying power, while they saw others rise and fall around them.

Bekir Arif, now into his fifties, is known as 'The Duke'. He is one of the seven brothers in the family and was convicted in 1999 of conspiracy to supply 100kg of heroin worth £12.5 million. He received a 23-year term in jail. For his part, Dogan was also jailed for drug smuggling, and it is said that he controls the family fortune from behind bars. Their family is said to maintain ties with relations in Turkey who oversee shipments in mainland Europe.

Today, the Arif brothers are still a common and feared name on the streets of London as they have been suppliers to many of London's street gangs, some of which include SUK and PDC.

The case against the Arif brothers came about with the arrival of Michael Boyle, an Irishman with Republican terrorist links, as a hitman on the streets of south London. His appearance would mark an alarming development in a murderous underworld vendetta. Over the next seven years, the ensuing feud was responsible for at least eight killings – three of innocent bystanders – and further shooting incidents. It was a tale, as writer John

Steele noted, 'punctuated by brawls and bravado in pubs and bars, fights with baseball bats and glass ashtrays and, in its later stages, a series of gun attacks.'

The feud was between the Daleys, the Brindles and others. It started around August 1990, when a group of men entered the Queen Elizabeth pub at 42 Merrow Street, Walworth, and threatened the landlord, John Daley, the brother of Peter. One of the group – in true Kray style – put a gun into the mouth of Peter Daley when he arrived.

The following month, a man called Ahmet Abdullah entered a drinking club and pumped seven bullets into one Stephen Galligan, a friend of the Brindles. Amazingly, he survived. 'Abbi' Abdullah was a violent criminal with a long list of his own enemies. He was also close to the Arif family. In March 1991, Abdullah was found shot dead in a William Hill bookies in Walworth. Anthony Brindle and his brother, Patrick, were charged with his murder and later acquitted at the Old Bailey.

The news of Abdullah's death was broken by two of the Arif brothers to their father, Yusef. He had regarded Abdullah as his son and, even today, his grief is held by the Arif clan to have contributed to his fatal heart-attack. Nevertheless, despite the fact that the Arifs were related to the Brindles by marriage, they are believed to have held a grudge against Anthony and Patrick thereafter.

In May 1991, Dennis Arif and his brother Mehmet were arrested following an abortive £1 million robbery of a Securicor van in Reigate, in which one raider was shot by police. It was this robbery that marked the demise of the family's dominance in south London. Then, in August of that year, another Brindle brother, David, entered the

Queen Elizabeth pub frequented by the Daleys, and became abusive.

As it turned out, David Brindle was severely beaten with a glass ashtray wielded by James Moody, a friend of the Daleys and a south London hard man, who achieved a degree of notoriety when he escaped from a prison with Gerard Tuite, then on remand as an IRA suspect. Now David Brindle began making threats to kill Daley and Moody, but he himself was murdered before August was out. Two men, armed with revolvers, entered the Bell pub in East Street, Walworth. An innocent Stanley Silk was also shot dead. Witnesses heard the gunmen shout, 'This one's for Abbi... ' – though this may have been mischief-making to link the shooting to the Arifs. Moody was among those suspected and, in March 1993, he too was shot dead in the Royal Hotel, Hackney.

Further incidents followed until, in August 1994, two other innocent men, Peter McCormack and John Ogden, were shot dead in Cavendish Road, Balham. One of the deceased bore a striking resemblance to Peter Daley. At this stage, Boyle, an armed kidnapper with lengthy prison terms behind him in Ireland, entered the equation.

Boyle had been recruited in the Daley cause by George Mitchell, a well-known Dublin criminal and friend of Peter Daley's, a London property dealer. Boyle said that Daley had been described to him as a criminal who was having financial difficulties and 'problems' with the Brindles.

Some of south London's most violent criminals, with their own scores to settle and drug-related turf to protect, became embroiled in the feud. For Scotland Yard and the South East regional Crime Squad, which would handle the Boyle case, the indiscriminate violence was deeply worrying.

Boyle's first involvement in the Daley–Brindle feud is in dispute. It is known that, within days of the McCormack/Ogden shooting, another Brindle sibling, George, was shot and injured while visiting his parents. After his arrest for the Anthony Brindle shooting, Boyle called DI Steve Farley to his cell in Belmarsh High-Security Prison in south-east London and, among other things, claimed to have been responsible for the George Brindle shooting. Ballistic tests showed that a second gun, a Magnum found in Boyle's 'surveillance van' at the time of the shooting of Anthony Brindle, had also been used on George. However, though Boyle has agreed at various stages that most of what he is said to have told Farley is true, he now claims the George Brindle admission is false.

For Farley and other crime squad officers, Boyle represented an unexpected disruption to Operation Partake, launched in May 1995 to investigate Peter Daley and others. Within days, Daley was arrested in a park in Luton with Mitchell and others. Nearby, police found more than £500,000 in cash. Enquiries into the facts behind the haul continued and no one was charged.

Another area of London in which significant gangs operate is Lewisham, where the Ghetto Boys are arch rivals to the neighbouring Peckham Boys and the Younger Peckham Boys, all black gangs. Most members of the once-competing African Crew have now been jailed.

The Ghetto Boys are based in New Cross and Deptford. The gang was formed on the Woodpecker and Pepys Estates and is primarily of Afro-Caribbean origin.

Most of the members hail from the London borough of Lewisham, and some members of the gang are known to carry firearms such as the Mac-10 submachine-gun. A member of the Ghetto Boys fired a shot at the 2004 Urban Music Awards, injuring accountant Hellen Kelly. Fortunately, the lady was wearing a sturdy bra; the bullet hit the underwire, preventing fatal injury.

The Peckham Boys was formed in the North Peckham estate, and its members are primarily of black origin. The gang is split into 'tinies', 'youngers' and 'olders', according to age group, and membership runs into the hundreds. The teenagers convicted of the high-profile murder of Nigerian schoolboy Damilola Taylor on 27 November 2002 were members of the Young Peckham Boys.

Born in Lagos, Damilola had travelled to the UK in August 2000 with his family to allow his sister to seek treatment for epilepsy. He moved on to the North Peckham Estate and began to attend the local school.

On Monday, 27 November 2000, the lad set off from Peckham Library at 4.50pm on his way home; he was captured on CCTV as he made his way along the route. On approaching the North Peckham Estate, he was cut in the left thigh. Running to a stairwell, he collapsed and bled to death in the space of 30 minutes. He was, however, still alive in an ambulance en route to the hospital.

There were two conflicting accounts of how he sustained his injury. The theory accepted by the Metropolitan Police is that Damilola was attacked and stabbed with a broken bottle. The alternative theory is that he fell on broken glass in an accident.

Subsequently, in 2002, four youths, including two 16-year-old brothers, went on trial at the Old Bailey. They were all acquitted of murder. Despite this setback, the police vowed to keep the investigation open and new DNA evidence techniques led to a re-examination of the evidence obtained at the time of the murder. In 2005, fresh arrests were made. Hassan Jihad, 19, and two brothers aged 17 and 16, were brought in.

The second trial in 2006 again ended without any convictions. On 3 April, the jury returned a 'not guilty' verdict on Jihad for the charges of murder, manslaughter and assault with intent to rob. The jury was unable to reach a verdict on the charges of manslaughter against the other two brothers, so they were found not guilty, but with the possibility of a re-trial on those charges. On 6 April, the Crown Prosecution Service announced that the two would, indeed, be re-tried.

On 9 August 2006, Ricky and Danny Preddie, after a 33-day re-trial, were convicted of the manslaughter of Damilola Taylor. When the verdict was given, Ricky Preddie was dragged down to the cells by prison officers after swearing at the court and saying, 'You're all going to pay for this... '

Mr Justice Goldring said, 'Take him down.' After a brief pause, when shouting could still be heard in court, he added sternly and loudly, 'Take him RIGHT down.'

On 9 October 2006, the judge sentenced the Preddie brothers to eight years' youth custody. They will be eligible for release after serving four years. However, since neither brother has shown even a trace of remorse for the crime, it is hard to say when either may actually be freed on parole. In the unlikely event that they are released *before* their four-year tariff expires, it will be on licence, any breach of which will see them packed off back to prison to serve the remainder of their sentence.

Should they commit another serious act of violence, they face the possibility of a very long sentence indeed. With the normally tight-lipped Probation Service anxious to not comment on such offenders, this time they have made an exception, stating, 'They [both brothers] pose a high risk of harm to others.'

In 2006, the Peckham Boys were involved in a widely reported gang war against the Ghetto Boys street gang based at the Pepys and Woodpecker Estates in Deptford and New Cross respectively. In the conflict, one innocent man was shot dead in New Cross, having been mistaken for a Ghetto Boys member by the Peckham Boys. He was shot at by a group of around 50 youths on mountain bikes, who had cycled from Peckham to Deptford.

Shortly after this murder, another man was shot and stabbed in Deptford by the same group, but survived. In a revenge attack, several members of the Ghetto Boys shot at youths in Peckham several days later. During the conflict, police seized handguns and submachine-guns. The dispute between these rival gangs has been ongoing for over 20 years.

Brixton is where 200 or so hardcore Yardies are based in the borough of Lambeth. Some of them are members of the Firehouse Posse or Brixton's Cartel Crew.

Gun crime is reaching almost epidemic proportions and is beginning to spread within the Tamil, Sikh, Indian, Pakistani and Bangladeshi communities and the murder rate has tripled over the past decades. There were 40 murders involving south Asians and 228 kidnappings in 2003. And it was in 2003 that Scotland Yard created a specialist squad (The Tamil Task Force) to deal solely with the rising gangland violence in Sri Lankan Tamil communities following thirteen gang-related murders centered round the Tamil areas of Ilford, Walthamstow and Wembley.

This rise in violence among the Tamil communities first started to cause serious concern in the later 1990s following a spate of stabbings and street fights with rival factions across London. The first homicide attributed to the Tamil gangs to be given media attention was in 2002 when a young Tamil was murdered and left to burn in Roe Green Park, Kingsbury, north-west London. He was killed amid a dispute involving local Sri Lankan gangs in the area.

Around the same time, a killing in Merton focused more attention on Tamil violence, and police concluded that the attacks were part of longstanding vendettas originating from Sri Lanka itself.

The incidence of violence among London's Tamil communities seemed to be escalating, as Croydon's Tamil immigrants, numbering around 3,000, voiced concern over the violence in the community. In 2002, three Tamils were charged with attempted murder in a matter of two months.

The Tamil Snake gang was the first of the organised Tamil gangs to have been created, allegedly by members of the Tamil Tigers who sought asylum in the United Kingdom. The gang's leader has not been found, but several members have been sentenced for various crimes, from extortion and fraud to murder.

In 2003, the Snake Gang shot a young man dead in a feud after trying to assassinate a relative. He was executed in his house and one of the killers also tried to shoot his father-in-law. Just hours before this incident took place, the gang had attempted to kill the deceased's brother-in-law in a drive-by shooting in Lyon Park Avenue, Wembley.

Following this, two other Tamil murders were committed in 2003. A 23-year-old Sri Lankan was attacked in Wembley. An hour later, an 18-year-old Sri Lankan was involved in a dispute between rival gangs in Ilford. Both men died from their injuries in hospital. In 2004, Sugandthan 'Shanthan' Nadarajah, a member of the Tamil Snakes, killed a young man in his car with an axe in Croydon in revenge for having been hit by a car driven by a member of the victim's gang two years earlier.

Shanthan, also known as 'Master', is affiliated to a number of south London organised gangs. Categorised as an 'enforcer', or a 'soldier', he earned the alias 'The Mad Axe Man' and was he was directly involved in a variety of co-ordinated attacks against other gangs in the region. One example was the aforementioned London Road Street Murder, where a fellow Tamil was hacked to death with an axe inside his car in front of his friends.

Although Shanthan's blood was found on the murder weapon, the court was unable to prove that he had actually committed the murder, but was able to convict him for manslaughter and he was sentenced to life imprisonment, along with Shanthan Tharamalingam, Sasikaran Selvaratnam and Ranjan Shanmughanathan who were part of a four-man team which was a sister group to the Tamil Strike Team who regularly targeted victims in Croydon for their attacks.

London is now home to over 100,000 Tamils. The

highest-density areas are East Ham, Ilford, Tooting, Wembley, Harrow and Walthamstow. Early in 2004, a teenager was attacked, this time by the Tamil Ari Ala Gang, brandishing samurai swords, hammers and axes. Following a number of murders, the newly formed Tamil Taskforce arrested 24 suspects in attempts to curb the violence. Scotland Yard arrested thirteen, and 500 officers searched homes in Newham, Waltham Forest, Redbridge, Harrow, Brent and Croydon. Officers seized a pistol, ammunition, swords, axes, baseball bats and pickaxe handles. In Newham, credit card cloning equipment was found and five men were arrested on suspicion of deception. 69 credit cards and a £30,000 Mercedes were also seized in Waltham Forest.

Greenwich is the turf of the Cherry Boys. The gang was formed on the Cherry Orchard Estate off Charlton Road, from which the gang derives its somewhat effeminate name. Members are of Afro-Caribbean origin and it is one of the three largest gangs in the borough of Greenwich (nicknamed 'Green Borough'), along with the Woolwich Boys and T-Block from Thamesmead.

The Cherry Boys have had a long-standing dispute with the Woolwich Boys, and it often boils over into skirmishes, one of which occurred at 4.00pm outside Kams Convenience Store in Charlton Road, on Wednesday, 27 June 2007. This mass brawl resulted in three people being stabbed, and 21 people from both gangs being arrested. Some were charged with attempted murder, with the 34 police officers finding an unhealthy collection of golf clubs, cricket bats and knives at the scene.

This incident had been precipitated when Ben

Hitchcock, 16, died after he had been stabbed in a fight in Southend Road, Beckenham, on 23 June. Eyewitnesses described youths wielding metal chains, poles and pick-axe handles in the fight, thought to have involved two gangs from Penge and Lewisham. In the early hours of the morning, youths believed to be members of the Woolwich Boys and T Block fought outside the Mermaid club in Woolwich High Street. Two 16-year-olds were stabbed and gang members then took part in a running battle across General Gordon Square in Woolwich town centre, using metal rods and rubbish bins as weapons. One victim was stabbed multiple times and was left with a punctured lung. Two people were arrested on suspicion of causing an affray and released on police bail.

14

Triads UK

*'The highly secretive nature of Triad dealings
makes it difficult to filter myth from reality in
judging the full extent of their activities.'*

MARTIN BOOTH – THE DRAGON SYNDICATE

British law enforcement agencies have identified the main Triad gangs as 14k and Wo Shing Wo, but they are challenged by the Snakeheads, mainly from the Fujian province, who operate networks bringing illegal immigrants into Britain. 14k is at its most potent in Birmingham and the north of England. Shui Fong dominates in London, Glasgow and the south coast, and Wo Shing Wo has its power base in Manchester. Large-scale immigration of Triad members from Amsterdam occurred following the death of their leader, Chung Mon, in 1975, in addition to those who came from Hong Kong during the 1980s.

Historically, the Triads (meaning 'groups of three') engaged in counterfeiting, and have done so since the

1880s. During the Sixties, they moved into copying expensive books and selling them on the black market. More recently, Triad counterfeiters have turned to watches and designer apparel such as handbags and clothing.

The real money for the Triads of late, however, has come from computers. Not only are the Triads effective smugglers of pornography, but they have cornered the market when it comes to computer software piracy. Obviously, since computers and the Internet became a staple of the modern household, the gangs have made more and more from pornography and piracy by employing the most ingenious computer technicians. In fact, the Triad gangs have also been known to make counterfeit films and, not content with that, have exerted their influence on the Chinese film industry. These guys have a network and influence that extends much further than many might think.

The Triads first arrived on our shores during the post-war era with the 14k Triad emerging in Chinese communities in London, Birmingham, Liverpool and Manchester. 14k is one of the largest groups to come out of Hong Kong. Formed by nationalists fleeing communist China, it has around 30 sub-groups, more than 20,000 members and a well-organised leadership. Although illegal gambling dens, brothels and mah-jong schools have developed in rundown Chinese communities since the late 1940s, authorities largely turned a blind eye and ignored the minor criminal activities from a generally law-abiding and industrious segment of British society, particularly as the Chinese takeaway became as popular as fish 'n' chips. However, with the large scale of immigration encouraged by the Labour Party in 1964, there was a huge influx of Hong Kong immigrants, some of whom were affiliated to particular Triad groups, who, in turn, were eager to expand drug-trafficking networks into Europe. Although nearly all the Triad groups operating in Britain were affiliated with 14k, each operated independently of the Hong Kong 14k and generally viewed each other as rivals.

As well as in Hong Kong, they are active around the world and the 14k Triad engages in a wide array of criminal activities such as credit card fraud; its worldwide reach allows it to gather credit card information globally. The 14k Triad fought a bloody turf war with the smaller Shui Fong Triad in Macau during the mid-1990s.

Shui Fong, also known as Wo On Lok, originated from a workers' union formed as part of the Hong Kong soft drink company, Wo On Lok – literally, it means 'water room'. Over the course of the conflict, more than 30 people were killed in gun battles, fire bombings and knife fights. Even Portuguese colonial authority figures were targeted, a car bomb almost killing the Chief of Police. The police decided to crack down on Triad activity and, in 1998, gang boss Broken Tooth Koi was arrested and charged with various criminal activities and sentenced to fifteen years in prison the following year.

Wo On Lok are no slouches either. On Sunday, 25 July 1999, a Chinese man died from multiple injuries after being attacked with a variety of weapons in Colchester. A fight had broken out between rival Triads, a car chase followed and the victim's vehicle crashed on a roundabout, where he was murdered. It is believed that Wo On Lok was responsible. Indeed, much earlier, in

1991, Hong Kong businessman Lam Ying-Kit was shot four times after he tried to take over the Wo On Lok in the UK.

It is unclear which Triad was responsible for first importing heroin into Great Britain, although authorities believe it was originally transported from Hong Kong, via Amsterdam, by the Ng Sik-ho, and received by either the 14k or the recently arrived Wo Shing Wo, the original Wo group, which operated as the longest established Triad in Hong Kong. With corruption within the Hong Kong Police Force at an all time high, many of Hong Kong's Triads turned to Great Britain where a narcotics task force was non-existent and their activities were largely unknown by British officials. It proved to be a perfect solution for the Triad gang masters.

During the 1980s, the power of the Chinese underworld was constantly shifting from one Triad to another in an attempt to control Britain's drug trafficking trade. Triads soon began expanding into other criminal activities, including VAT fraud, using innocent loanshark and extortion victims to provide a business front. The Triads also began to eschew heroin as well, turning instead to less serious drugs such as cannabis and designer drugs, which were smuggled by Triad couriers from the Netherlands and Germany as they competed with rival European outfits.

Following the signing of the Joint Declaration between Great Britain and China in 1984, the news of Hong Kong's return to China caused many Triads to flee to Great Britain. These newer Triads were far more organised and professional and, as many of its members were respected and prominent Hong Kong businessmen, they were easily able to use their legitimate businesses as fronts for tax evasion and money laundering on a huge scale. The Wo On Lok soon established themselves in London and Southampton and, maintaining links to similarly exiled groups in Ireland, France, the Netherlands and Germany, they engaged in 'lesser' crime such as illegal gambling, counterfeiting and video piracy, although they also still continue extortion activities on Chinese residents.

British authorities finally woke up to the problem and began to crack down on Triad activity during the early 1990s and, although law enforcement had been battling the Triads for some time, their first insight into the Triad structure and influence on British society came during the 1933 trial of George Cheung Wai-hen, an assassin for the Wo On Lok, who had become a government informer. He testified at the Old Bailey against six Chinese immigrants who were charged with possession of a firearm with intent to cause grievous bodily harm. Their target was the rival Triad member Lam Ying-Kit after a failed a failed attempt on his life on 7 September 1991.

According to Cheung's testimony, he described his traditional induction ceremony into the Wo On Lok, which took place around 2.00am in the basement of the Princess Garden Restaurant in Greyhound Road, Fulham. During the ceremony, he claimed to have paid his sponsor and dai lo, actor Tan Wai-Ming, a fee of £36.60 to operate in Great Britain. As the result of his whistle-blowing, Cheung was given a reduced sentence of five years in jail.

Today, the authorities consider the Wo Shing Wo to be the largest Triad operating in the country. Although largely based in Manchester, it also has affiliated groups in Birmingham, Glasgow and London and smaller groups in Bristol, Newcastle and Cardiff. Although members are recruited in the traditional manner, many members include prominent businessmen who either maintain links with the organisation for their own protection or act as full participants in their criminal activities. Although they abide by the territorial urban districts of other Triad organisations, often centred around a Chinese cultural club or martial arts association, they have been involved in extortion activities over an area as far scattered as Truro and Great Yarmouth.

14k Triad has seen a decline of its power since its appearance in the early 1950s, yet it still remains the oldest-established group in the underworld, and is still the second-largest Triad operating in the country. Based primarily in London and Liverpool, the 14k continues its traditional activities of loansharking and extortion of Chinese businesses, although they have also had a history of targeting other immigrant groups, such as Indian and Pakistani-run corner shops and small factories.

In terms of opposition to the Triads, the West Indian community has been more likely to report incidents of harassment and intimidation than its Asian counterpart, and with its own ethnic gangs to turn to, the West Indians are well able to put up stronger resistance, if not actually to retaliate themselves. Much of 14k is made up of teenagers or illegal Chinese immigrants, although there have been reports of non-Chinese members as well.

The San Yee On is an influential Triad organisation which, like its Hong Kong affiliates, is a highly organised criminal syndicate involved in white-collar crime. It also owns legitimate businesses, specifically in the entertainment industry, which arranges concerts and theatrical plays from the Orient.

The San Yee On is an influential Triad organisation which, like its Hong Kong affiliates, is a highly organised criminal syndicate involved in white-collar crime. It also owns legitimate businesses, specifically in the entertainment industry which arranges concerts and theatrical plays from the Orient.

As late as 2005, the Gaming Board started to investigate allegations that Chinese gangsters had been using the Napoleon Club casino, at Queen's House, in Leicester Square, London, which draws a significant proportion of its members from the Chinese and southeast Asian community living in nearby Chinatown. The gangsters were suspected of using the venue to launder vast sums of illicit cash from extortion, vice and people-smuggling operations.

Associated with the Triads, moneylenders carried large amounts of cash to loan to gamblers who had lost their stakes and wanted to carry on at the tables. As much as £25,000 was handed out in a single evening. If the loans were repaid using gaming chips or cheques drawn on casinos, these could be used to disguise the source of income, thus allowing drug and vice money to be laundered.

The Gaming Board's investigation had come hard on the heels of a June 2004 inquest into the gunning down of money lender and Chinese illegal immigrant, You Yi He, who had been shot dead in broad daylight at 5pm, Tuesday, 3 June 2003, outside the Bar Room Bar (BRB), at 32 Gerrard Street, Westminster. He was hit in the hand and the chest. The dead man had been a member of 14K as well as a long-standing member of Napoleon's casino, where, according to staff, he was part of a team lending there regularly. Police learned that You Yi He lived with his brother in Mare Street, Hackney. A married man with two children, he had left them behind in the Fujian province of south-west China and entered the UK in 1997. No one has been arrested for the killing which was believed to have been carried out by the rival Snakeheads Triad.

15

Our Journey Through Gangland UK

'Organised crime constitutes nothing less than a guerrilla war against society.'

LYNDON BAINES JOHNSON, FORMER PRESIDENT
OF THE UNITED STATES

During the research and the writing of Gangland UK, a gang was jailed for Britain's largest credit card fraud. It was a £17 million deal led by a Russian, an illegal immigrant called Roman Zykin, who was living in Paddington, central London.

The gang was uncovered by chance. A British Transport police constable on anti-terrorist patrol stopped Zykin at Victoria Station on 29 September 2005, and discovered he had 40 mobile phone top-up cards on his person. The cards were later examined and found to contain thousands of stolen American credit card numbers.

An eighteen-month investigation took officers and banking officials on a money trail to Poland, Estonia,

Russia, the United States and the Virgin Islands. A total of 32,000 credit card numbers were eventually found stored on computers.

Zykin, aged 38, was later sentenced at Southwark Crown Court and imprisoned for five-and-a-half years after pleading guilty. Along with the rest of the gang, he admitted conspiracy to transfer criminal property and having a 'false instrument with intent'. Jailing him, Mr Justice Stone said, 'This was a substantial organised crime. It was carefully planned and was executed in a sophisticated way.'

The gang led a lavish lifestyle – one gang member owned a £900,000 home in Hertfordshire, while others splashed out on a Spanish villa, a converted east London church and other properties in the capital. They also enjoyed first-class travel and five-star holidays in Spain, Russia and Poland. They shopped exclusively at Selfridges, and squandered fortunes on designer clothes and shoes. The other members of the gang were 30-year-old Polish national, Dariusz Zyla, of Haringey Gardens, Wood Green; 31-year-old fellow countryman, Krystof Rogaliski, who lived in Claude Road, Plaistow; and an important Estonian 'link man', Hannes Pajasalu, 34, of no fixed address. They received four, three, and two years respectively. Zykin's wife, Malgorzata, 41, who also admitted taking part in the scam, was jailed for four months. They have all been recommended for deportation upon their release, although with the slackest border controls of any European country, this crew will probably be back in the UK before we know it.

I began this book with a warning – a portent of what will become of British society if we, and the Government, or any successive government, do not wake up to the effects of the social disease, the pandemic which is spreading globally, known as gang culture and 'organised crime'. And, as things stand today, there is no antidote or known cure.

The Introduction to this book illuminates the ever-increasing anti-social behaviour of some 200,000 youngsters/yobs/thugs who commit street crime. Teenagers, and many kids as young as nine or ten, are prepared to resort to violence on a whim, and see its use as a perfectly viable means of getting what they want. These are children and young adults with little to no parental controls, and they are the budding serious villains of tomorrow, many of whom will spend much of their lives going from youth offender institutions to Borstals, before graduating to 'proper' incarceration. They will then be released back into society as fast as is expedient to do so because of prison overcrowding and a determined lack of will by society to do much about it.

We cannot say that the writing has not been on the wall. Gangs have always been a fairly consistent feature of the urban landscape of Britain. In the seventeenth century, British gangs routinely vandalised urban areas, were territorial, and were involved in violent conflict with other gangs. From time immemorial, wherever there have been dense populations, there have always been groups of ill-doers who prey on the law-abiding and innocent.

The obvious fact that cannot be ignored is that most home-grown British gangsters have come from rundown inner-city conurbations, and most were in trouble shortly after they started school.

The Gunn brothers have been used as an example of

organised crime flourishing within our council estates. Of course, the Bestwood Estate is merely an example because the problem exists on most large estates – it always has done and it always will. And at a time when British law enforcement is potentially about to be drastically reduced in manpower, to be replaced by an amateur task force of Neighbourhood Watch do-gooders, with no powers of arrest, where will this take us? Backwards, naturally. Reporting a bunch of out-of-control yobbos to the police is one thing, but the issue the present Home Secretary seems to have missed is that there will not be enough underpaid 'real' police around to attend such incidents – a bit like today really, yet far worse.

The book also tries to dispel the notion that many of our home-grown gangsters have a romantic edge to their lives and criminal activities. I have used the example of Robin Hood and compared how the Gunn brothers stacked up against the man in green tights – they were, after all, compared to the legendary hero of Sherwood Forest by some of the residents of the Bestwood Estate themselves.

Kenneth Noye, a short young man, bullied at school, certainly grew up to become a master criminal. In many circles, he is admired for that. Cunning as a fox and just as secretive, his big mistakes were not only to have killed a brave and defenceless police officer, but also an innocent young man, whom he stabbed to death in a road-rage incident – both crimes shocked a nation. Had he not committed manslaughter, for that's what it boiled down to with the killing of DC John Fordham, and had he not committed murder most foul, for that's what it boiled down to with Stephen Cameron, he might still be enjoying the fruits of his crimes today.

During the writing of this book, I spoke to several police officers who remembered the night when John Fordham died. They all told me that every British policeman was sickened to their stomachs and all of them couldn't wait to get their hands on the vile cop-killer. And, of course, both killings brought about the utter disgust of the public and media at large. From then on, Kenny Noye's fate was sealed – he would have to spend the rest of his life behind bars.

And so to the Krays. Their names still live on as criminal icons of years gone by. Two tough lads who came from deprived nothingness to rule London's underworld for many years, but, in today's terms, were they really so hot? The area for which they deserve a modicum of respect is how they dragged themselves out of poverty and created a world in which they mixed on an equal footing with the rich and famous. Their downfall was Ronnie, a psychopathic, delusional 'nutter' who started to think that he equalled any Italian mafia godfather. His brother, Reggie, certainly had his business wits about him but, influenced by his devotion to Ronnie, he allowed murders to be committed and their downfall was soon to follow. Had the Krays not killed, they might have gone on to stay 'legit', and prospered. As we have seen, that was not to be.

Of course, today we should regard the Krays in almost prehistoric terms, extinct dinosaurs of a long-gone criminal era which could never thrive in modern gang-driven, crime-ridden Britain today.

By comparison, I have compared the Richardsons with

the Krays. A couple of more mentally stable thugs, or 'Jack-the-lads', who vied for control of London's underworld. As arch enemies of Ron and Reg, their only real claim to fame was the 'Torture Trial', proving merely that Charlie Richardson was a sadist and not much more.

Things heat up for us when we travel north to Scotland; Glasgow became the stamping ground of some of the best-organised and most brutal gangsters ever to live on British soil. It was the home of the Ice Cream Wars and Thomas 'Tam' McGraw, a millionaire mobster-turned-police informer, who stayed in business because the police were bought and sold. They were tough, unforgiving, old-school types, these gangster Scots and, if the truth were known, they were always more than a match for the Krays.

The Adams family also caught our attention, and particularly their leader, Terry, who was at the top of his profession and controlled his empire with such ruthless efficiency that he could have run a major multinational company. Yet Terry, who made Tony Soprano look like a wuss, was the godfather of the nearest underworld network Britain had to the Mafia. He was the Capone of his time and, like Alphonse Capone, it was the taxman who finally nailed him.

One has to give Terry respect. He was ever the dapper gent in his velvet-collared overcoats. He lived in a £2 million house in north London crammed with stolen antiques, a far cry from his upbringing on the rough Barnsbury council estate in Islington. His family and close associates were reputably worth about £200 million, and they were feared far more than the Krays ever were.

The Wembley Mob was a gang at large throughout the 'Swinging Sixties', which was an era when gang-driven armed robberies and daylight smash-and-grab raids proliferated. By the summer of 1972, the Metropolitan Police were at their wits' end, but seemed powerless to stem the tide of violence and mayhem. The Wembley Mob simply went about their business – ruthlessly, efficiently and successfully.

The gang's downfall was a 'grass', the most infamous supergrass in British criminal history – Bertie Smalls.

Grasses, snitches, songbirds and bent coppers abound as well. But there were some decent, determined, hard-nosed detectives, too, determined to redress the balance despite limited resources, and this is why I have introduced Bert Wickstead to offer a wider perspective on gang culture. Known as 'The Gangbuster', his name will live on with others, such as 'Slipper of the Yard', both dedicated policemen whose names brought nightmares to scores of the country's gangsters for decades.

Moving closer to the present day, the Securitas Crew could not be ignored, nor the success of their brilliantly executed heist. It was perfect, having been signed, sealed and delivered with military precision. If only the after-crime laundering of the cash had been planned with as much ingenuity.

How do you make £53 million in untraceable currency disappear? Unfortunately for the gang, the brilliance of the raid was only matched by the incompetence of the aftermath. Most of the gang were caught within a heartbeat, in criminal investigation terms, with one female accomplice ambling into a bank dressed as a

Salvation Army nurse and trying to deposit thousands of pounds with the distinctive Securitas logo still wrapped around the notes. You couldn't make it up.

Equally as incompetent were the Great Train Robbers. Although, again, it has to be acknowledged that they did pull off one of the most remarkable heists in world history, and we have to give them a great deal of credit for that. Having accomplished the near impossible, one might have thought that dividing up the cash between them would have been a simple task, one that should have been completed easily within a day.

But what did our robbers do? They rented a farmhouse at a location that was bound to draw attention from the nosy locals with nothing better to do. They came and went as if they owned the place, just a 20-minute drive from where the world's largest robbery had taken place. They left their fingerprints all over the place, yet were very surprised when they were arrested.

In commenting on their lengthy prison terms, the word 'disgraceful' often comes to mind. Apart from whacking the train driver over the head – and Jack Mills had resisted, after all – the robbery was non-violent, so perhaps they should have been rewarded for their ingenuity and their reluctance to resort to more direct, violent means.

Perhaps one of the most unnerving aspects of Gangland UK is the chapter on street gangs. It brings into stark reality the problems facing decent society today. And it is not just the indigenous, white population who are the perpetrators of gang-related crime – far from it. We have brought upon ourselves, through sublime and convenient sweep-it-under-the carpet ignorance, a social disease that will never go away. We have, in truth, imported gangsterism from all corners of the globe – and particularly Asia and an impoverished Eastern Europe. It is the same old, sad story – lack of effective border controls, insufficient policing... although the authorities are probably doing all they can to stem the tide. It's just that they're losing the battle.

For decades, both of the major British political parties have formed governments on their phoney 'get tough on crime' law enforcement tickets. There have been promises after promises after promises... ad infinitum. Yet, today, the problem is far worse than it has ever been, and Government guidelines issued to the judiciary are advising fewer custodial sentences for the young hooligans. Their parents have lost all control, oblivious to – or tacitly allowing – their offspring to run amok with knives and baseball bats, terrifying decent people on their local streets.

With the CPS willing only to take on prosecutions that will result in cast-iron convictions, the police and the general public are hopping mad, and they have every right to be. But will the decent citizen take back the streets? Of course not. Merely raising a hand against one of these yobs brings down the wrath of the law, so why bother?

Vast swathes of our inner-city areas are run by street gangs. No-go areas are policed by hoodies and hammer-wielding thugs who strive to mark out their territories like hyenas fighting over scraps of meat and bragging rights. One might say that, as long as they only maim and kill their own, then so be it; however, as this book highlights, they not only do that, but they maim and kill innocent people as well.

I finished this book with the Triads. Seemingly, they keep very much to themselves and Chinese-related street crime is relatively rare.

There are costs to gangland crime in the UK, and they are enormous costs, too, and not just in financial terms – misery, terror, unsafe streets and businesses, injuries, deaths... Who bears those costs for Gangland UK?

You!